THE ABSOLUTE VIOLATION

The Absolute Violation

Why Torture Must Be Prohibited

RICHARD MATTHEWS

McGill-Queen's University Press
Montreal & Kingston · London · Ithaca

© McGill-Queen's University Press 2008
ISBN 978-0-7735-3422-3 (cloth)
ISBN 978-0-7735-3451-3 (paper)

Legal deposit third quarter 2008
Bibliothèque nationale du Québec

Printed in Canada on acid-free paper that is 100% ancient forest free
(100% post-consumer recycled), processed chlorine free.

This book has been published with the help of a grant from the Canadian
Federation for the Humanities and Social Sciences, through the Aid to
Scholarly Publications Program, using funds provided by the Social
Sciences and Humanities Research Council of Canada.

McGill-Queen's University Press acknowledges the support of the Canada
Council for the Arts for our publishing program. We also acknowledge
the financial support of the Government of Canada through the Book
Publishing Industry Development Program (BPIDP) for our publishing
activities.

Library and Archives Canada Cataloguing in Publication

Matthews, Richard
    The absolute violation: why torture must be prohibited / Richard Matthews.

Includes bibliographical references and index.
ISBN 978-0-7735-3422-3 (bnd)
ISBN 978-0-7735-3451-3 (pbk)

    1. Torture. 2. Torture – Moral and ethical aspects. 3. Torture victims.
    I. Title.

HV8593.M355 2008   323.4'9   C2008-901695-5

Typeset in Sabon 10.5/13
by Infoscan Collette, Quebec City

In memory of my father

DR KEITH MATTHEWS

Contents

Acknowledgments   ix

Introduction   3

1   Understanding Torture   31

2   What about the Ticking Bomb?   68

3   Why Utilitarians Must Oppose Torture   100

4   Torture, Tragic Choices, and Dirty Hands   139

5   On Neither Excusing nor Justifying Torture   186

Conclusion   203

References   221

Index   233

Acknowledgments

Having finished this book, I now understand why no author writes a book alone. Without the friendship and the intellectual and moral support of a lot of friends and family members, I could never have finished this book. To be honest, I doubt that I would ever have had the courage to start. Some read drafts of chapters, others contributed insights through conversations, and all simply believed in me and the importance of the project.

Heidi Matthews (LLB, LLM cand.) is one of the brightest individuals I've had the good fortune to befriend. She convinced me to start the project and contributed much valuable critical commentary and moral support. Dr Sean McGrath of Memorial University of Newfoundland read a draft of the introduction and provided enthusiastic debate and encouragement throughout. Dr John Scott taught me the first philosophy course I ever took. He convinced me early of the necessity for politically engaged philosophy and continues to mentor me now, having read drafts of the introduction and the fourth chapter. He has never turned down a request for time or aid since I first sat in his class. In spite of two very young children and a busy job, Jordan Furlong (LLB) managed to find time to edit the chapter on law and torture. His expertise both as an editor and in the field of law was a wonderful gift to me. Additionally, I was very angry at the time, and he patiently convinced me to tone down some of the more impassioned remarks. We have been friends for a very long time, and he demonstrated friendship's virtue once again.

My colleagues and friends at Mount Allison University, Dr Paul Bogaard and Dr Roopen Majithia, both supported me through dialogue and provided me with the opportunity and the peace to devote myself to the extensive research needed to pursue this project. Their encouragement was crucial. As well, Mount Allison University provided me with the office space and library facilities to carry out my work.

I had the good fortune to test each of the central theses on a lecture tour of Australia in February 2007. Dr Barbara Hocking and the Association for Canadian Studies in Australia and New Zealand were kind enough to provide me with a grant; the graduate students and faculty of the Queensland University of Technology warmly hosted me. In particular I want to thank Ms Jenny Jones, Ms Eleanor Milligan, Dr Peter Isaacs, Mr David Massey, and Dr Trevor Jordan. The experience and criticisms strengthened the book considerably.

I would also like to thank two anonymous reviewers for their extensive and constructive comments on the manuscript. It has been enriched considerably by their expertise. Likewise, I wish to express my deep appreciation to Philip Cercone, Robert Lewis, Ligy Allakattussery, Joanne Pisano, Joan McGilvray, and the other staff at McGill-Queen's University Press.

My family, Dr Kathleen Matthews, Dr Clare Matthews, Katy Matthews (LLB), and Keith Matthews (MBA), enthusiastically backed me throughout a very long and challenging period. I hope they understand how much their belief in me continues to mean.

Three friends have offered me particularly important support. I've shared many doubts and conversations on politics with Michael Jacobs, who consistently offers great insight. And Sean Windsor and Raymond Hartery have each contributed vitally as well, notably by helping me to appreciate the institutional realities that govern military decision making.

Above all, my partner, Emma Woodley, has been essential. A book of this nature is occasionally painful to research and write. As important as it is, a week spent reading nothing but human rights reports and the consequent horror stories does little for the spirit. At every key moment, she literally held me together and gave me the strength to continue. Not only did she offer me love, strength, and emotional support, but she also offered me the benefit of her considerable radical feminist insights into gender issues and patriarchy by criticizing the crucial first chapter of the book and suggesting important additional texts for inclusion, such as one by

Susan Brison. In addition, she is the best editor I've ever worked with and has provided invaluable help proofreading the book. I am blessed by her.

To the extent that the book works, it is because of them. Any errors, of course, are mine.

THE ABSOLUTE VIOLATION

Introduction

This is a question of serving the dignity of man [*sic*] by methods that remain dignified in the midst of a history that is not.

Camus 1991, 76

Prior to 11 September 2001 those unfamiliar with human rights work would probably have accepted the commonplace that torture had been eradicated from the civilized world. It was reserved for violent Third World dictatorships and communists, something that "they" do, not "we." Anyone with a more nuanced knowledge of recent history and politics will be aware that the reality is rather uglier. Even so, there seems to be little awareness of the extent to which modern torture techniques were in fact developed by the most powerful industrialized states. There is also widespread ignorance of the extensive evidence demonstrating the use of torture by the United Kingdom, the United States of America, France, and other democracies since the end of the Second World War.

Alfred McCoy's (2006b) fascinating history of the Central Intelligence Agency (CIA) and torture explores in great detail the psychological research on torture performed in Canada and the United States in the 1950s and 1960s. These programs resulted in methods that were then field-tested and revised in Vietnam and in numerous Cold War counter-insurgencies across the globe over the past forty years. Darius Rejali (2007b, 8) traces the development of stealth tortures in modern democracies from early in the twentieth century. Analyzing the "unnerving affinity between democracy and stealth torture," Rejali argues that exploration of stealth tortures is a consequence of governmental desires to escape public monitoring and accountability. The French developed their own theory of counter-insurgency warfare, with torture as a centrepiece of the program, in the Algerian War of the 1950s and then sent staff officers to

Argentina and the United States to further disseminate their knowledge (Robin 2006, 46–7). The United Kingdom maintained at least one torture facility during the Second World War and immediately afterward, mainly, it seems, to gather intelligence about the Soviet Union in the early days of the Cold War (Cobain 2005). It also took advantage of American and French experience in torturing suspected Irish Republican Army (IRA) members in the early days of the "troubles" in Northern Ireland.

But torture practices were typically concealed, denied, or masked by euphemism. That same post-Second World War period also saw the creation of various conventions on civil and human rights, many of which explicitly and absolutely prohibited torture. Public awareness seemed to have been growing concerning the appalling torture practices of governments, and along with this, there emerged an international consensus of opposition to torture.

The decision of President George W. Bush's administration to declare war on coherence following 11 September 2001 marked the turning point. Prior to 9/11 almost nobody would defend torture. In philosophy classrooms such questions might have arisen but only for the sake of testing moral intuitions or the possible limits of moral theories like utilitarianism. Serious public advocacy of torture rarely occurred. An exception was Israel's Landau Commission (1989), whose inquiry resulted in a defence of the use of "moderate physical pressure" by the Israeli General Security Service. Ostensibly, it was a means to deal with bomb threats. More precisely, it was a tactic used in pursuit of perceived Israeli security interests. The Landau Commission's recommendations were highly criticized and ultimately overturned by a 1999 decision by Israel's Supreme Court, which emphasized that the methods of moderate physical pressure constituted torture and thus forbade them. It thereby reenforced the absolute ban against the use of torture. Michael Levin's (1982, 1990) libertarian defence of torture is another rare argument for its use.

However, since 2001 discussions and defences of torture have multiplied, most notably in legal circles, newspapers, magazines, and similar media but also in applied ethics. Alan Dershowitz, Oren Gross, Sanford Levinson, Andrew Moher, and Richard Posner explore legal arguments for torture. Each theorist sanctions torture, but they are divided on just how to handle it. Dershowitz (2004, 266), for example, argues for a system of torture warrants in order to place political and administrative controls on its use. Gross (2004, 1489) defends preservation of the absolute prohibition against torture. He thinks the public is better served by an absolute prohibition, even though he concedes the moral imperative that will drive some public officials to use torture in order to prevent a catastrophe and argues that torture is therefore sometimes permissible. Miriam Gur-Arye (2004, 183) argues that "in rare situations the use of interrogational force may be justified under the limited boundaries of self-defense rather than necessity." Andrew McCarthy (2005, 10) argues that people will oppose torture in the abstract, but when confronted with "real world cases" they will support it as justifiable. He believes that the absolute opposition to torture results only from thinking in a moral vacuum. This is of course only a subset of the protorture literature.

In applied ethics, Michael Gross and Fritz Allhoff actively defend torture. Gross offers a communitarian defence of torture in an essay in the journal *Bioethics* (2004) as well as in a chapter of his book *Bioethics and Armed Conflict* (2006). Allhoff has published several recent essays arguing in favour of torture.

Probably, the emergence of these arguments is spurred by national-security fears. Public outrage and the demands that anything be done to ensure public safety have spurred reflection on the means necessary to achieve this. It is not surprising that public figures might turn to torture as a quick fix for a complicated political problem, but it is unjustifiable nonetheless. Fearful reactions do not encourage careful reflection on moral problems. This is reflected in the odd way defenders of torture fail to closely investigate the precise harms of torture and thereby construct skewed cost-benefit calculations of its utility.

But independently of the utility considerations, the defences of torture are pernicious. This is not an abstract conceptual debate: it has political impacts on individuals, their families, larger communities, those who execute torture, and the countries that condone its use. These arguments for torture do not merely lurk in the bowels of arcane academic journals; they influence policy makers to devote economic, political, and institutional resources to the practice of torture that would be better directed elsewhere.

Furthermore, torture is and ought to be revolting. Its consequences for victims and survivors are terrible. Its impacts on interrogators and cultures are enormous in their own right. Following the American-led invasion of Iraq in 2003, the photos and evidence from the torture of Iraqis and others at Abu Ghraib, Bagram Air Force Base, and Guantanamo Bay were an important and appropriate shock to the conscience. Unfortunately, for many – if not most – they do not seem to have been much more than that.

In this, protorture arguments function to pacify such uneasiness. Revulsion is the correct moral reaction, yet we are encouraged to suppress our feelings and support state torture conducted supposedly on our behalf. The arguments for torture legitimize practices that are not, on careful reflection and examination, justifiable. Every such argument, each episode of the Fox Network's television series 24, and each cynical euphemism and denial is another dose of soma. Torture is essentially filthy, yet the arguments that require or permit torture sanitize it. We thereby become increasingly comfortable with evildoing.

Moreover, defenders of torture neither examine nor understand torture at all. Consequently, they frequently contribute to the recurring myth that practices like water-boarding, stress positions, exposure to heat and cold, control of diet, and other forms of "pressure" are not torture. This clears a space for cynical attempts to define torture as all those acts that "we" do not do in our prisons, interrogations, counter-insurgency, and counter-"terror" operations.

One odd feature of the debate is that even defenders of the absolute prohibition of torture sometimes concede an abstract justification for torture. It is not uncommon to find critics who oppose torture in practice echoing Henry Shue (1978, 141) in arguing that torture might be justifiable in the hypothetical case, even though they maintain that such cases do not happen in the real world. Therefore, for all practical purposes, they conclude, torture can never be justified. My argument is more ambitious: I demonstrate that even the hypothetical cases are weakly constructed and unsound.

The point of this book is to provide a comprehensive defence of the absolute moral prohibition against torture. I reject each of the contemporary arguments for state-sanctioned torture and provide a philosophical and moral case in support of the absolute prohibition of torture. In current international law, torture is forbidden absolutely, even in a state of emergency. There are good reasons why international law excludes exceptions, and providing philosophical support for the nonderogability clause of the United Nations Convention against Torture is one of the goals of this book.

To further specify my intent, I should emphasize that I concentrate on the political uses of torture by states against the agents of other states as well as against perceived internal opponents or other non-state actors. I intend to argue that none of the existing arguments in favour of the state use of torture supports their conclusion and hence that the arguments are ultimately invalid. I also believe that torture should be excluded in other cases, but most of those are uncontroversial, and in the remaining cases some different arguments would have to be employed in addition to those that I develop here.

WEAKNESSES OF EXISTING
DEFENCES OF TORTURE

A centrepiece of much protorture argumentation is the "ticking-bomb" hypothesis. Here, we are asked to envision what we are morally required to do in the event that an enormous bomb has been set in a major metropolis. We have a suspect whom we know to have planted the bomb and who refuses to tell us its location or the time of detonation. We have tried all other measures to find out the location of the bomb. All have failed. In that event, torture advocates claim, surely we are obliged to torture the suspect in order to prevent the terrible harm that will be inflicted on all of the innocent people who will be killed if we allow the bomb to go off.

The reasoning is consequentialist, for the costs of refusing to torture are believed to be worse than torturing the suspect. However, we can further subdivide protorture arguments into two classes. The first consists of utilitarian arguments. These maintain that torture is justifiable if – and only if – it is happiness-maximizing. If you can show that a state is better off under the right circumstances if it uses torture, then torture is the morally required option. This provides a cost-benefit analysis in which the admitted harms imposed by torture are weighed against any benefits. If torture proves to better a community by improving its security or providing some other benefits, and if the harms are not excessive in comparison to the benefits, torture is morally required.

The second class is the so-called "dirty-hands" argument for torture. Here the reasoning is still consequentialist, but the argument has to do with the nature of the role that a public official occupies. There are occasions, so defenders argue, when public officials are obligated to dirty their hands. They are required to deliberately do something that they know to be evil because the consequences of refusing to do evil are so much worse. Public officials may therefore be morally obliged to torture someone in order to prevent a bomb attack or other terrible threat to their nation.

These arguments share a number of weaknesses. Notably, most of the arguments in the debates about torture do not carefully explore the history of torture. In the rare cases where history is mentioned at all, it is usually to support a claim that torture has worked at least once. Alan Dershowitz (2002, 137) and Michael Gross (2006, 220) both cite instances of allegedly successful torture. However, neither author looks closely at the cases to establish whether it was *torture* that made the significant difference. In the one case of "successful" torture that Dershowitz cites, he fails to note that the necessary information was on the laptop of Abdul Hakim Murad, a nonstate actor who had planned to destroy several airliners and to bomb CIA headqarters but was captured by the Philippine security forces in 1995 before the plan could be carried out. McCoy (2006a) also argues that the publicized intelligence details were fabrications fed to Murad under torture. It does not help that the other evidence of successful torture provided by defenders of torture consists only of anecdotes given by security personnel who have an interest in presenting their successes and defending their practices. This is not surprising given that the cases where torture may have been effective are those where it has been used far more violently and indiscriminately than any defender supports. No real case of torture has or could fit their models.

Therefore, this book is historically and empirically informed. Where I use historical events, statements of public officials, and other historical data, it is to achieve several goals. I identify classes of historically real actions to ask whether the arguments for torture can successfully exclude them. I briefly consider how reasonable military and intelligence officials interpret the arguments made by defenders of torture to show that they use the same reasoning employed by defenders of torture to extend torture much further than torture advocates desire. I show that the historical evidence does not suggest that torture is controllable, as defenders hope. I use historical examples to support certain deductive conclusions about the inevitable and probable consequences of the implementation of torture policies. Finally, the historical evidence provides useful counter-examples and cautionary evidence to suggest that the ways torture policies will play out must be quite different than torture advocates suppose.

Many essays on the subject of torture, both for and against, share a weakness: they rely too heavily on the United Nations Convention against Torture (UNCAT). While I concede the fundamental legal importance of the convention and accept that it is essential in the struggle against torture, it is a mistake to think that we understand the nature and structure of torture simply by knowing the UNCAT definition by heart. It tells us nothing about the specific kind of wrong done by torture, for example. Nor does it help us to identify the victims of torture or the extensive harms that it causes. It presupposes these, and justifiably so, given the specific human rights purposes that it serves. But we still need to understand them in order both to appreciate what is at stake in the debate over the justifiability of torture and to appropriately consider the ethical issues that torture raises.

In part because they rely so heavily on the UNCAT definition, the arguments for torture pay no attention to the physiological, psychological, medical, social, gendered, phenomenological, and other properties of torture. Yet if we are to avoid pseudo consequentialism, we must closely investigate its real harms and consequences. To appreciate these, it is necessary to carefully assess the specific nature of torture. One must understand what it means to say that torture is an attack on dignity and identity. We must investigate the theatricality of torture and the perverse intimacy of the relations between torturer and victim. By understanding these, we can begin to appreciate the inevitable resulting harms.

Additionally, many arguments about torture are oddly individualist and consider only the relation between interrogator, victim, and a threatened population. The harms are strangely described as inflicted on isolated subjects, and torture defenders display no understanding of human intersubjectivity. In consequence, the debates become unacceptably abstract and misleading.

As I have mentioned, all the relevant arguments for torture are consequentialist, yet strangely, they never closely analyze the specific empirical consequences of torture. Given that advocates of torture typically claim to be consequentialists, this is surely odd. But the medical, psychological, economic, sociological, and gendered aspects of torture might as well be invisible for all of the attention paid to them in the literature.

Furthermore, as a rule, defenders of torture curiously focus on the ethics of specific decisions or acts of torture, whereby a public official, an interrogator, or perhaps an interrogation team, as representatives of a state, responds to an emergency by choosing the discrete act. They wrongly concentrate on the behaviour of individuals, for in reality, state-sanctioned torture is both deeply institutionalized and a form of group violence. It is inflicted on the bodies and minds of individuals and their social networks, but the ethical issues can be appropriately conceived only as group-on-group violence and oppression.

Both the absence of a careful empiricism and the dearth of attention to questions of gender, race, and cultural difference are deeply problematic for reasons following from the consequentialist point that I have just identified. The abstract character of defences of torture hides precisely torture's most problematic feature: its attack on mental, physical, economic, political, and cultural properties.

METHODOLOGICAL NOTES

Initial Remarks on Consequentialism

Of the three ethical traditions emerging from classical Greece, I consider the arguments for torture that emerge from the utilitarian and virtue-ethical traditions. I do so because the arguments that concern me are all either utilitarian or virtue-ethical.

Michael Gross (2006, 228) and Fritz Allhoff (2005a, 250) both suggest that deontologists could create an argument for torture by defining a set of individuals ("terrorists") who sacrifice their right not to be tortured by virtue of their participation in violent actions. But this case is rarely explored and for good reason: there could not be any of the fair procedures such as due process and competent defence to ensure that only the people who actually belong to this set are tortured. The victims in this case are always suspects and therefore do not demonstrably belong to the set of persons who have sacrificed such a right. The apparatus of deontological politics and ethics is ill-suited to practices and states of affairs that are a priori unfair, as state torture must be. Consequently, theorists must twist deontological principles into an unrecognizable consequentialist shape to support torture.

In any event, the rare cases that do take this line are in reality consequentialist: they invoke state-of-emergency reasoning to permit or excuse the violation of specific rights. Where this happens, however, the theory becomes consequentialist, not deontological. In consequence, the arguments I make in the rest of this book come to bear.

Although by temperament I sympathize with deontological opposition to torture, my strategy is to show that a careful consideration of the consequences of implementing torture *entails* its prohibition in all cases, not its permissibility or justification. Nor can there be any obligation to torture someone else even under emergency conditions. The absolute deontological prohibition of torture is supported by empirical and consequentialist considerations.

No Appeal to Human Rights

In following this strategy, it might seem strange that I do not oppose torture by appealing to human rights. There are reasons for this. The first is that defenders of torture typically accept that every human being has a right not to be tortured, and they agree that this should be enshrined in international law. The debate is not about whether there is such a right but about whether such rights may ever be overridden. Since this is the centre of the debate, we miss the point if we appeal to the human rights of the victims alone in defending the absolute prohibition against torture. Such a defence would be question-begging.

W.D. Ross (1930, 19–20) introduces an important distinction that is relevant here. He speaks of prima facie versus absolute rights. A prima facie right is one that holds provided all things are equal but that may be violated if the appropriate conditions hold. An absolute right, if there is such, would hold come what may and could never be overridden for any reason. Torture advocates explicitly or tacitly maintain the view that the right not to be tortured holds prima facie but may be overridden if needed.

When such a need arises, defenders of torture insist that consequentialist considerations must determine which of the different actions are to be chosen. Hence to absolutely oppose the use of torture, opponents of torture must also be prepared to offer consequentialist arguments as well. Fortunately, there is a great deal of empirical evidence about the extremely destructive effects of torture, and opponents of torture should be prepared to use it to support their case.

This is a useful place to identify a pernicious piece of rhetoric that haunts the debate. Jean Bethke Elshtain (2004, 85) and

Michael Walzer (2004a, 36), among others, speak disparagingly of "doctrinal civil libertarianism" and "absolutism." They argue that there are plenty of people who are so concerned with the purity of their own souls that they are prepared to allow thousands of people to die rather than sully themselves by doing something wrong like torturing. The assumption here is that defenders of the absolute prohibition are morally naive and display no regard for the consequences of their views. Typically, Immanuel Kant is the whipping boy, one frequently regarded as the thinker who so prizes individual dignity that he will allow an entire community to die rather than sacrifice a single individual.

This is a tired caricature of an extremely sophisticated moral position as well as of the absolutist positions opposing torture that derive from Immanuel Kant's work. Its inadequacy can be demonstrated simply by reflecting on the impossibility of forming a categorical imperative to ignore the consequences of one's actions. The first formulation of the categorical imperative requires that "I ought never to act except in such a way that I could always will that my maxim should become a universal law" (Kant 1998, 15). It must be a maxim according to which everyone could act simultaneously. Logically, nobody could desire a law that ignores consequences, for this would be a practice incompatible with human survival and hence could not produce a law for all rational beings. It need hardly be said that such a law would be harmful to human dignity.

It is not that Kant and Kantian deontology reject consequences but that such theorists believe the consequences always have to be subordinate to the highest good. As Thomas Nagel (1979, 58) notes, absolutism sets limits to consequential reasoning. For human rights advocates, especially those influenced by Kant, this greatest good is human dignity. Since torture cannot be reconciled with such a good, it can never be justifiable. But this conclusion is a far cry from a naive concern for the purity of an individual soul.

Absolute opponents of torture share, albeit in quite varying ways, this sense that human dignity is the highest good and not justifiably or excusably violated for any instrumental purpose. But dignity matters consequentially as well as intrinsically. Dignity is minimally a property of individual human beings and their communities, and its violation has far-reaching harmful effects.

In any case, the deep concern that those absolutely opposed to torture have for the consequences of torture is demonstrated by the careful empirical work over the past forty years in systematically working them out. This work is absent from the arguments in favour of its use, apart from a few oblique references. Antitorture literature is generally far more aware of the consequences of torture than any of the essays that defend its use, for it studies and cites the historical and medical cases and uses those to build its position rather than relying on a priori philosophical or legal argument. What marks the work of human rights advocates, then, is not a concern for their own souls but an argued and empirically supported conviction that torture must stop.

I, too, will consider consequences and, in doing so, will employ a level of empirical support that does not occur in any of the defences of torture. In such work, you will find occasional references to the violation of individual dignity, the brutalization of the torturers, risks to civil liberties, and the like. However, you will not find any analysis of dignity. Hence we do not get any conception of what is involved in attacking it. The conception of dignity is curiously and disappointingly individualist as well. Once we abandon the individualist assumption and replace it with a sense of human dignity as culturally and intersubjectively determined, then the consequences of torture are far-reaching and terrible. They are certainly far worse than defenders of torture realize. Their work also provides little or no analysis both of brutalization and of the specific ways torture threatens and inevitably undermines civil liberties. These are serious weaknesses, especially given the gravity of the subject.

My first task, therefore, will be to explore the nature of torture. I offer some reflections on the definition of torture given in the United Nations Convention against Torture. I look at what torture attacks – its targets, its political purposes – and show how the nature and practice of torture entail complex medical and psychological sequelae as well as moral and political damage to individuals, institutions, communities, and societies. The damage that torture inflicts is inevitable and far more serious than defenders of torture appreciate.

Hypothetical Imperatives and Logical Inevitability

Here, some defence of my use of the term "logical inevitability" is necessary since I will regularly claim that certain consequences are

inevitable. Appreciating this requires a brief foray into Kantian ethics, especially the concept of a hypothetical imperative. Unlike a
categorical imperative, a hypothetical imperative is an "if-then"
expression in which the antecedent of the conditional is something
that, considered by itself, need not happen. The reality could be
otherwise. However, in the event that the antecedent of the conditional holds, and in the event that the conditional itself is true, the
consequence inevitably follows.

In Kant's specific discussion, the idea is that if you will a given
end or objective, inevitably you will the means to that end. In Kant's
(1998, 25) words, hypothetical imperatives "represent the practical
necessity of a possible action as a means to achieving something
else that one wills." In the context of torture, these assumptions
include the policy decisions surrounding the decision to employ torture. Suppose the goal is intelligence gathering. If the state requires
some intelligence, and if it decides that torture is a means by which
to acquire the desired information, it will try to find the means that
best ensure success. The state will not just torture but will try to
do so as effectively as possible and will devise strategies to maximize
that outcome. This in turn inevitably generates the institutionalization problems that I discuss in chapters 3 and 4. It is not an accident
that states pour research funds into studying torture. Nor is it an
accident that they suborn medical personnel and others into partic-
ipating. The less institutionalized the torture, the greater the probable
ineffectiveness of its use.

But I also utilize conceptual necessity, especially in chapter 1. I
work with the empirically supported assumption that identity is
intersubjective and infer an inevitable range of consequences that
torture must inflict. The medical literature is rich with accounts of
these effects. Given that torture is designed to break human identity,
and given that all the strategies are different means to achieve this
goal, a vast range of consequences will inevitably follow. Few of
these consequences are even mentioned by protorture literature.
When they are mentioned, little attention is paid to the problems
that these effects pose for any consequentialist calculus. The ethics
of torture, however, require both conceptual and empirical consideration, and thus the medical, psychological, psychosocial, and
political consequences ought to play a crucial role in the debates.

Public officials and policy makers are aware of the points that I
raise here. They know that one cannot just institute a torture

campaign but that it requires considerable institutional and logistical support. Laws either have to be changed or subverted. Torturers have to be trained in their trade and must be able to practise in order to get good at it. Propaganda has to be employed to get public support for violent practices – campaigns in which the public becomes predisposed to support violent and reprehensible means.

Torture is a tactic. It is employed because public figures believe it can help them to achieve various goals. But the instrumental and tactical rationality of torture and its supporting policies should not be confused with moral legitimacy. Although the implementation of torture policies may offer certain tactical advantages for policy makers, the policies nonetheless cause far greater general harms than any benefits that are achieved. Indeed, one of the points I emphasize concerning torture is that it might offer specific tactical benefits for specific individuals or groups but that the political and moral harms to institutions and societies are far greater than defenders of torture realize and inevitably morally outweigh the tactical benefits.

I also intend to demonstrate that, whereas the above general harms are certain and whereas specific harms are probable, the hoped-for good consequences are highly dubious. Not only are they deeply uncertain, but we have absolutely no hard evidence that torture has ever had anything like the success for which torture defenders hope (Wahlquist 2006, xxi). Whatever limited tactical success torture campaigns have achieved is in the context of counter-insurgency and counter-terror campaigns and accompanied by the repression and oppression that these inevitably require.

Prohibition, Obligation, Permission, and Excuse

In the debates about torture, we find frequent discussion on whether torture ought to be absolutely *prohibited*, as human rights activists maintain. We also find some authors like Oren Gross (2004, 1487) arguing that if the circumstances are extreme enough, consequentialist reasoning *obliges* public officials to torture. Gross offers a pragmatic defence of the absolute prohibition but thinks that exceptional circumstances can require its violation. Gross suggests, for instance, that while torture should be absolutely forbidden, a plea of necessity or self-defence might be considered in order to mitigate the sentence of the interrogator. Allhoff (2005a, 246) also speaks occasionally, if perhaps inconsistently, of torture as *permissible*. Or finally, we might consider *excusing* a public official who tortures to prevent a catastrophe.

There is a conceptual tangle here, so I intend first to focus on *prohibition* and *obligation* as the core of the debate. I will define each of these logically and then provide a brief argument for why the issue in the torture debate is prohibition and obligation rather than permission.

Logician Jaako Hintikka (1981, 63) defines *prohibition* in the following way: "Obviously, saying that acts of a certain kind A are forbidden is to say that no act under consideration may be of this kind. In other words, every act under consideration ought to be an omission of A, i.e. every act ought to be an instance of the negation ~A of A." In less formal language, to say that an act is forbidden is to claim that we may never perform such an act. Saying that torture is prohibited entails that we are always obligated not to torture.

By an *obligation,* Hintikka (1981, 63) understands the following: "we are obligated to do A only if *every* act of ours ought to be an instance of A (where 'A' may be replaced by any attribute of acts). There are attributes of acts for which this is not unnatural. For instance, one can say that 'you ought to abstain from stealing' means 'every act of ours ought to be an instance of abstention from stealing.'" To take a Kantian example, we are obligated always to keep our promises. Saying that I am under an obligation to keep my promises entails that I am never permitted to break them. The point is not that I ever have an obligation to make a promise but rather that if I do so, I ought always to keep it.

And finally, Hintikka (1981, 65) defines *permission* in the following way: "The most natural way of explicating the notion of permission seems to be to say that acts of a certain kind are permitted if, in every particular situation, one is allowed to perform an act of this kind." If I am permitted to do something, the action is open to me to perform or not as I desire. When we are permitted to do something, we do not thereby lie under an obligation.

Although Oren Gross, Allhoff, and others who defend torture occasionally talk about the permissibility of torture, their arguments are much stronger than this. They argue for an obligation to torture. I maintain that this is in fact the case for a number of reasons.

Notably, the consequentialist calculations that support arguments for torture do not generate the inference that public officials are permitted to torture a suspect if they have one in custody and an explosion is imminent. The claim is that public officials *ought* to do so. Now, it follows logically that if they are obligated to do something, they are also permitted to perform the same act. But the consequentialist calculations employed by torture defenders are a form of lesser-evils reasoning, which asserts that public officials are morally obligated to choose the lesser of the two evils. This is an a priori truth for those who accept such reasoning. A failure to choose the lesser evil (in utilitarian terms, a failure to maximize the "good") counts as a wrong and is blameworthy.

If the debate were about permissibility, torture advocates would consider it legitimate for a public official to refuse to torture, even though 10,000 lives could be lost as a result. None of the defenders of torture thinks that this would be acceptable. They would blame such an individual for failing to live up to his or her public responsibilities. Furthermore, even in the cases where theorists speak of interrogators having permission to torture, they do not argue that they are permitted to torture if alternatives are available. Rather, this is an issue of necessity and, once again, concerns a supposed obligation to torture.

Another way to consider the point is with reference to the abortion debate: defenders of a woman's right to choose argue that abortion is morally permissible. This means that women ought to be free to choose whether to have an abortion. On the assumption that abortion is permissible, whichever choice they exercise is legitimate. It is clear that nobody argues that women are generally obligated to have an abortion. That would be as much a violation of female autonomy as would be an absolute prohibition against abortions. What this suggests is that if an action is permissible, one is both allowed to do the act and allowed to refrain from carrying it out.

But the arguments for torture are not like this. They all generate a "correct" answer, namely that in certain circumstances torture is morally required to prevent an even greater catastrophe, for they consider the prohibition against torture to hold prima facie. This means that, all things being equal, torture is forbidden. Since it is right to maximize benefits and minimize harms and wrong to maximize harms and minimize benefits, in the relevant emergency circumstances a public official is obligated to override the prohibition and thus to order torture. But "permission" is irrelevant here, and the debate concerns a moral obligation to torture.

Permissibility does come into the torture debates when a given state decides to employ torture and is then confronted with a further dilemma about which techniques, or kinds of torture, are permissible. But this presupposes that torture is both justifiable and in certain situations obligatory. In any event, the torture debate is not fundamentally a debate about technique, even if defenders will typically call for the use of minimally violent techniques. The core debates over torture address whether there ought to be an obligation to torture or whether it is absolutely forbidden no matter what.

On the matter of excusing torture, in chapter 5 I discuss various legal arguments that defend torture. I explore whether it makes sense to speak of an excuse for state torture or whether a society should offer its torturers a self-defence option. I also explore Dershowitz's torture warrants as an alternative proposal for dealing with torture, working with the assumption that moral reflection is primary and that laws ought to follow the ethical arguments. Consequently, my moral argument that torture is never justified and should never be permitted ultimately entails the impermissibility of any laws justifying torture. My aim is to leave no possible space for any moral or legal justification of torture.

Vagueness

In debates about torture, one occasionally encounters worries surrounding the vagueness of the concept. The following remark from Duncan Forrest (1996, ix) is fairly typical: "There is no clear distinction between torture and the limits of legitimate interrogation. What some would regard as normal treatment others would regard as excessive use of force, physical or psychological. This depends to a great extent on the culture in which one is brought up."

A brief excursion into vagueness will help to clarify what is at stake and help us to appreciate the implications of vagueness for thinking about torture. The following is a typical logical definition: "A linguistic expression is said to be vague if there are borderline cases in which it is impossible to tell if the expression applies or does not apply. Vague expressions often allow for a continuous range of interpretations" (Hurley 2003, 75).

The vagueness problem is associated with a classical logical paradox called a "sorites paradox," or the "paradox of the heap." The idea is that if I have a pile of sand consisting of 10,000 grains in front of me, we are entitled to call it a heap. If I remove one grain of sand, we can still legitimately call it a heap. If I keep removing grains of sand from the pile, at some point it will cease to be clear whether the heap remains. Clearly, when I get to the last remaining grain, the pile is no longer a heap. However, if I have two grains of sand, that is obviously not a heap either. If I had a hundred grains of sand, that would be unlikely to be a heap as well. The problem is that there are no clear rules or principles by which we can unambiguously identify when a group of grains of sand constitutes a heap.

Vagueness and sorites considerations are important problems in the debates about torture. The problem has to do with determining where legitimate interrogation practices shade over into torture. It should be pretty clear to just about everyone that burning a captive with a blowtorch over every inch of his or her body would constitute torture. If we played Pantera or some other form of heavy metal music at 130 decibels for twenty-four solid hours to a bound and hooded captive in a room too small to stretch out in, would that count?

If we consider some of the scenes from Michael Winterbottom's film *The Road to Guantanamo* (2006) in company with medical and psychiatric evidence, we realize that compelled exposure to exceptionally loud heavy metal music for extended periods is clearly torture. However, six, five, four, three, or even fewer hours of exposure is also torture, especially if used in combination with other techniques. For example, it is torture to be subjected to such music while having one's hands chained behind the ankles and while being forced almost to kneel in darkness with extremely bright lights flashing intermittently.

A number of appropriate worries arise from vagueness and sorites considerations. One is pragmatic: the boundaries of vagueness can be exploited by public figures for cynical political reasons. This is semantic cynicism, which public figures commonly use to exclude methods that are appalling in their own right from the characterization of torture. Recent US restriction of torture to those methods causing excruciating pain, organ failure, and death is an example (Greenberg and Dratel 2005, 172). In cases like this, the vagueness of the concept is interpreted in an arbitrarily and ignorantly narrow fashion. Doing so offers political advantages to the group employing torture, for it helps them to hide their torturing behind a semantic illusion.

Semantic cynicism is a real problem, but as Christopher Tindale notes (1996, 352), there are also problems of good-faith misinterpretation. In this case, someone might inadvertently torture another or treat him or her in a manner that is cruel, inhuman, or degrading simply because the torturer does not appropriately understand how it is that some borderline practices will count as torture. These are important concerns, but they have to do with empirical application and judgment. They are the difficult and exceptionally important domain of the working human rights activist, the lawyer, the judge, the nurse, the doctor, the psychologist, and others who work with torture.

Although no principled line can be drawn for borderline cases, we in fact have considerable resources and expertise upon which we can draw to make the relevant decisions. A well-staffed human rights committee that was well versed in the aetiology, physiology, and phenomenology of suffering would be well placed to make these judgments. Such a committee's expertise would also require an expertise both in human rights and in international humanitarian law, along with sociological and historical expertise. Moreover, this committee would require the medical and psychiatric expertise of nurses, physicians, and psychiatrists who work with survivors of torture. It is perfectly possible to put together such groups to make the relevant judgments, and human rights nongovernmental organizations and the UN Committee against Torture, which monitors international compliance with the UNCAT, have in fact done so. Borderline cases are an inevitability, however, and the debate about practices is likely to be ongoing and the judgments fallible. They will be open to criticism in light of improved future understanding of torture and its consequences.

However, since the purpose of this book is to refute the arguments for torture, I am content to count as instances of torture the set of practices defined by the United Nations Convention against Torture and interpreted by competent, independent, and honest human rights groups or commissions with appropriate expertise. Vagueness, then, poses no specific problems for the arguments presented here.

In any event, Fritz Allhoff, Michael Gross, Oren Gross, Alan Dershowitz, Richard Posner, and others are arguing for *torture*, not for aggressive interrogation practices. They pay little attention to vagueness problems and thus curiously argue for more than even

Donald Rumsfeld permits in the famous memos documented in *The Torture Papers* (Greenberg 2005, 357–9).

Nevertheless, vagueness is much more problematic for those who advocate torture, for they need to be able to determine which torture techniques their arguments entail and which ought to be excluded. Moreover, they have to worry about a further host of dangerously vague concepts that they also associate with torture. These include, among others, vague classifications like "enemy," "suspect," "victim," and "terrorist."

Vagueness also becomes a major problem once we start worrying about the consequences of torturing people and when we start trying to determine whether it is in fact possible to limit or control the methods and harmful effects of torture. One worry is that vagueness problems may constitute *a priori* barriers to the possibility of control of torture. Such loss of control and other tragic consequences emerge once state-of-emergency reasoning and torture justifications are married to vague concepts. It becomes even more inevitable when we recall that torture policies will have to be applied according to the judgments of local interrogation teams. Since this will vary a great deal from person to person and team to team, the likelihood of unintended and unforeseen suffering becomes probable, if not unavoidable.

The problem is in part that categories like "enemy" are hopeless. Who is the enemy in any given situation? Is it someone who has planted a bomb? Perhaps, but that person is a foot soldier and unlikely to know a great deal. Is it the planners? Most certainly, but how do you find them? They are not the individuals who typically get caught prior to an explosion. What about the person who runs a safe-house? What about family members who might have tacit knowledge? What about family members who know nothing at all but provide necessary protection, emotional aid, food, and logistical support? The sorites sequence becomes particularly tragic when applied in emergency situations and *inevitably* leads to an extension of the class of individuals targeted. A consistent reaction to this logical problem in counter-insurgency warfare is expressed by General Iberico Saint-Jean of Argentina: "First we kill all the subversives; then we will kill their collaborators; then their sympathizers; then ... those who remain indifferent; and finally we will kill the timid" (Marchak 1999, 151). This response simply resolves the problem by drawing the net of complicity broadly.

It is impossible to eliminate vagueness from torture methods or from the categories of those to whom states apply them. Their vagueness, in the context of the prosecution of a counter-insurgency war or some other perceived state of emergency, entails that interrogators will inevitably violate far more people than they might intend. General Saint-Jean's remark is simply one of many historical instances demonstrating that working intelligence officials draw the conclusion that doing so is necessary.

The vagueness of these terms renders it inevitable that those who torture will draw their nets more widely than torture advocates desire. Hence once we recognize the logical status of hypothetical imperatives and the problem of vagueness, we will also recognize the logical inevitability that torture will be widespread, that it will capture a large number of third parties and the irrelevant in its net, and that the restrictions torture advocates place on justifiable torture will fail a priori.

There is an additional kind of vagueness that raises additional problems. This is the problem of the fog of war, which is a different kind of epistemic problem. It is not an issue of conceptual indeterminacy but a consequence of one's having to make decisions under pressing temporal constraints and usually with vastly inadequate information. These conditions make it extremely difficult in practice to distinguish true from false information. Fog-of-war considerations matter because weak or nonexistent information makes it even more difficult to control the use of torture. The fog of war guarantees an increase in the margin of error for torturing individuals who know nothing and further ensures a failure to control torture.

The vagueness problem is acute for torture advocates for an additional reason: the order to torture and the implementation of policies governing torture will have to follow a chain of command that begins with the initial policy maker, passes through a sequence of subordinates, and concludes with the interrogation team. Each member in the sequence will have to make his or her own judgments about the borderline cases, and there are no rules that can be invoked to ensure that the policy maker and the torturer will have the same understanding of the intended torture. The risk of chaos is high, and the probability that the policy maker will order actions that turn out quite differently from anything he or she envisions is similarly enhanced – all because of a basic logical problem married to complex and indeterminate sociological and political circumstances.

CHAPTER OUTLINE

Chapter 1 is the foundation upon which everything else in the book depends. I begin by looking in detail at the definition of torture given in the UNCAT. I discuss the purposes that the definition is intended to serve and examine some criticisms. I argue that it provides a politically essential definition but is nonetheless insufficient for understanding torture. I then establish the essential points about torture. Although they might seem so obvious as to be scarcely worth noting, in the debates they tend to be mentioned and then cast aside without analysis. First, torture is violently coercive. Second, it is an attack on human dignity. Third, an attack on dignity is not an attack on a body per se, or a single subject, but on human intersubjectivity. The consequence of this is that the individualist assumption that motivates the ticking-bomb hypothesis and much of the debate in favour of torture is simply false. It is one of a number of simplifying assumptions whose consequences are pernicious in concealing the real consequences of torture. Fourth, I argue that to properly understand the attack on dignity, we have to appreciate that torture is first and foremost an attack on human identity. In consequence, gender and ethnicity are inevitable targets of the attack. That such large proportions of female and male torture victims and survivors are raped must be wedded to the truth that 100 per cent of torture victims are sexually assaulted. It is essential to understand this given that the medical and psychiatric communities consistently emphasize the break down of the person as a central aim of torture. Sexuality is a cornerstone of human identity and thus an inevitable target of attack. Similar considerations govern the attacks on ethnicity and race. To speak then of torture as anything other than sexist and racist is to completely misunderstand what torture attacks.

Following the discussion of torture as an attack on human dignity, I provide an extended treatment of the political purposes that torture seeks to achieve. One of the main reasons I explore these purposes concerns the work I do later in chapter 4 on the "dirty-hands" problem. An important issue in the torture debates centres on questions of limits. Are there any limits to what state-of-emergency thinking may justify and/or obligate a state to do? Identifying the various purposes served by torture sets the stage for this question by identifying an incomplete but large set of historically real purposes. In chapter 4, I then show how it is that the problem of dirty hands can entail every one of the possible purposes for which torture is used.

By identifying these purposes and pointing back to the discussion about the coercive nature of torture, I also begin the process of undermining a central but incorrect distinction often invoked in the torture debates – the idea that we can speak coherently of a justifiable "interrogational" kind of torture. Having worked through the nature of torture, I demonstrate that the terroristic properties are intrinsic to torture. These abstract distinctions do nothing but sanitize a practice that in reality exceeds any such classification. The same reasoning that licenses the "interrogational" use of torture also supports terroristic and other uses as well, provided the cost-benefit calculations add up in the appropriate way. Consequently, interrogational torture is a vacuous category.

Chapter 2 decomposes the ticking-bomb hypothesis into each of its elements and then analyzes these to demonstrate their conceptual and empirical inadequacies. I argue that every single element of the hypothesis is misconceived and empirically empty and that its ability to generate a conclusion in favour of torture works only as a consequence of its artificiality.

To defend these points I argue the following:

1 That the abstraction of the concepts in the ticking-bomb hypothesis automatically eliminates possible empirical reference.
2 That none of the key terms in the hypothesis are appropriately defined or explored. For example, we do not know what interrogation is or what torture is, nor do we know what it means to call someone an interrogator or a "terrorist."
3 That the language is already so emotionally loaded as to beg the question in favour of the desired conclusion – including words like "terrorist," "innocent," and the like.

I conclude that the ticking-bomb hypothesis is either a purely formal logical game or a source of invalid inferences from a set of nonempirical assumptions that lead to conclusions about moral and political practice that are unjustifiable. In the former case, there is no empirical reference at all, and the argument is unsound and irrelevant for the human rights debates. The latter case is just an instance of bad reasoning.

Chapter 3 explores utilitarianism and torture. I begin by giving an account of three different versions of utilitarianism. I locate utilitarian defences of torture specifically within one of these three versions: the act-utilitarian tradition, which stems from Jeremy Bentham.

I analyze the ways that utilitarians are divided on questions like torture and then devote most of the chapter to carefully mapping the consequences of torture in order to demonstrate that *all* utilitarians ought to oppose the practice. Defenders draw support for torture from act utilitarianism because they pay little attention to the historical realities of torture. That is, they do not study its full consequences. As a result, they draw the range of consequences far too narrowly and thereby skew the calculations in favour of the invalid conclusion that torture can sometimes be justifiable on utilitarian grounds. In contrast, I provide both conceptual and empirical analysis of the specific consequences that state torture entails.

I build on the analysis of harm in chapter 1 by first providing an analysis of the problem of qualitative differences in pain and then deepening our appreciation of the harms of torture. The utilitarian arguments offered for torture reduce all forms of pain to one qualitatively identical kind. But the medical and psychiatric literature emphatically rejects this approach and suggests that the pain-pleasure calculus that utilitarian defenders use to justify torture is simply inadequate.

However, I allow the possibility that utilitarians might find a way to deal with this objection and show that other considerations combine with the problem of qualitative differences to suggest that the inevitable suffering is far worse than torture advocates recognize. For example, I examine some of the empirical evidence supporting the harms that the use of torture imposes on the torturer. I also analyze various ways that the choice to torture entails a wide range of institutional and political changes that themselves are instances of serious political harms.

The harms mentioned in the preceding two paragraphs are, as a class, inevitable, even if specific effects will vary depending on individual psychology and physiology, gender, ethnicity, culture, historical circumstance, economics, and other relevant factors. But I also examine a set of probable harms – morally unacceptable effects that are relatively likely to happen. The probability of these harms could be assessed statistically and historically.

In contrast to the entire set of consequences that I explore, I also note that the consequences that defenders of torture avow to be goods are in fact, on their own account, deeply uncertain and improbable. It is a commonplace even for defenders of torture to accept that its ability to produce reliable results is highly uncertain. Posner's (2004, 294) point is that in the absence of more reliable alternatives, a very uncertain practice is better than nothing. Yet given the certainty of one set of the harmful consequences that I detail, and the more or less high probability of the other set, there is no reason to believe that the hypothetical benefits of using torture could ever outweigh the harms that inevitably result. It also does not help this specific utilitarian case that it is difficult to calculate the consequences of events that have not happened and may never happen. By contrast, we do have considerable empirical evidence to help us to consider the consequences of implementing the state torture of suspects.

In effect, this kind of consequentialist calculation fails to distinguish between harms that are certain or highly probable and those that are vague and uncertain. It treats them all on a par, even though a sophisticated calculation must recognize such differences. It is odd that utilitarian defenders of the use of torture never explore whether it matters that the cost-benefit calculations take into account these logically significant distinctions. On these grounds, I conclude that even act utilitarians ought to reject the use of torture unconditionally, even in states of emergency.

Chapter 4 explores a different kind of consequentialist reasoning. The "dirty-hands" problem emerges from virtue ethics, and although it is also consequentialist, there are a number of significant differences from utilitarian consequentialism. Among other things, the dirty-hands problem makes no appeal to a universal sense of the good and does not invoke the greatest-happiness principle so central to all utilitarian thinking. Rather, the dirty-hands position is concerned with what it calls "tragic-choice" or "lesser-evils" reasoning. The idea is that public figures occasionally and perhaps inevitably find themselves in situations where they have to deliberately perform an evil act in order to prevent some further evil from happening. Given that the consequences of torturing the individual are deemed less horrible than the consequences of failing to meet the needs of public security, dirty-hands theorists argue that there are contexts in which the public figure is morally obliged to torture a suspect.

The work done in chapter 3 has already begun the counter-argument to this position through a careful detailing of consequences. But it is not sufficient to refute this position. Indeed, my strategy is not to deny that tragic-choice situations ever happen. I am prepared to concede that they might. What I intend to show is that even if they do happen, they do not entail the justifiability of torture.

To establish this case, I explore the ways the dirty-hands position, when generalized in the absence of nonderogable human rights, is actually violence-maximizing, not -minimizing. I also explore and criticize some of the proposals that dirty-hands theorists invoke in their attempts to limit the use of torture to solely "necessary" cases, showing in each case why the suggestion is inadequate.

Chapter 5 analyzes and criticizes various specific legal arguments for torture and the suggestions they envision for controlling and limiting torture to only the necessary cases. I consider four specific legal arguments: (1) that it should be excused on grounds of necessity; (2) that interrogators should have available to them the defence of self-defence; (3) that torture should be legalized and controlled; and (4) Oren Gross's (2004) "official-disobedience" model for torture. I maintain that all these arguments fail to understand state torture. In particular, they fail to appreciate its institutional character. Furthermore, I note that state-of-emergency thinking is far more corrosive than torture defenders realize. It builds in a priori the conditions for the violation of the rules and policies established in an attempt to control it. Hence, in the event that one accepts the kind of state-of-emergency thinking on which the arguments depend, all actions might come to be perceived as necessary. The notion that a state can both institute torture policies and morally control them is thus indefensible.

CAUTIONARY REMARKS

The debates over torture are often highly charged and vulnerable to name-calling, *ad hominem* attack, and other unacceptable tactics. I want to emphasize at the outset that I intend to avoid such demonizing. Although I fundamentally disagree with torture, I am not interested in making anyone out to be a moral monster simply because they argue for an evil practice. Torture defenders invoke rich and long-standing moral traditions and deserve fair and charitable treatment. This is especially important since they are aware that the practice they defend is ugly, but they fear that refusing to perform such acts will permit acts to happen that are even more vicious and reprehensible.

Consequently, defenders do not believe that torture is a good thing and are quite emphatic that, all things being equal, they believe it should never be done. The problem is, in their view, that occasionally it is just false that all things are equal. In such circumstances, the normal prohibitions against torture have to be overridden.

I refuse to demonize torturers. Although it is clear that some historical torturers have been sadistic sociopaths, it is also the case that many of them are ordinary human beings caught by terrible circumstances and that others fit the banality-of-evil thesis so beautifully articulated by Hannah Arendt (1977). In the course of torturing, they end up committing extraordinarily evil acts. In turn, some of them have their characters destroyed and become sadists. It is also clear from the medical and psychological evidence, as well as from interviews with former torturers, that they often suffer greatly as a result of their actions. To be sure, they do not suffer to the extent of their victims, but suffer they sometimes do. Given that they implement the policy decisions of others, responsibility and blame do not attach to the torturers alone. Nonetheless, in their own way, they also bear the terrible costs of the evil policy decisions of their superiors.

Furthermore, I do not use loaded language like "terrorist" or "fanatic" because of the demonizing function such terms play in popular discourse as well as in the literature on torture. They scapegoat complex historical individuals and oversimplify difficult historical events and circumstances. The terms are irredeemably vague and are unacceptable in a careful philosophical or political discussion of torture. They conceal complicated socio-political realities such as oppression as well as longstanding political struggles, economic grievances, and the like of real people. They also function tacitly to beg the question of right in favour of those who want to torture.

My own chosen terms are the more neutral "state actor" and "nonstate actor." One of the unfortunate features of the arguments for torture is that they are available to both state and nonstate actors, especially once one concedes that states do not have any prior moral or political privilege to commit extreme violence. This is especially pressing in the context of the oppression of ethnic groups and minorities, which generates so much of the violence for which torture is then considered a solution. Once that happens, both Jean-Paul Sartre (2004, 233) and Michael Walzer (2004b, 64–5) can use the same argument for extreme violence, even though the former speaks on behalf of the oppressed and disenfranchised of the world, while the latter defends the use of torture by public officials of states tasked with a responsibility to protect their public from exactly the downtrodden and disenfranchised who commit counter-state violence.

I distinguish between home, target, and third-party populations. The home population is the group of which the torturer is a member and that the torturer perceives him or herself to be defending. The target population is the ethnic, political, or other relevant group that the torturer believes poses a threat to the home population. Third-party populations are any group that is neither a home nor target group.

THE ROLE OF HISTORICAL EXAMPLES

When I introduce extreme cases for discussion, I do so not to suggest that defenders of the use of torture would defend these events. In fact, I am confident that they would be horrified by them. However, I introduce the cases both to help deepen our understanding of the nature and structure of torture as well as to reflect on its targets. It is also worth asking whether the arguments that torture advocates employ actually exclude these cases or whether such horrors are in fact logical consequences of the employed reasoning. I argue that the reasoning used in the first place to justify torture also entails the most extreme cases provided that the right empirical circumstances obtain. Indeed, I employ such cases because they help to demonstrate that the arguments for torture are far more permissive than defenders realize.

Additionally, the historical examples play a cautionary role. They help to demonstrate the unsoundness of the arguments for torture. The historical details display the grim reality of torture. The history of implementation provides no evidence that it is successfully controlled at all. There is no significant evidence of torture ever having been carried out under the conditions that torture defenders envision. Given that state and other political torture must be institutional, it can never be conducted according to its defenders' ideals. But the argument that it is possible to limit the violence of torture also collides with harsh empirical evidence that this has in fact never been the case as well as with plenty of evidence to suggest otherwise. The history suggests that in the absence of an absolute ban on torture accompanied by effective monitoring of police and intelligence practices, it will spin out of control.

I do not consider other arguments for torture, such as Steven Kershner's (1998) position that we ought to introduce torture as a technique of punishment. Nor do I explore older theological arguments that torture might be necessary to save the soul of an individual. The former belong to the theory of punishment and raise the question of what, if anything, a person convicted of a crime may be said to deserve to suffer. The latter are theological arguments and equally not relevant to the subject matter of this book. I think both are bad arguments, but this stance requires another discussion.

I do not address a central, and perhaps even more pressing, moral problem: that of the torture of inmates in police custody or in prisons. Amnesty International (2000, 12) notes that as a matter of fact the greatest amount of torture that happens in the world takes place in prisons under lawful custody (even though such torture is usually illegal). At least as important a moral issue in its own right, the ethics of the torture of police suspects and convicted prisoners is thankfully not a popular subject of debate. Kershner is the only exception of which I am aware.

Occasionally, I am critical of "slippery-slope" arguments against torture – not because I think that their conclusions are wrong but because they are insufficiently strong to generate an absolute prohibition. As inductive arguments, they will always leave open the illusion that some new regulation or policy, as yet undiscovered, might be able to prevent the slide into uncontrolled violence.

There is a great deal at stake morally, politically, and legally in this debate. The nonderogability clause of the UNCAT is undermined by the protorture arguments. Similarly, the worldwide struggle to reduce and ultimately put an end to torture is lost if there are moral arguments in favour of its use.

1

Understanding Torture

So what is torture? I have already noted some logical worries about
the concept – that it is vague, for example. Nonetheless, a considerable amount of conceptual, medical, historical, and legal expertise
has been devoted to the subject. Consequently, we have excellent
resources with which to work.

To narrow the subject, I want to address an important remark
by W.E. Twining (1978, 158). He warns us to be wary of thinking
that there is a simple single problem that definitions of torture
attempt to capture, noting that it refers in fact to a variety of serious
human rights infringements. Too much emphasis on any of the classic properties taken to be essential to torture will lead us to miss
other cases of political torture that we need to be able to understand. So even what might seem like the obvious claim that torture
is against the interest of its victims still encounters the historical
and occasionally still-existent assertion that the suffering is inflicted
for the good of the victim. In the medieval era some people believed
this would save the soul of the individual from eternal damnation.
But even today, some officials apparently claim that at least part of
their violence is inflicted for the sake of those they harm (Carlson
2006b, 68).

Twining is right to emphasize the complexity of the problem and
the risks of definition. But it is important also to recognize the
necessity of narrowing a definition. Any given attempt is going to
be vulnerable to counter-examples of cases that we would recognize
as torture but that do not fit the definition. Michael Davis (2005,
163), for example, worries that the United Nations Convention
against Torture (UNCAT) is too narrow because it excludes torture

by illegal organizations and nonstate actors and does not recognize the torture of animals. Likewise, Catherine MacKinnon (1993, 25) warns us against refusing to consider as torture the abuse of women and other misogynist violence merely because it is not carried out by state agents. Such abuse is torture, and she is right to point to various forms of state involvement in it. She also gives us reasons for treating with great care the distinction between state torture and that committed by nonstate actors. We cannot treat any of these as apolitical: "A reason often given or implicit in considering atrocities to women not human rights violations, politically or legally, is that they do not involve acts of states. They happen between non-state actors, in civil society, unconscious and unorganized and unsystematic and undirected and unplanned" (26).

I agree with MacKinnon that all torture is political and that all acts of torture are human rights violations, just as I agree with Davis that there are other forms of intersubjective abuse that can legitimately be regarded as torture. But the specific debate here is one concerning the behaviour of state agents. Alan Dershowitz, Fritz Allhoff, Richard Posner, and the others who defend torture have in mind only those cases in which a state agent tortures for the sake of national security. A narrower definition of torture is needed to fit the scenario they envision.

Since the concern of this book is state torture, it is appropriate to exclude from consideration other abuses that are legitimately defined as torture, like the torture of animals. The latter issues introduce additional important political complications and deserve additional analysis.

An appropriate understanding of torture has to respect the structure and practice of torture if it is to be adequate to the subject matter of human rights work. The distinction between torture and cruel, inhuman, and degrading treatment is a useful starting point.

THE DISTINCTION BETWEEN TORTURE AND CRUEL, INHUMAN, AND DEGRADING TREATMENT

We have to be precise about the nature of torture and pay attention to a wide range of sources in order to appreciate its consequences. But we also have to be wary of the distinction between torture and cruel, inhuman, and degrading treatment. It is not uncommon to hear people remark that torture is more severe than inhuman and degrading treatment. "Severity" is vague in its own right, so this is not a good way to distinguish between torture and cruel, inhuman, and degrading treatment. The latter can be just as violent and even cause more suffering than some forms of torture. Sir Nigel Rodley (2006, 111), a former United Nations special rapporteur on torture, describes a visit to a Russian jail in 1994 in which between 90 and 120 people were imprisoned in a cell designed to hold 30 at most. The sufferings experienced by those prisoners over a multiweek or multimonth period may well match or exceed those inflicted during torture, even though the neglect is a consequence of inadequate resources and institutional indifference rather than intent. In any event, we should be cautious in even placing these two on a common severity scale. Both categories include extraordinary violence. The wisdom of international law is clear here, as the UNCAT forbids both.

There are further problems associated with this distinction. John T. Parry (2006, 8) warns of the danger that the distinction allows public officials to permit reprehensible interrogation practices precisely because there is no nonderogability clause for cruel, inhuman, or degrading practices. To do so, they simply take advantage of the semantic vagueness of the distinction between torture and cruel, inhuman, or degrading treatment. Once we recognize that the two classes of evil acts cannot be defined in terms of such a severity scale, it is a little more difficult morally to support such cynicism.

Here, we should recall that we are dealing with concepts whose borders are murky. The lesson to draw is that we should be cautious about a priori generalizations about horror. Judgments as to whether it is worse to be tortured or treated in a cruel, inhuman, or degrading manner are difficult and are in any case not important. They are two related yet distinct classes of evils, and both are wholly immoral and unacceptable.

UNDERSTANDING TORTURE EMPIRICALLY

If we want to understand torture, we need to understand the practice fully. There is no point in either defending or opposing it if we have no idea what we are talking about. We need to be able to identify the properties essential to torture and be able to distinguish them from those that are accidental. Once we understand the essential properties of torture, it is possible to show how its historical consequences are inevitable rather than accidental. By showing this, we can begin to grasp why the cost-benefit calculus used to defend torture fundamentally fails to understand either torture or its consequences.

Existing defences of torture universally neglect to examine the medical or psychological literature. Furthermore, they examine only anecdotal historical evidence if they look at it at all. This leads defenders to construct conclusions about torture and its harms that are simply false. By carefully examining such sequelae, I utilize widespread and unified empirical support for my analysis of the nature of harms as well as for my claims about the extensive consequences of assaulting human dignity. One conclusion I draw is that torture is to be understood not only in terms of the violence of the torture chamber but also in terms acknowledging that the suffering inflicted extends across the communities to which torture victims and survivors belong and into subsequent generations.

Moreover, although defenders of torture concede that it is an assault on human dignity, lack of attention to psychology and sociology means that they do not understand what it means to assault dignity. In the analyses they provide, they focus only on the dignity of an abstract human subject. But this is a weak fiction bearing no relation to the violence inflicted by actual torture. Torturing one person simultaneously inflicts terrible suffering on entire communities. It is not the case that the only victim of torture is the person who sits in the chamber. To be sure, he or she is the primary victim and suffers more than others, but the others are severely tormented as well – in a host of identifiable and carefully documented ways. Yet the consequential calculations of the usual arguments for torture give the impression that it is a matter of the harm of one against the harm of many. The reality is far uglier than that.

Consideration of the sequelae and purposes of torture provides additional evidence against the claim that absolute opponents of torture display a naive concern for the purity of their own souls. The work detailing the consequences of torture has been done by human rights activists, not by those who support torture. Far from worrying about the state of their own souls, they are deeply concerned for the wellbeing of their society, for potential victims within their society, and for the suffering of third parties.

I need to introduce an important caveat here. I do not develop a full-blown theory either of human dignity or of self-hood. Both these subjects are closely related and crucial in their own right. But they require a distinct meta-ethical and anthropological analysis that is beyond the scope of this book. Consequently, I am going to allow the intersubjective and social consequences simply to emerge from anecdotes, witness statements, and medical and psychological evidence.

CAUTIONARY REMARKS ON THE UNCAT DEFINITION OF TORTURE

In arguments both for and against torture, it is not uncommon to find authors introducing the subject of their papers, quoting the convention definition, and then providing analyses of the definition itself. I do not want to suggest that it is wholly wrong to do this. Nonetheless, there are limitations to the UNCAT definition. It does not help us to understand the nature or structure of torture. Hence if we do not explore torture more deeply, we will fail to investigate additional morally crucial issues.

Article 1 of the United Nations Convention against Torture defines torture as follows:

> The term "torture" means any act by which severe pain or suffering, whether physical or mental, is intentionally inflicted on a person for such purposes as obtaining from him or a third person information or a confession, punishing him for an act he or a third person has committed or is suspected of having committed, or intimidating or coercing him or a third person, or for any reason based on discrimination of any kind, when such pain or suffering is inflicted by or at the instigation of or with the consent or acquiescence of a public official or other person acting in an official capacity. It does not include pain or suffering arising only from, inherent in or incidental to lawful sanctions.

I want to highlight several points. Notably, the convention requires intent on the part of the interrogator. Torture is not something that happens inadvertently but must be planned and carried out for some specific purpose. The list of possible purposes is brief and not intended to be exhaustive. But it tacitly acknowledges that public officials torture one party to get at others and thus presupposes the sociality of the victims of torture. It is not concerned with sadistic tortures, where pain is inflicted for its own sake. It also highlights the role of public officials or persons acting in official capacities. This allows the convention to include the activities of mercenary interrogators paid by governments to perform actions that, for various reasons, these governments do not wish to be seen performing themselves. Furthermore, the convention does not cover the punitive sanctions that specific governments may inflict on lawfully convicted individuals.

Article 2 of the convention states that the prohibition against torture is nonderogable. Hence no exceptional circumstances whatsoever – whether a state of war, a threat of war, internal political instability, or any other public emergency – may be invoked as a justification of torture. The debate about torture, in many ways, is really about article 2 since defenders of torture both accept the UNCAT definition and agree that torture should be generally prohibited. But they reject the nonderogability clause and thus disagree with the claim that public emergencies cannot be invoked to justify the use of torture.

I should emphasize that the UNCAT definition is a theoretical definition designed to help human rights activists, lawyers, public officials, and other interested individuals to identify cases of torture and distinguish them from other related acts such as those involving cruel, inhuman, and degrading treatment, acceptable forms of interrogation, and the like. It thus serves an ostensive function by aiding in the specification and identification of prohibited acts. But it does not tell us about the nature of torture, how it functions, or what it attacks, nor does it identify any of torture's structural properties. We need a great deal more than this definition if we are to understand the harms that torture inflicts. But reflection on the UNCAT definition alone will not help us to understand these harms and hence will not allow us sufficiently to understand why torture is so repulsive and why it should always be forbidden. For example, the UNCAT definition presupposes that it is wrong to attack human dignity but does not tell us anything about the nature of dignity. Without an appropriate understanding of dignity, we will draw false conclusions about the kinds and extent of harms.

If we are not careful to recognize that human beings are fundamentally social and that personal identity is intersubjectively constituted, we will to fail to identify the range of inevitable and probable harms that result from torture. Furthermore, since political torture is fundamentally an attack on individual identity, no amount of study of the UNCAT could tell us what happens to the victim or the torturer. Nor can we learn anything about the nature of the wrong that is done in breaking down an individual's identity. These are important considerations and indicate why the UNCAT definition is insufficient for generating arguments for or against torture. One must be aware of it as an important and essential human rights tool, but it presupposes the arguments against torture rather than shedding light on them. Hence in addition to understanding the UNCAT, a great deal more work has to be done to understand the moral complexities surrounding torture.

Moreover, although the UNCAT definition aims to be comprehensive by including all purposive torture, it cannot help us to rank the different aims (as defenders of torture wish to do in their hope that interrogational torture can be morally acceptable). It is neutral on all these different reasons, rightfully condemning them all. But without examining at least some of the purposes for which torture is utilized and without exploring the possibility that there might be an acceptable type of torture, we will be unable to determine whether it is coherent to define torture in terms of a given purpose. By exploring both the structure of torture and its properties and by examining the historical purposes for which torture is used, I demonstrate that there is no such preferred class of torture. This analysis is thus crucial to undermining the concept of purely interrogational torture.

ESSENTIAL PROPERTIES OF TORTURE

Prior to examining these properties, I believe it is essential to take account of two important remarks by Susan Brison. In her remarkable book *Aftermath: Violence and the Remaking of the Self* (2002, 6–7), she explores the violence and harms of rape and warns against the too-hasty assumption that they are easily comprehended or calculated. She criticizes utilitarian philosopher Ross Harrison for making such assumptions, arguing that it is, in fact, an extremely complex issue. She insists that such comprehension requires conceding the moral significance of first-person narratives (29). Otherwise, the specificity of the harms cannot be recognized. This criticism also applies when we seek to understand the harms of torture.

In exploring the ways torture harms specific torture victims and survivors, as well as in examining the intersubjective relational networks within which victims and survivors live, I do not maintain that the account of suffering is complete: it is not, and I doubt that it could be. Nor do I suggest that the experience of torture and its aftermath is identical for every torture survivor. But I do insist upon the inevitability of wide-ranging suffering for the victim of torture, the torture survivor, and broader communities, even though the precise experience of suffering may vary considerably depending on individual and cultural factors.

I also want to emphasize that just as harm is a complex matter, so is the closely related concept of dignity. Everyone concedes that torture is an assault on dignity, but there is no sustained analysis of it and, consequently, no understanding of the intimate relation between assaults on dignity and the harms that result. Although I do not have the space to analyze first-person anecdotes in detail, I also accept Brison's point that they matter philosophically. Where possible I integrate first-person accounts and witness statements and provide an interpretation of salient details. First-person accounts provide examples of harms that are unavailable elsewhere and thus help us to have a richer sense of the damage inflicted by torture.

Forensic human rights anthropologist Eric Stener Carlson (2006b, 54) asserts that torture is first and foremost coercive, an act of domination and self-assertion performed by members of one group on others under conditions of political uncertainty. Political torture is, as the UNCAT definition suggests, always purposive. It does not include the kinds of tortures that might be the random products of a deranged mind but is always carried out for the sake of the achievement of some political goal. Since such torture is inevitably nonconsensual, torture is essentially coercive. As everyone will concede, this is absolutely incompatible with respect both for autonomy and for dignity.

Here, we should resist the temptation to reach for some claimed larger moral goal as a justification and to think that the justification is part of the nature of torture. It is not. Such justifications explain why some governments and nonstate actors use torture. But the question of what torture is must be distinguished logically from the question of why torture might be used. "Moral" justifications do not alter the fact that torture essentially involves an act of domination in which the will of an interrogation team is imposed on the mind and body of a suspect. Defenders of torture recognize this.

What they fail to concede is that the coercion is far more complicated and that it involves struggles between competing political groups. Coercion is exercised on the entire opposing community, not simply on the specific victim.

Quite often in public and academic discourse, we encounter a debate about the distinction between physical and psychological torture. Richard Posner (2004, 293), for example, maintains that we should "respect the line that separates psychological from physical coercion, and permit it to be crossed only *in extremis.*" He believes that physical torture is worse than psychological torture yet displays no evidence that he has studied the medical or psychological impacts of torture or even read any survivors' accounts or witness statements. Similarly uninformed is Jean Bethke Elshtain (2004), who incorrectly believes that psychological torture is "torture lite" and who cites Mark Bowden, again incorrectly, to the effect that these do no lasting physical harm (85). She also believes that allowing shouted insults to count as torture undermines "those distinctions on which the law and moral philosophy rest" (79). She displays the same lack of awareness of the medical, psychological, and survivor literature as Posner. It is striking that her analysis is couched in terms of everyday experience of insults, whereas the use of insults in torture involves a shattering of the everyday world. She seems unaware of the differences that context makes.

Andrew Moher (2004, 484) displays a similar misunderstanding in believing that it is possible to isolate a torture technique that lacks long-term consequences. He envisions as an example "the insertion of a long needle under the finger nail, intended to cause excruciating pain but no lasting damage." He can make this claim only because he is unfamiliar with the medical literature on the impacts of torture. Like the other authors I have mentioned, he fails to understand the central point that torture is an attack on identity with inevitable long-term consequences, regardless of whichever specific techniques one decides to employ. Just like Posner, he provides no argument to support his assertion. They both tacitly invoke the vagueness problem. Neither pays any attention to the context and structure of torture. They treat torture ostensively, defining it in terms of specific techniques, and thus fail to understand that it is far more complicated.

These falsehoods and oversimplifications have spin-off harmful effects. Wrongheaded debates arise over whether physical is worse than psychological torture and whether psychological methods

should even be considered torture at all. From the standpoint of
the violence and suffering that torture inflicts, this is not a meaningful distinction. Since political torture is fundamentally an attack
on the mind of the suspect, these categories merely distinguish
between the different ways public officials try to destroy the human
mind. Hence both are psychological. But likewise, since psychological methods have physiological consequences, they are both examples of physical torture as well. Before I defend both of these claims,
I will provisionally distinguish between the two forms of torture.

PHYSICAL TORTURE
AND PSYCHOLOGICAL TORTURE

Physical torture attacks the surfaces and internal organs of the body.
It inflicts direct and identifiable damage on the neurological system,
the genitals (both internally and externally), and the extremities.
Physical torture tends to leave easily discernible medical sequelae.
If an interrogator burns a victim's genitals with a cigarette, the scars
will remain for the rest of the individual's life. Falanga attacks the
feet of a victim with blunt objects, producing bruising, broken
bones, scarring, neurological damage, and other assessable effects.

In popular culture, when people think of torture, they imagine
such visceral cases of physical torture. Psychological torture, by comparison, attacks the mentality of the victim. It must involve a certain
amount of physicality as well (after all, interrogators have to use
force to restrain and shackle victims into stress positions or to compel
them to stand for long periods of time), but above all, psychological
methods aim at the person's psyche and seek to destroy the psychological world of the victim. The so-called "five techniques" employed
by the British army in Northern Ireland and by other military and
intelligence services the world over are instances of psychological
methods. Prolonged hooding, enforced stress positions and standing,
exposure to extremes of heat, cold, and/or loud noise, inadequate
food provision, and sleep deprivation are all psychological methods.
And so is enforced isolation of the victim.

Physical and psychological methods are often combined, and
many forms of torture such as rape and sexual assault attack both
at the same time and consequently do not fit clearly into either
camp. While the distinction is vague, people seem intuitively to
recognize physical methods and to treat them as worse. But can

we really defend this claim? Are physical methods "worse" than psychological methods?

The answer is negative. Tom Malinowski (2006, 140–1) notes that stress positions were among the most feared among survivors of North Korean Gulags. They were simply compelled to stand absolutely still for hours until they collapsed from exhaustion. Lois-Ann Lorentzen (1998, 194) reports that one consequence of long-term hooding, experienced by Ana Guadeloupe Martinez in El Salvador, was a series of eye infections. John Conroy (2000, 6) remarks that combinations of psychological torture created a state of psychosis with long-term psychological impacts on the torture victim. Torture survivor Jim Auld claimed that the recurrent loud noise was the worst feature of his situation. And Paddy Joe Mclean, "a schoolteacher from County Tyrone, heard funeral hymns, saw his own casket and a firing squad, and at one point forgot who he was, believing himself to be a farmer from Enniskillen whom he had met only once. His tongue was so swollen from lack of water that he thought he would choke on it, and he later described trying to 'vomit his tongue'" (8).

Michael Ratner and Ellen Ray (2004, 39) remark on the devastating effects of hopelessness among the victims of Guantanamo Bay. The worst problems are not the physical violence and abuse but the belief that they will never escape the prison:

The Red Cross has said one of the most psychologically devastating things happening to people in Guantanamo is the notion that they have reached a dead end, that there is no way out. The psychological harm is horrendous. In fact, one of the threats employed to make prisoners in Iraq talk, even after they had been subjected to abuse and torture, was to threaten them with Guantanamo, because everybody understood that there was little or no chance of ever getting out of there.

Inge Lunde and Jorgen Ortmann (1992, 322) note that the use of swearing was particularly devastating for some of the clients of their clinic:

Our experience shows that underneath these words often lurks psychological sexual torture which the client felt was the worst torture: "Your mother is a whore, you are not a man, you are homosexual, everyone will be disgusted with you."

Ana Guadeloupe Martinez (Lorentzen 1998, 197) also stressed that verbal references to rape and other sexual abuse were some of the most horrific experiences she had, a point echoed by Gill Hinshelwood (1996, 191). Eric Lomax (1995, 138) describes how his imagination of torment was a worse tormentor than his torturers could ever be.

Mike Jempson (1996, 67) cites a particularly horrific case of psychological torture – one that shows the vagueness of the distinction between physical and psychological torture. It also shows that both physical and psychological methods, insofar as we can pragmatically distinguish them, are perfectly compatible and occur in the same act:

> Soldiers from a counter-insurgency brigade in Colombia broke into a house in Sabaneta, Santander department, during November 1992. While her husband was being beaten, Sonebia Pinzon was taken outside and raped in front of her three year old son. She could hear her two year old daughter Marcela screaming inside. The toddler was found semi-conscious and bleeding: she too had been raped.

The torture survivor in this case was violated in multiple ways. The husband received an undetermined physical beating. Ms Pinzon's suffering was exceptionally complex. Her own beating and sexual assault were one violation. The damage done to her three-year-old son by being compelled to watch the sexual assault was his own special psychological torture. She was additionally psychologically devastated by the knowledge that her son had to witness this. She underwent further hell in hearing the suffering of her daughter. The attempt to clearly distinguish physical from psychological torture, as well as to determine who was "really" tortured, is vacuous. All of them were tortured – in multiple vicious ways.

Dinah Pokempner (2006, 160) identifies some of the reasons behind the increasing use of "psychological" torture methods. Non-physical methods leave no marks and thus are easier for governments to conceal. This is the case even though they can psychologically destroy and occasionally kill the victim. In any event, we should not be surprised at the emergence of psychological methods because the point of state torture is to break the will and identity of a person. Since political torture is above all an activity aimed at compelling a person against his or her will, refined torture methods are just additional weapons in a torturer's arsenal.

If nothing else, this evidence demonstrates that psychological methods are at least as bad as physical ones. If the testimony of torture survivors as well as of the doctors and psychologists who treat them is not sufficient to refute the belief that only "physical" methods count as torture, I doubt that anything could be sufficient. The available evidence demonstrates as conclusively as is imaginable that psychological methods are at least as bad as physical ones. The testimony both of torture survivors and of their doctors and psychologists refutes any counter-claim. But we also have to recognize that *all* torture is psychological. The medical and psychiatric literature displays quite a remarkable unity here (Kordon et al. 1992, 440; Bustos 1992, 333; Carlson 2006a, 19; Somnier et al. 1992, 57; Seelmann 1991, 33; Jaffe 1991, 59; Fabri 2001, 453; Skylv 1992, 38; Denford 1996, 155; Salimovich, Lira, and Weinstein 1992, 78). Political torture, the kind that is at issue in the current debate, is always an attack on the mind of the individual. It does not matter whether the torturer uses a hood or a kick in the genitals. All methods attack the mind. Again, this is what distinguishes the political torture of human beings from the sadistic torture of animals. To attack the individual politically is to attack his or her entire personality. I will further explore this later in this chapter, but suffice it to say at this point that the distinction between physical and mental torture designates little more than that some tortures leave discernible surface scars on their victims and some do not.

THE THEATRICALITY OF TORTURE

That torture attacks the mind explains what might otherwise seem a curious universal feature of torture – its theatricality. Elaine Scarry (1985, 27–8) remarks on the strange performative features of torture: it is something that is always acted out. It is intensely symbolic and metaphor-laden. William Cavanagh (1999, 12) describes it as a "perverted liturgy" that transforms a true community into an atomized aggregate. Marcelo Suarez-Orozco (2004, 385) emphasizes that torture is never merely an instrumental act but always laden with symbolism, a polysemantic ritual. For both Scarry and Suarez-Orozco, the use of torture plays an inverting role in transforming the fear born by the interrogators into an assertion of their power over the suspect. Torture happens because of some cluster of fears – perhaps of terrorist threats, of pressure from higher up for intelligence, of inadequate performance leading to reduced possibility of promotion. There can be many reasons. The assertion of power through torture, in their view, is a way to combat such fears and impotence.

Metaphors describing the interrogation chamber as a "production room," "cinema," or "stage" are prevalent. Considerable preparations are needed if one is to organize an effective torture chamber. In order to best exploit the fears and weaknesses of specific suspects, the chamber needs to be arranged much as a stage is arranged in theatre to generate some desired symbolic effect. The political fear of "terrorists" and "subversives" is eliminated through a symbolic reduction of the suspect. In the Argentinean case that Suarez-Orozco describes, much of the specific symbolism surrounds the castration and resulting impotence of the male suspect.

Given that torture is psychological by nature, even if the means can vary from overtly physical to non-skin-damaging methods, we need to recognize the inevitability of such symbolism and theatricality. Torture is intended to manipulate emotions and produce fear for some specific political purpose(s), so the productive element of torture is essential to its nature.

THE ASYMMETRICALITY OF TORTURE

Torture is essentially psychological and theatrical. A further relevant structural property is its asymmetricality. Intuitively obvious, this point is echoed in the medical and psychological literature. It has important consequences for thinking about the nature of torture. Mary Fabri (2001, 453) describes how the torturer "dictates every aspect of the victim's life, stripping the individual of his or her personal integrity or agency." Michael Davis (2005, 164) notes that the powerlessness is displayed in two ways: through physical restraints and through the creation of an intellectual helplessness in which nothing the suspect does can make any difference to the outcome or end of the interrogation. Susan Hawthorne (2005, 41) describes the helplessness of the torture victim epistemically: "But the thing about torture is that you do not know whether you will be alive at the end of the day. You do not know when it will end. It is more than just 'powerlessness'; it is subjugation, degradation, abandonment, and dehumanization." Whatever the torturers might say to the victim, he or she is in no position to judge truth or falsehood. The judgments he or she might make are irrelevant to any determination of when the torture will end, so the torture situation severs any possible epistemic link between knowledge and the victim's power to escape the torture situation. The torturers exploit the powerlessness and ignorance of the victim for a range of purposes, but the victim can do nothing to end the torture.

I do not mean to say that the asymmetricality of torture means resistance is impossible. Quite the contrary, resistance to torture seems to be fairly common. But the point is not that the torturer is all-powerful and capable of imposing his or her will on a completely empty and helpless suspect; rather the "choices" a suspect makes about how to respond to the torture, whether to resist or to comply, have no causal role whatsoever in the determination of when the torture will end. Such decisions are entirely at the whim of the torturer. Furthermore, as John T. Parry (2004, 154) notes, any attempt at resistance by a torture victim entails the possibility of an escalation of the violence. Whether victims acquiesce early in the torture or resist, they are tortured, and the torture does not cease because of any act of theirs. It is a decision solely of the torturer.

Even compliance with the stated wishes of the interrogator is not causally relevant to determining when the torture will end. The power to end torture lies solely with the interrogation team. Neither yielding apparently desired information nor behaving in some way believed likely to end the torture is necessary or sufficient. It is perfectly possible for the torture to continue regardless of the behaviour of the victim. The interrogator may doubt any yielded information. The interrogator might have further goals in play of which the victim is unaware. The interrogator might be sadistic and torture further regardless of any acquired intelligence. It is false to think that by any intention or action the victim causes the end of the torture. This is determined only by satisfaction of the desires and interests of the torturer and interrogation team. As Jose Saporta Jr and Bessel van der Kolk (1992, 155) remark, there is an essentially arbitrary and uncontrollable aspect to torture that is completely beyond the torture victim's control. The victim is incapable of predicting what will happen and wholly at the mercy of the torturer. The suspect is powerless to end the torture; whatever resistance is available has to do with the preservation of character and personal integrity against the assaults. The torturer alone has the power to determine the length and kinds of torture.

In addition to creating a theatrical situation involving an extreme power imbalance, the torturers also seek to structure the situation so as to maximize the confusion and disorientation experienced by their victims. Saporta and van der Kolk (1992, 152) observe that "The experience of torture is incomprehensible, which is compounded by the fact that the torturer structures the environment to maximize confusion. Unfamiliarity of the environment, unpredictability, blindfolding, and seclusion all undermine the victim's ability to make sense of the experience. As prior schemas of the self and the world are shattered by torture, the torturer can impose new organizing schemas of the self and others." Other properties can easily be added. Isolation is essential to torture, as the victim is purposefully separated from friends and family. Even the victim tortured in front of family and friends is relevantly isolated, as no aid or meaningful communication is possible. Commonly, torture victims have no idea of their location and are stripped of their sense of time. They often have no idea of the identities of their torturers. All of these add to the disorientation and destruction of the world. Successful use of torture takes advantage of such world-destroying properties to wreck the will of a victim.

These reflections on fundamental properties of torture add up to empirical and conceptual support for Elaine Scarry's most crucial contribution to our understanding of torture: that it is by nature an attack on the entire structure of the torture victim's world. It is psychological and symbolic by nature. It creates a fictional structure, a reality or world completely different from any of the usual associations, norms, and values that define the life of nontortured individuals. By design it undermines the victim's world through disorientation, isolation, and the infliction of specific forms of suffering – all for the sake of the destruction of identity and the imposition of new schemas of self and others.

ATTACKING DIGNITY

I have already mentioned that defenders of torture do not closely analyze what it means to attack dignity. They are aware that torture violates it, but their failure means that they are unable to recognize the extent of the violence that torture involves. They also implicitly adopt anthropologically indefensible individualist assumptions about human beings. Although I reject such individualism in favour of an intersubjective model of human being and dignity, I will begin with the primary victim of torture – the individual actually imprisoned and tortured – and explore some of the ways that torture attacks his or her identity. The victims of torture suffer the worst effects and are the primary subjects to whom we are morally responsible. But the suffering and evil generated by torture extend well beyond them. We are responsible for preventing the additional suffering as well.

Individual Considerations

Political torture is an attack on human identity. It seeks to break down a personality and reconstruct it in a fashion suitable for the realization of the desires of the torturing agents and institutions. But what is going on? What does it mean to say that torture attacks individual identity? We have already seen that political torture is fundamentally aimed at the mental. Being essentially coercive, it involves the deliberate and systematic violation of the will, desires, and choice of the torture victim. Everyone will concede that political suspects are not tortured consensually. Hence anyone in the Kantian tradition will already be opposed to torture on this ground alone. As a dignity and will violation, torture cannot possibly be justified to the person on whom it is inflicted. But those who defend the use of torture concede this. So simply acknowledging that torture violates an individual agent and cannot be reconciled with this agent's will or desires is not, by itself, sufficient to generate a refutation of the arguments for torture.

To achieve this aim, we need to examine carefully the consequences of assaulting dignity by torturing. As mentioned, torture assaults the body of the victim in various ways. Among other things, it attacks the senses and seeks to strip those senses of their normal worldly references. In doing so, torturers seek to produce the illusion that the body is the source of the harm to the mind. It creates an odd mind-body split in which the victim's own body is perceived as the origin and cause of the suffering. For example, in some stress positions, the torturer does not lay a hand on the victim once he or she has been compelled into it. For short periods of time, no suffering is endured. But as the seconds turn into hours and longer, the whole body starts to suffer. If a victim is compelled, for example, to hold the arms out for long periods of time, then the entire body will quickly begin to ache. The longer the arms are held out, the worse the suffering becomes. If the victim is handcuffed, stripped naked, and placed on a narrow length of pipe with his or her feet unable to reach the ground, then a perception arises that the suffering is caused by the prisoner's own body rather than by the torturer. Such tortures do not even require the immediate presence of torturers, who can come and go at their pleasure.

To further deepen our understanding of what is attacked in an assault on dignity, consider that the infliction of suffering, especially physical suffering, also assaults the voice of the individual and the capacity to speak (Scarry 1985, 19–20). The experience of extreme suffering reduces the individual to moans, screams, and similar animal noises. It temporarily or permanently destroys the properties that make us human. Jean Amery (1995, 131), describing his own torture by suspension from a hook, says that "Only in torture does the transformation of the person into flesh become complete. Frail in the face of violence, yelling out in pain, awaiting no help, capable of no resistance, the tortured person is only a body." Torture treats the human being as nothing more than meat. Either it attacks the body to reduce the mind or it attacks the mind directly. This generates a sense that the body is responsible for the suffering and creates a strange guilt arising from the sense that one is inflicting the suffering on oneself and hence is responsible for the suffering. Guilt weakens the psychological resistance of the torture victim by making it more difficult to assign blame for the suffering to those responsible. In addition to the psychological consequences, such "noninvasive" practices have pernicious physical sequelae as well. Grethe Skylv (1992, 47) identifies the following:

> this maltreatment causes over-stretching of the stabilizing
> ligaments and joint capsules of the spine, giving segmentary
> instability and other segmentary disfunctions. These lead not
> only to back pain, but, in accordance with our ontogenic
> development, may also give a sensation of pain corresponding
> to the dermatome, myotome, or sclerotome of the strained
> segments as well as affecting the vessels and viscera belonging
> to the corresponding segment ... The visceral symptoms, caused
> by the irritation of afferent sympathetic nerves going from the

truncus sympathicus via the dorsal root-ganglion to the dorsal root, may simulate cardiac disease, gastrointestinal, genital, or other conditions, depending on which spinal segment the dysfunction is localized to.

There are additional psychological methods. Hooding cuts off eyesight and thereby contributes to the disorientation that is so essential in torture. The hoods are often designed to be foul and reek of urine or vomit; they partially constrict breathing and can induce panic. Solitary confinement, sometimes in cells too small to lie down in, cuts off the suspect from social contact with other human beings other than guards and torturers. It may also pervert the contact with other human beings so that the best one gets is the screams from down the hall or a hurried whisper at an opportune moment.

Torture victims also experience spatio-temporal distortion – that is, they have difficulty determining where and when they are. Many noninvasive torture techniques are designed to wreck the capacity to make such judgments. Since judgments of time and locations are an essential element of personal identity, spatio-temporal orientation is one of the earliest casualties of torture.

Further, since torture is an attack on identity, it is inevitably gendered. Unless one has an abstract and nonsociological concept of the person, one has to recognize that the identity of a specific human being is a complex matter, one of the most central components of which is gender. As torture is an attack on identity, torture will inevitably attack the gender of the victim. This point is not always recognized by opponents of torture either. Consequently, feminist research on torture is extremely important. For example, Ximena Bunster (1993, 103) argues that human rights advocates have not addressed the problem that torture attacks women as *women*. As torture is first and foremost a coercive attack on identity and as gender is an essential component of identity, the consequence is that torture of women political prisoners is inevitably sexist, gendered, and patriarchal.

Consideration of the sexual nature of torture reinforces this claim. Kate Millett (2007, 165) argues that "The sexual is invoked to emphasise the power of the tormentor, the vulnerability of the victim; sexuality itself is confined inside an ancient apprehension and repression: shame, sin, weakness. The victim tortured sexually is tortured twice as it were, first by being deliberately harmed, second by being harmed in a way regarded as the most humiliating of all humiliations." In fact, although it is difficult precisely to establish the numbers, very large numbers of female and significantly large numbers of male torture victims are raped. Bunster (1993, 99) claims that 80 per cent of female torture victims in Latin America and 50 per cent of males are sexually tortured. Moreover, we have to resist the temptation to identify sexual assaults solely with penetration. Carlson (2006a, 16) argues, for example, that kicks aimed at the testicles are sexual assaults. Such kicks are a common and prevalent form of torture and can be inflicted only on a man. Such a method takes advantage of the physical and psychological features of the male victim to break down his identity both through extreme pain and through the denigration associated with literal and symbolic castration of the male. If we recognize that sexual torture includes such blows and other assaults on sexual organs, as well as verbal sexual threats, then the number of sexually tortured victims must reach 100 per cent. Once we understand that torture attacks the identity of the individual, all cases of torture have their sexual component. To torture people is to sexually assault them. This is a matter of inevitability, not probability.

Certainly, Cherie Booth (2006, 120) and others draw this conclusion. In her view, the psychological reality of torture and of war makes sexual violence inevitable. Given that gender is one of the essential constituents of personal identity and given that political torture involves the deliberate destruction of an individual's identity, her conclusion is coherent. Any given torture sessions will be adapted to the unique personality of the torture victim. Since part of this specific reality includes gender, the selected torture techniques will inevitably be gender-specific and hence will create the sexual violence that Carlson and Booth observe.

Furthermore, these gendered aspects of torture hold regardless of whether the torturers realize it. It might not even occur to them that they are acting in a sexually violent manner. They might even think they are preventing sexual violence (by prohibiting penetration, for example). But regardless of the specific torturer's perception, the torture will still attack the gender of the individual and the violence will be sexual. If an individual also happens to be lesbian, gay, or transgendered and the torturers somehow discover this, the torture will be further refined to account for these facts.

Given the extreme asymmetry in the power dynamics, victims must live in fear of sexual assault. It makes no difference whether they are shown policies prohibiting sexual assault. The documents might be false or the interrogators may violate them. Nor does it mean anything if a torturer makes a promise. In the torture situation, the power is so asymmetrical and the desires of the victim so irrelevant, that the policy and the promise cannot count as meaningful. The conditions for trust simply do not obtain.

If identity is gendered and if torture is a deliberate attack on personal identity, it is inevitable that the torturer will attack the gender of the victim. The medical and psychiatric evidence, along with sociological and anthropological reflection on human being, demonstrates that identity is gendered. The literature also demonstrates that torture is a deliberate attack on personal identity. Hence torture will inevitably attack gender. Precisely how the torturer attacks it is an empirical question. Many different tactics can be utilized to break an individual. But all of these will inevitably involve some form of gendered violence. Often this will include rape and other forms of easily discernible sexual violence. But the other violence will inevitably have its gendered component as well. The point here is that *all torture is sexually violent and gendered*, even though the specific means used and forms of gendered violence may vary considerably. Defenders of torture never discuss the issue of gender. But the idea of gender-neutral torture is revealed as oxymoronic once we understand some of the basic facts about personal identity and dignity as well as important facts about the nature and structure of torture.

To this point, I have focused only on the individual as the target of torture. I have remained entirely within the parameters of normal discussion of the harms of torture. I have analyzed some of the ways torture attacks individual dignity and shown it to involve complications not addressed by defenders of the use of torture. There is little analysis of any of these considerations in any existing defences of torture. There is merely the unanalyzed concession that torture violates dignity. This already demonstrates that the analysis of suffering is far more complicated than anything they offer. However, that human beings are social and that their identities are intersubjectively constituted creates further problems.

Intersubjective Considerations

At this point, it is therefore necessary to challenge outright the assumption that torture attacks only an individual. It is a common assumption in defences of torture, a particularly explicit example of which can be found in the defence offered by Mirko Bagaric and Julie Clarke (2005, 584): "ultimately, torture is simply the sharp end of conduct where the interests of one agent are sacrificed for the greater good." This is false, but to show this I will begin with an examination of the reasons for isolating individuals in torture. Individuals are isolated precisely to cut them off from support networks. Human beings are social, and a central component of any torture involves separating them from their communities. This is the omnipresent first step in any state assault on identity. Consequently, it becomes difficult to think of torture in terms solely of a relation between torturer and victim.

As many authors indicate, torture has an isolating and disorienting function. The torture cell is a kind of theatre or stage designed to create an atmosphere of terror for an individual. What is so important about creating such a strange context? Why is it so important to cut off the normal involvement of torture victims with their own bodies? Why isolate them in torture facilities? Why hood them or cause them to disappear, as so many governments do?

There are a number of reasons for these tactics, but the most pressing one at this juncture is that part of what it is to be a human being is to have a range of social and normative attachments with family, friends, and other members of an immediate community. But as Saporta and van der Kolk (1992, 154) note, in attacking personal identity, torture does not merely strike the body and mind of a given individual but is a sustained assault on his or her social attachments and belief systems. This plays out both through the systematic isolation of the individual from his or her larger community and in the threats made to the individual victim about harms that might be inflicted on his or her family. Torturers seek to sever these communal bonds precisely because they are additional essential components of individual identity. They then seek to replace the healthy social connections and ties with a perverted bond to the torturer. The torturer will deliberately try to create a state of dependence for the torture victim. This state is similar to that observed in hostages, abused spouses, and abused children.

Furthermore, if the victim is lucky enough to receive any contact with family members, this occurs in the threatening and distorting context of the prison. The mere presence of family members is a risk and a threat to their wellbeing and therefore a further opportunity to terrorize and coerce the tortured individual. Family members are more vulnerable to sexual and physical coercion, abduction, disappearance, and their own torture simply by visiting their loved one and communicating with him or her at all.

What this means is that since torture attacks the social attachments of individuals, the kind of self that it seeks to break is social. Torture interrogators understand this and take advantage of the fact. The self is not an atom existing independently of relations to a broader community but exists in various emotional and normative relations to others. By disparaging parents, children, lovers, and friends, these emotional relations are undermined. This has as a consequence the victim's long-term alienation and diminished capacity to maintain relationships (Gorman 2001, 446). The suspicion that the torture survivor may be perceived to have betrayed others adds an additional common complicating factor. It further entrenches disorientation and uncertainty in the mind of the torture victim and contributes to increased isolation from his or her community.

In considering torture as an attack on identity and dignity, we also need to be aware that torture is not experienced by its survivors as occurring only in the torture chamber. Amery (1995, 131) asserts that those who have been tortured remain so for the rest of their lives. Such anecdotal analysis is supported by the therapeutic literature. The consequences of torture extend over the lifetime of the survivor. Lunde and Ortmann (1992, 318) assert that "Many torture survivors feel that torture is a perpetual state and experience it in the present tense. To reach a point where torture is placed in the past, and is now finished, is a difficult process." That torture attacks social attachments suggests that the restriction of our understanding of torture simply to the isolation of a prison cell is insufficient. The individual is separated from the community and isolated. But the reverse holds as well. The community is separated and isolated from the individual. Both are thereby harmed. Not only that, but examination of the consequences of the attack on identity reveals that the torture does not just attack the individual now but also imposes terrible harms on the future life possibilities and relationships of tortured individuals.

An assault on the identity and dignity of the individual harms or outright destroys his or her possibilities for maintaining social relationships now and into the future (Vesti and Kastrup 1992, 361). As a result of torture, survivors often have trouble pursuing a meaningful career or even holding down a job (Kagee 2004, 630). It also undermines the possibility that individuals might pursue meaning-giving projects such as sports or other hobbies. If aware that such hobbies are important to the identity of victims, the torturer may choose to damage specific parts of the body to make it impossible for them to do something they find meaningful. Irreparably crushing the fingers of a pianist will challenge his or her identity as a musician, reduce if not destroy future professional possibilities, and perhaps make it difficult for the victim to appreciate and enjoy music for the rest of his or her life.

To attack individual human beings through torture entails assaulting their social attachments as well. Human individuals exist in complex nests of social relations and attachments. In isolating the torture victim and damaging or destroying these relations, the attack extends well beyond the primary torture victim – for the same harms that I have indicated with respect to the primary victim can also be experienced in varying ways by those to whom the tortured individuals are related, including entire extended families.

Hector Timerman (2006), son of Argentinian journalist, editor, and torture survivor Jacopo Timerman, describes the hell experienced by his family in dealing with his father's disappearance and torture. His story deserves some presentation in detail:

> If thinking about someone being tortured is painful, it is not as terrible as to see the result of it. My mother and I waited two hours in the Central Police Department. We were allowed only three minutes with my father. He was a man destroyed, both physically and mentally. Saying goodbye as if for the last time, he told us he would never be set free and to reorganize our lives on that basis. My mother sobbed uncontrollably as she saw what had become of my father. She stroked him, as if he were a child, and kept asking, "What did they do to you? What did they do? Why are you so ill?" (72)

Their suffering extended far beyond their visit:

> For the relatives of the tortured, it was very hard to go on living a normal life, going to one's job, enterprise, or university thinking about the people who were being thrown out of airplanes into the sea or tortured to death. Our reality was its

own hell. When the media reported on the struggle against terrorism or the international campaign against Argentina, when people took to the streets to celebrate sports triumphs or entered a restaurant, laughing and kissing, it was impossible not to feel confusion, anger, and emotional isolation. It was difficult even to embrace my fiancée, Anabelle, thinking at that moment that somebody was hurting my father. (73-4)

Notice the parallel experiences of the family and the torture victim: psychological terror and suffering on the part of the family; stress for the family as a result of the suffering inflicted on their loved one; confusion, anger, emotional isolation; difficulties in maintaining healthy social relationships. These are all variations of the suffering experienced by primary torture victims.

Torture inevitably has a host of secondary victims as well since torture inevitably also inflicts terrible suffering on family and friends. In the medical and psychological context, Diana Kordon (1991, 29) likewise notes the inevitable harms inflicted on the families of torture victims. Finn Somnier and colleagues (1992, 63-4) identify breakdowns in the functioning of family units and the survivor's inability to work as consequences of torture. At least as disturbingly, the children of torture victims experience very high rates of anxiety, nightmares, fear, nocturnal enuresis (bedwetting), withdrawal, depression, irritability, aggressiveness, generalized fear, excessive clinging to and dependence on the parents, and diminished school performance.

Torture does not just harm an isolated individual for a discrete period of time but also has impacts extending across generations. The children of torture victims are deeply impacted by their parents' suffering and carry this harm into at least the second generation. But as an attack on personal identity, torture inevitably takes advantage of discrete cultural differences, norms, values, prohibitions, and taboos. This is a way of saying that torture will have its racist elements as well, for just as gender is a central focus of attack, so torturers will single out the racial and cultural aspects of an individual's identity. Consequently, Barbara Chester's (1990, 170) description of the suffering experienced by torture victims as both personal and communal is well established.

I hardly need point to specific aspects of the tortures at Abu Ghraib and other places to note the ways that these tortures have targeted specific perceived Muslim norms and values. The use of guard dogs to exploit a cultural fear of dogs, enforced nudity and rape, threats to sexual organs, and the other explicitly gendered aspects of the torture at Abu Ghraib all work in concert with the racist and ethnic elements of the torture. The selection of these techniques is no accident. Some individual or group had to choose the methods using a combination of existing expertise in torture, greater or lesser knowledge of Muslim culture, trial and error, and judgment.

Sister Dianna Ortiz (2002, 253), reflecting on her own torture at the hands of the Guatemalan army, muses that she was not attacked because she was a subversive; rather, in attacking her, the army attacked the Catholic Church in Guatemala in a bid to undermine its support for the oppressed of the country. What this suggests, along with all of the other evidence I have described, is that torture is never solely about assaulting individual minds and bodies. Once we recognize that community and ethnicity are essential components of identity, we also have to concede that torturing individuals and trying to break down their identities is simultaneously an assault on their entire culture. This assault is reflected in the rage with which members of such cultural groups react to the torture of specific members, for they are perfectly aware of the cultural and racist nature of the assault carried out on specific individuals. We should not be surprised at such responses because they lie at the heart of questions of individual identity and dignity. Given that dignity and identity are culturally defined as well as gendered, an attack on identity is also an attack on various cultural norms and belief systems and hence on the culture itself.

As with my remarks on gender, this is not idle speculation. The medical and therapeutic literature provides a host of empirical support. The specific means for torturing a given individual will vary depending on his or her specific cultural identity. T.L. Dowdall (1991, 51) draws attention to the specific racism of torture in South Africa under apartheid. In South Africa torture "emerged as a logical development within an abusive social control system. This system – widely known as apartheid – was intended legally to entrench power and economic advantage in the hands of the white minority."

Here, torture was explicitly pursued for the state's racist goals, but it is inevitable that torture will attack aspects of the culture and race of specific individuals unless torturer and victim share a common ethnic and racial background. In that case, the torturer will select other relevantly different features of the victim's identity. It is not an accident that Jacopo Timerman's torturers attacked his Jewish identity (Timerman 1981, 73–5). It is inevitable given what torture attacks, just as the racist aspects of the Abu Ghraib tortures are not incidental. Any specific racism overtly espoused by the torturers will just intensify the racist qualities of the assaults. Since torture is an attack on identity, wherever race is an issue it will be a focus of attack.

These assaults also have fracturing effects on the target communities. Dowdall (1992, 462) also notes that, in consequence of having been tortured, the victims of the South African police were frequently treated as collaborators and subjected to further violence and murder by members of their own communities. The use of torture unavoidably introduces division into a community and thereby increases the experiences of threat and suffering. In any case, the way that ticking-bomb hypotheses and arguments for torture tend to focus on a "terrorist" or other isolated individual inevitably conceals this complex nest of intersubjective social relations. Furthermore, governments know this. They understand that the institution of a policy like torture is not about attacking specific individuals. It has much more to do with the pursuit of broader tactical and strategic aims, such as divide and conquer, even if torture policies are always implemented on the minds and bodies of the governments' individual victims (Suarez-Orozco 2004, 386).

The divisive nature of torture is historically well supported. Michael Taussig's (2004b, 173) following personal anecdote is one powerful example. After his friend Roberto had disappeared, been tortured, and then released, he sought help from Michael. Taussig vividly portrays the fear:

> Then he sprung it on me. "Could I stay in your apartment when you leave?" My heart sank. I so much wanted to help but to have him use the apartment would be to endanger a whole bunch of other people, beginning with Rachel and the three kids. I felt the most terrible coward, especially because my cowardice took the form of not being able to tell him that I thought his situation was too dangerous, for that would tear open the façade of normalcy that I at least felt we so badly

needed in order to continue being, and being together and that he needed to survive. In so many ways I too was an active agent in the war of silencing.

This is further evidence, Taussig notes, of how the torture survivor is victimized by his or her experiences. Not only does the survivor have to deal with horrific personal suffering, but his or her social networks are terribly damaged. Friends and family members have to demonstrate exceptional courage just to associate with the torture survivor. These are also additional grounds to support the idea that the torture does not end simply because the survivor escapes the torture chamber. Torture makes it difficult for an entire community to function and maintain cohesion.

This evidence demonstrates that the consequences of torture extend across entire communities. They are society-wide and indiscriminate. Torture may look like a precise means to inflict suffering, but it is not and cannot be. Not only do its effects spread spatially across a society at the time that it is implemented, but its harms are also intergenerational, harming the psychological and physical wellbeing, prospects, and possibilities of children as well. This additional violence and suffering cannot be avoided even if there is political will to avoid it.

Jean-Paul Sartre (1968, 82) is therefore correct in his assessment that torture inevitably attacks the group. This analysis further clarifies and supports Scarry's observation that torture attacks the entire world of the victim. Ron Baker's (1992, 86) psychosocial analysis of the impacts of torture is pertinent as well: "refugee and torture experiences will affect the sense of identity, trust and security felt by the person, which in turn will impact on roles of parent, spouse, employee, employer, citizen, etc. In turn, the obstacles and successes the individual meets in the environment will affect the psychological state, well-being and sense of identity being experienced."

Torture does not attack the personality and dignity of an isolated individual. Such an attack is far more complex. Focused on the bodies of discrete individuals, it assaults the humanity of entire communities along gender, cultural, ethnic, familial, occupational, and generational lines.

It is important to inject a note of hope at this point. Although the damage that torture causes is enormous and in many cases irrevocable, Dowdall (1992, 462) cautions us against despair. Even when torture occurs, it is not inevitable that the individual will be destroyed. Even in its most central aim – the destruction of identity – torture is not inevitably successful. There are numerous cases of individuals managing to preserve their dignity and integrity in spite of the violence done to them.

SUBCONCLUSIONS

It is useful to briefly summarize the results achieved so far.

First, political torture is essentially coercive. Whatever else we might say about it, torture essentially involves the violation of the will of an individual for the sake of some aim of the torturer and the government or nonstate entity that supports him.

Second, torture is essentially an assault on the identity of the individual. It seeks to break down and restructure that personality to make him or her submissive and amenable to other political aims. Consequently, there is no important distinction between physical and psychological torture methods. All state torture is psychological, even if some of the means used to torture an individual are more visceral than others.

Third, to achieve this, policy makers and planners create an institutional environment aimed at the production of fear, terror, and suffering in the individual torture victim.

Fourth, the sociological, medical, and psychological evidence demonstrates that torture involves far more than simply assaulting one person. Personal identity is constituted intersubjectively. Torture techniques inevitably play on this fact. For example, capture and isolation are involved in all political torture. By design, this has disorienting consequences. It severs the individual from his or her normal social ties and is the first step in creating the terrible situation of dependence.

Fifth, since identity is a complex combination of gender, ethnicity, economics, and racial history, among others, the destruction of identity will inevitably attack these in combination. The interrogator will study the victim in detail over time to determine weaknesses in identity and will exploit these. Gender in particular is inevitably attacked. The ubiquity of sexual assault in torture supports these a priori considerations. If we understand what torture is and we understand the complexities of identity, then we realize that torturing someone inevitably sexually and racially assaults them.

Sixth, and finally, since identity is intersubjectively constituted, torture inevitably assaults entire communities. The effects torture has on those wider communities can vary significantly, just as the specific effects can vary widely from individual to individual. But the harms are nevertheless inevitable. So torture is not simply an attack on one person but always an attack on many.

THE AIMS OF TORTURE

An understanding of torture is insufficient if we do not pay careful attention to the range of purposes for which it is used. In the context of the debate about torture, this concern is especially important. Defenders of torture typically forbid almost all cases of torture and attempt to identify a small class of tortures that they hold to be legitimate. They believe some purposes can legitimate torture, even if the vast majority of reasons are indefensible.

Commonly, torture is divided into two classes: interrogational and terroristic (occasionally sadistic is included). Those who defend torture seek to isolate interrogational torture from the others and to defend its use (Moher 2004, 469; Michael Gross 2004, 189; Allhoff 2005b, 252). The groundbreaking examples are Henry Shue's classic definitions. Shue (1978, 132) defines terroristic torture in the following way: "Terroristic torture is a pure case – the purest possible case – of the violation of the Kantian principle that no person may be used *only* as a means. The victim is simply a site at which great pain occurs so that others may know about it and be frightened by the prospect."

Terroristic torture involves the infliction of extreme suffering simply for the sake of spreading fear and terror. Ultimately, in terms of the strategic aims of states and nonstate agents, such use of terror is designed to compel some population to fall into line with the relevant desires and policies.

In contrast, interrogational torture is intended to extract information from the victim (Shue 1978, 133). Shue asserts that such torture has a built-in endpoint: the acquisition of the desired information. An important distinction between the two is precisely that there is, at least in principle, a clear point at which interrogational torture ends: the point at which the subject yields the desired information or at which the interrogator acquires the information by other means (141). However, we have to be careful in making the distinction. Shue points out that there are very few pure cases of interrogational torture and that such things are almost always mixed in practice (140). I am going to go further and argue that a pure concept of interrogational torture is incoherent and that the distinction between interrogational and terroristic torture cannot be maintained in principle. Rather, torture is, as Enrique Bustos (1990, 143–4) describes it, essentially a strategy of domination used to enhance control in the face of a crisis.

On the grounds of one possible interpretation, we understand terroristic and interrogational torture to reflect the possible intentions held by individual interrogators or by the institutions that sanction the torture. This seems to be Shue's view since he explicitly frames the two types in terms of the specific goals of an interrogator or policy maker. In that event, if I am engaged in interrogational torture, I intend to get information. I do not intend to spread terror. To show why this suggestion does not work, recall the discussion of the nature and consequences of torture. Torture is essentially coercive. In its political uses, it is by nature an attack on human identity. Torture seeks to demolish the identity of a person for specific political goals. These points are essential to whatever further purposes one might seek to achieve in torturing someone. Furthermore, the structure of torture is such that, by nature and design, it must disorient and create fear and terror in the mind of the given victim. To whatever extent torture can succeed in achieving certain goals, it does so precisely through the infliction of confusion, fear, and suffering.

What this means is that Shue's remark about the use of torture to spread fear is not sufficiently strong. The way he describes terroristic torture makes it seem as though the spreading of terror is a *possible* feature of torture, but in fact, to whatever meagre extent that it succeeds, it can do so only by virtue of its terroristic qualities. Terror is essential to torture, not accidental. Hence it does not matter whether "interrogational" torture has a clear end point. The terrorism holds regardless and is the condition for a successful interrogation.

It means further that Shue is also not sufficiently strong in describing terroristic torture as the ultimate case of a violation of the Kantian principle that no person may be used as a means. Since all torture is terroristic, there are no exceptions. They are all pure cases. It makes no difference whether there are additional goals such as saving lives, winning counter-insurgency struggles, or anything else.

The intersubjectivity of identity is important as well. In attacking personal identity through torture, interrogators may have the specific goal of acquiring information from a given individual and may not specifically desire to spread terror in the broader population. But they deceive themselves if they think that they do not thereby spread terror more widely. To attack the dignity and personality of a single individual is to assault a far wider set of individuals and communities than the individual because all of those who are relevantly related will suffer in a multitude of ways as well. Since identity is intersubjectively and relationally constituted, this is not something that can be avoided. Humans are social beings. To attack one human thereby entails attacking whole complexes of social relations, all of which are harmed by the use of torture. The experience of fear by all socially connected individuals is inevitable. Taussig's story should remind us of this. But third parties are also justifiably terrorized by the use of so-called interrogational torture since they have every reason to fear that the same acts will be performed on them.

We should be aware of an important caution written by psychologist Ervin Staub (1989, 25). In a discussion of evil actions, he explicitly repudiates the relevance of intentions to our appreciation of evils: "We cannot judge evil by conscious intentions, because psychological distortions tend to hide even from the perpetrators themselves their true intentions. They are unaware, for example, of their own unconscious hostility or that they are scapegoating others." They may be unaware that they are torturing women *as* women, for example, or lesbians *as* lesbians, or Muslims *as* Muslims. They could be unaware of the ways their training, both formal and on the job, has created hostile and vicious dispositions toward their victims – their "enemies." Consequently, they might deceive themselves into thinking there is no sexist or racist element. Moreover, they might deceive themselves into thinking that their acts are justified.

The consequence is that the subjective intentions of specific interrogators play no role in understanding torture's terroristic properties. These obtain regardless of the beliefs of specific torturers. Where they do matter is at the level of implementation. They are one factor in explaining why torture happens, but they have little to do with what torture is. Intentions are likely to contribute to choice of technique and torture strategy. They may also help to shape the course of specific tortures. For example, it seems plausible to believe that the impact of torture might vary quite significantly if the interrogator is naturally sadistic versus hesitant.

The essential properties of torture include its coerciveness and its terrorism. Absent these properties, it would not be torture. Furthermore, it is essential to political torture that it be an attack on personal identity and dignity; it cannot be understood independently of what it attacks and of the ways it impacts its victims. Hence to focus on interrogation in torture is to confuse an accidental property of torture with something essential. Interrogation has to do with a specific purpose that a torturer may or may not pursue in the course of political torture. It has to do, therefore, with a specific intention. But because this specific intention can be realized only through the infliction of terror and the destruction of identity and dignity, the concept of purely interrogational torture is nonsense. The aim can be realized only through terror. Hence the initial disjunction between subjective intention and empirical practice and impact is irrelevant. Only the impacts matter here, and they are necessarily terroristic.

Furthermore, there might be multiple purposes at play in the execution of a torture campaign. The various purposes for which torture is used can be consistent. So while torture always terrorizes, the gathering of information is a possible tactical goal. Terrorism is compatible with the gathering of information. Control of sexuality as a torture goal is compatible with the prosecution of a dirty war. So is the destruction of communities and all the other purposes for the sake of which torture is applied. But we should never forget that torture policies and acts of torture are part of the tactics of some state struggle. They serve larger strategic aims to do with achieving victory over an opposition. There is nothing incoherent in the suggestion that there might be multiple compatible and incompatible subordinate desires and purposes simultaneously in play and all driving the use of torture.

Michael Hardt and Antonio Negri (2004, 57) describe environmental deprivation strategies for counter-insurgency warfare – a specific useful model for helping to display this plurality of values:

> This strategy recognizes that its enemy is not organized like a traditional army and thus cannot simply be decapitated. It even accepts that it can never know the enemy and its organizational

form adequately. Such knowledge, however, is not necessary to implement the method: the sovereign power avoids being thwarted by what it cannot know and focuses on what it can know. Success does not require attacking the enemy directly but destroying the environment, physical and social, that supports it. Take away the water and the fish will die. This strategy of destroying the support environment led, for example, to indiscriminate bombings in Vietnam, Laos, and Cambodia, to widespread killing, torture, and harassment of peasants in Central and South America, and to mass repression of activist groups in Europe and North America.

There are multiple possible strategies that governments and policies can pursue, but we should never forget that torture is a tactic, an instrumental means for pursuing strategic aims. It concerns the assertion of state power (Holmes 2005, 126; Evans and Morgan 2007, 39; Marks 2004, 375). Furthermore, the overall strategic goals are perfectly compatible with a wide range of subordinate tactics and intentions. The choice of specific torture tactics is itself also perfectly consistent with a wide range of different subjective intentions of agents. The consequentialist calculations employed by torture defenders pay no attention to the plural goals of torture and thus fail to appreciate the incoherence of the concept of interrogational torture. This further contributes to an oversimplification of the consequentialist calculus by assuming that one possible value (the prevention of a bomb attack) could be the only value driving a torture policy. Since torture is essentially terroristic and inevitably harms populations, this assumption is false. The idea of a purely interrogational torture is bizarrely utopian.

Nothing I have said rules out the possibility that torture might and sometimes does yield information. Indeed, insofar as there are questions asked in torture, it *always* yields information, although we should never forget that "information" and "truth" are completely different concepts. To say that torture is terrific at yielding information tells us nothing about whether intelligence agents can successfully use it to gain knowledge.

What, then, is wrong with the concept of interrogational torture?

First, it sanitizes phenomena that are, by their nature, terroristic and repulsive. It creates the false impression that the terroristic uses can be hived off from our understanding of torture in favour of a more ethically streamlined and acceptable set of practices. Shue does not intend this outcome, for he is completely opposed to torture. However, he is prepared to concede that in rare hypothetical cases it might be possible to justify its use. But, as he says, "Hard cases make bad law" (Shue 1978, 141). His sophistication is evident in his remark that there are few pure cases. But my point is that this pure case is impossible in principle. These cases are not hard cases; they are complete fictions.

The incoherence of interrogational torture is a consequence of a failure to recognize that the terroristic elements of torture are essential to its nature and to its effectiveness. Interrogations, if they are used, are entirely accidental to torture and presuppose terror if they are to work. They presuppose the terror not just of the individual torture victim but also of the opposition groups to which the victim may or may not belong as well as of the extended families and communities of which he or she is a member. It terrorizes third parties because of the inevitable mistakes that get made in capturing suspects. This terroristic quality cannot empirically be avoided. Whatever else torture may do, it terrorizes.

Second, defenders of torture are too quick to exclude the other uses of torture as unjustified by their reasoning. Torture is typically an element of counter-insurgency and counter-terror campaigns. These are planned by more or less instrumentally rational public officials for specific reasons and for the sake of specific perceived goods. In introducing torture campaigns, public officials will use some cost-benefit calculation and will conclude that all the stated purposes satisfy their sense of the good of their communities. The only thing that is needed here is the belief that more good is created by instituting terror than by refusing to torture. The reasoning that supports torture in the one case also, in principle, supports it in all the others. That historical agents draw these conclusions is further reason to doubt that the arguments speak only in favour of a narrow class of tortures.

Since it is not possible to isolate a distinct class of morally approved tortures called "interrogational tortures," an individual who defends torture must worry about the other kinds and aims. The following is a list of other kinds of aims. It is not exhaustive, but it is a start. The guiding question is: What excludes any of these reasons? All of them have been in fact chosen by specific governments. Public officials seem to believe they can achieve desirable goals through torture – goals that are perceived to be better than the alternatives. When public officials institute torture policies, they do not claim to be acting for no reason. Indeed, they stress their own consequential rationality. Although I explore this issue in chapter 4, it is important to ask torture defenders why they think that they can exclude any of the following aims.

Whether torture is performed to coerce confessions, to break resistance of oppositional groups, for the sake of experimentation on human beings, to save their souls, or for whatever reason, it is always a means of power projection. In the case of liberal-democratic states, this typically has to do with controlling noncitizen populations (Asad 1997, 296). Because torture is essentially coercive, and since it essentially attempts to break down and reshape the identity of a victim in order to serve the goals of the torturing institution, it is by its nature oppressive and an act of domination. Whatever justifications may be offered in support of coercion and domination, it is undeniable that governments torture to project power and to dominate others. Governments that torture presumably believe that this serves some desired good, but this does not alter the centrality of power projection to torture.

This having been said, there are many different explanations for the projection of power. Torture can be used out of desperation. In times of crisis it is not uncommon for public officials to be desperate for results that will help them to meet their responsibilities. Desperation may cause them to put enormous pressure on subordinates, who then turn to torture as a quick solution. This is more likely if massive public outrage occurs. Emotional responses and public calls for revenge might convince an official that he or she has to react quickly and be perceived to be acting in a strong and vigorous manner (Matthews 1998, 187).

States torture to compel activists and political opponents to cease their dissent. For example, they often torture members of opposition political parties (Frey 2002, 49). They torture in order to blackmail victims (Booth 2006, 118). Torture is performed to create informants and spies. Lorentzen (1998, 194) notes that rape and other explicitly sexual tortures are particularly valued for this purpose. Torture is used to frame either the victims or third parties. In some cases it is inflicted to extract confessions or to bring about religious and political conversions. It is used as a designed strategy to create terror and divide and conquer various communities.

Torture happens as a means to recruit soldiers and supporters as well as sexual slaves. Torture is used as well to promote solidarity among soldiers and intelligence agents by creating group guilt and responsibility (Matthews 1998, 187). The establishment of torture camps – for example, the rape and torture camps that were created in the Balkans – was instituted to reward male soldiers for their efforts. Torture is also implemented to control the gender and sexuality of victims. States also torture in order to train torturers. Jennifer Harbury (2005, 95–6) reports, for example, that CIA agent Dan Mitrione brought in street people to carry out training sessions for torturers in Uruguay. The result was four deaths and enormous suffering. Patrick Lenta (2006, 56) suggests that some states employ torture as a spectacle by which an injured state displays the asymmetries of power between itself and those who have attacked it. Finally, I have already noted Carlson's (2006b, 68) observation that some torturers seem to believe they are acting "for the good of the victims." There are other possibilities, but this is a pretty good subset. The challenge for defenders of the use of torture is to demonstrate why their arguments can exclude any of these specific purposes or any of the others. Given that torture defenders reject absolute conceptions of rights and absolute prohibitions, their consequentialist arguments support all of these, at least in principle.

I want to conclude this chapter by emphasizing that the consequences of torture are far more complicated than defenders of torture recognize. The precise nature and severity of the harms vary depending on individual psychology and the culture to which a given individual belongs (Pakar, Paker, and Yuksel 1992, 72). This alone should give us pause and incite significant doubt that we can construct a consequentialist calculus that supports the use of torture.

2

What about the Ticking Bomb?

The simplicity of the device is attractive, and recurrent in all totalitarian ideology: to ignore the complexities of reality, or even eliminate reality, and instead establish a simple goal and a simple means of attaining that goal.

Timerman 1981, 12

Prevalent in so much discussion of torture is the ticking-bomb scenario. This thought experiment invokes some catastrophic threat, like the detonation of an atomic bomb or perhaps the release of weaponized anthrax or a similar weapon of mass destruction. It then asks us to consider whether we could justify refusing to torture a terrorist given that the consequences arising from the detonation of the device are so high. Here are several examples from the literature:

> There is a standard philosopher's example which someone always invokes: suppose a fanatic, perfectly willing to die rather than collaborate in the thwarting of his own scheme, has set a hidden nuclear device to explode in the heart of Paris. There is no time to evacuate the innocent people or even the moveable art treasures – the only hope of preventing tragedy is to torture the perpetrator, find the device, and deactivate it. (Shue 1978, 141)

Fritz Allhoff (2005a, 246) and many others offer their own variations on the ticking-bomb theme. More controversially, Alan Dershowitz (2002, 144) constructs a ticking-bomb hypothesis on the basis of the following report:

> Several weeks after September 11, our government received reports that a ten-kiloton nuclear weapon may have been stolen from Russia and was on its way to New York City, where it

would be detonated and kill hundreds of thousands of people. The reliability of the source, code named Dragonfire, was uncertain, but assume for purposes of this hypothetical extension of the actual case that the source was a captured terrorist – like the one tortured by the Philippine authorities – who knew precisely how and where the weapon was being brought into New York and was to be detonated. Again, everything short of torture is tried, but to no avail. It is not absolutely certain torture will work, but it is our last, best hope for preventing a cataclysmic nuclear devastation in a city too large to evacuate in time.

Dershowitz notes that the threat turned out to be false in this case but argues that it shows the plausibility of the scenario. He believes it is a possible historical situation that intelligence officials must confront.

Mirko Bagaric and Julie Clarke (2005, 584) offer another example:

A terrorist network has activated a large bomb on one of hundreds of commercial planes carrying over three hundred passengers that is flying somewhere in the world at any point in time. The bomb is set to explode in thirty minutes. The leader of the terrorist organization announces this intent on the internet. He states that the bomb was planted by one of his colleagues at one of the major airports in the world in the past few hours. No details are provided regarding the location of the plane where the bomb is located. Unbeknownst to him, he was under police surveillance and is immediately apprehended by the police. The terrorist leader refuses to answer any questions of the police, declaring the passengers must die and will do so shortly.

This example is manifestly not well thought out, as the conditions the authors establish in order to make the case pressing could not possibly occur in the real world. For example, if the bomb was really set to explode in thirty minutes, there would be insufficient time to apprehend the suspect, drag him to an interrogation centre, get the torture team into place, and then beat the details out of him. Following the introduction of this thought experiment, the authors defend the real practice of state torture on the grounds that fantastic examples play an important role in the evaluation of moral principles and theories. They believe, for example, that it allows us to test the strength of our commitment to principles such as the moral primacy of dignity.

Ticking bombs seem to be exploding everywhere in the literature, yet close analysis reveals that ticking-bomb hypotheses are deeply flawed both conceptually and empirically. If I am correct, Stephen Lukes (2005, 11) is simply wrong to suggest that those who "defuse" the argument are trying to escape the problem of torture. A bad argument should not convince anyone. If the argument is both structurally and empirically weak, the ticking-bomb hypotheses cannot do the work their advocates ascribe to them. If the argument is unsound, it does not support the conclusion that torture is justified, and torture defenders have to resort to something quite different and more challenging.

Ticking-bomb hypotheses are structurally weak; in attacking the ticking-bomb hypothesis, we undermine one crutch used to defend torture. Defusing the ticking-bomb justification is not sufficient since other arguments for torture can be and are advanced, but its inadequacies are sufficiently great that anyone who puts it forward is reasoning badly. As Lukes (2005, 12) remarks, it is of course possible to envision alternative and more plausible circumstances in which an argument for torture might be used. However, even as the historical and social circumstances under which states torture become more plausible, moral arguments for torture become increasingly implausible. The specific ticking-bomb hypothesis itself is unsound in its incapacity to account for empirical realities.

LOGICAL OBJECTIONS

The ticking-bomb hypothesis constructs a terrifying threat. It then appeals to an apparently simple cost-benefit calculus to infer the conclusion that, in the rare circumstances in which such calculations have to be made, we are morally obligated to torture the terrorist suspect – for how could we justify a decision to refrain from torture when we know that such a decision makes it inevitable that many people will die, be injured, and suffer economic loss or any of the other consequences of exploding bombs? For torture advocates, the calculation is simple: one person suffers from torture, but many people suffer from the exploding bomb. Hence, they claim, we are morally obligated to torture the suspect.

I have already demonstrated that this one-many calculation is indefensible, but it also contains some terrible logical sleight of hand as well. This logical weakness is important. If I were to construct a valid argument using nonsense terms, I could show that, given a premise set, the conclusion must follow. Every rational observer would have to accept the conclusion. But establishing the validity of an argument does not demonstrate the truth of any premise or conclusion. That they are nonsense terms or that the terms are patently false is a reason to reject them regardless of whether the argument is valid. To reason well about policies and practices, empirical historical and sociological considerations matter.

So, for example, I can construct an argument that the current administration's war policies are being dictated by little green men from Mars:

1 If there are little green men from Mars, they are dictating war plans to the current administration.
2 There are little green men from Mars. Conclusion: they are dictating war plans to the current administration.

If 1 and 2 are true, the conclusion follows. Are they true? This cannot be settled on logical grounds alone but requires empirical and conceptual analysis. No reasonable observer would accept the truth of either of those sentences. Yet *on the assumption that they are true*, the conclusion follows.

A major element of my criticism of the ticking-bomb hypothesis is that it uses nonsense terms just as this hypothetical case does, except these nonsense terms are far better disguised and carry the appearance of acceptability. But the appearances are deceiving. Recognizing that the elements of the ticking-bomb hypotheses are nonsense requires some unpacking of the scenarios that they imagine.

In consequence, the ticking-bomb hypothesis is unsound. The justifiability of torture is supposed to be the conclusion of the argument, but it cannot establish this because *every* one of its concepts is historically and conceptually indefensible. It does not describe any possible actual world scenario and is a horror fantasy. Hence it neither can nor should play any role in the debate about torture. Furthermore, the ticking-bomb hypothesis displays no understanding of torture and its consequences, and it does not reflect any of the possible empirical realities. This is not surprising because these realities are incompatible with the various formulations of the hypothesis.

The usual objections to the ticking-bomb hypothesis are inductive. Many opponents and some supporters of torture point out that they fear a slippery slope, in which a practice used to justify torture only of terrorists will eventually, because of vagueness and fog-of-war considerations, become extended to nonterrorists (Levin 1990, 92). Others, like Alfred McCoy (2006b, 195), also invoke historical examples in which the implementation of torture was subject to a modicum of control at the beginning but then turned out to be more violent and uncontrollable over the long term than advocates had envisioned. Edward Peters (1985) provides an excellent historical analysis of these trends.

While I accept that these fears are genuine and important, they are not sufficient to reject ticking-bomb reasoning. Part of the problem is that, as inductive arguments, they are probabilistic. They leave open the false hope that the control of torture might be just a matter of refinement in torture policy or law, the creation of a set of torture warrants, or the establishment of some kind of democratic oversight mechanism. But the objections to torture are a priori as much as they are empirical. Torture is uncontrollable and its consequences incalculable because of problems internal to the nature of torture. McCoy (2006b, 192) is rare in also being sensitive to the logical weaknesses in the ticking-bomb hypothesis: he describes how it invokes an "improbable, even impossible, cluster of variables." By deconstructing the ticking-bomb argument into its components, I explore this "impossible cluster of variables" and demonstrate that the ticking-bomb hypothesis is a dangerous piece of weak a priori obfuscation.

POLITICAL AND EMPIRICAL OBJECTIONS

Once we recognize that the ticking-bomb hypothesis is unsound and – if applied to real-world cases, invalid – a host of further problems arise. Not only is the ticking-bomb hypothesis a bad argument, but it is also morally repulsive because it eliminates all the features of torture that lead us rightly to condemn it. It is much easier for people to swallow arguments for torture when such arguments eliminate everything that might lead us to regard the torture victim favourably or compassionately. Hence its pseudo consequentialism results in the sanitization of a practice that is filthy by its nature. Such cleansing contributes to the normalization of torture in the minds of the public and thereby makes it more acceptable.

We can observe this sanitization in the elimination from the hypothesis of considerations of gender, personal history, family, political context, economic injustice, and oppression. In the "ideal" world of the ticking bomb, interrogators are neither sexist nor racist: they operate from pure motives and with a knight-like devotion to preserving the wellbeing of the innocent. And the "terrorists" are tortured because they are "terrorists," pure manifestations of evil apolitically pursuing violent ends. In ticking-bomb hypotheses they never seem to be tortured for the reasons that play out in the real world – that is, because they are female, gay or lesbian, Islamic, or Jewish. In ticking-bomb hypotheses nobody is tortured because he or she is a communist or a capitalist, and torture is never a part of a counter-terror or counter-insurgency campaign. Indeed, in ticking-bomb hypotheses the torturing state is never regarded as committing its own atrocities against those who resist it. In consequence, the hypotheses' treatment of torture is not only nonempirical but also apolitical. This is odd since even though ticking-bomb hypotheses are supposed to somehow inform political debate, they purposefully exclude considerations of historical context.

STRUCTURAL COMPONENTS OF THE TICKING-BOMB HYPOTHESIS

The ticking-bomb hypothesis works through a logical illusion. To break the spell, we need to explore each distinct component and to indicate what it is, how it works, and why it is unacceptable. The ticking-bomb hypotheses include some and often all of the following constituents. Often they do not do so overtly while tacitly presupposing certain dubious beliefs about each concept.

1 Imminence
2 Threat
3 Necessity
4 Epistemic state of the interrogator
5 Suspect/source

Imminence

Every ticking-bomb hypothesis presupposes an imminent threat. It is not hard to see why: the greater the time available to an interrogator, the more likely it is that intelligence methods alternative to torture will be available to resolve the dilemma. Furthermore, given that no defender of torture likes such practices, he or she would rather establish conditions to ensure that torture is utilized only when absolutely necessary.

I imagine people would generally concede that torturing an individual because of the fear of a bomb threat five years in the future would be wrong. It would be unacceptable because, with that temporal distance, there is no real reason to believe that a bomb will be set. There is still plenty of time to use standard intelligence methods to detect and prevent it. The problem is that imminence is vague. Recall that vagueness is a problem for those who defend torture. Imminence is one of the places where vagueness is particularly disturbing. Just as there is no principled way to determine when a heap of sand transforms into a set of grains, so there is no principled means to determine whether a threat is imminent. Since defenders of torture want it to be employed only in those cases where imminence considerations leave no alternative, principled difficulties in identifying when a threat is genuinely imminent become a problem.

Some threats are obviously immediate. If a bomb is about to explode in five seconds, that is clearly imminent. If the bomb will go off in an hour, that counts as well. What about a day? It may be plausible to count that as imminent. But the problem should be apparent: one day is imminent, but is a week imminent? If so, why? Just as important, if it does not count as imminent, then why not? Suppose we stipulate that a week is close enough in time to count as imminent, should we then say that a month is not? On what grounds do we assert that the former is imminent and the latter not? At some moment the period of time should be clearly nonimminent. But the sorites paradox shows that there is no principled way to distinguish the imminent from the nonimminent period of time.

What is the problem here? The more imminent is the threat, the less likely torture is to succeed in providing the desired information. Torture takes time to work. The amount of time may vary between interrogation teams as well as depending on the individuals being tortured. Suppose the threat is five seconds – then there is insufficient time even to begin the torture, let alone to get the desired information. By the time the interrogator has contemplated whether to torture, the time has already expired. The same point is true of a minute, an hour, and probably even several hours. I will discuss the issue more in chapters 3 and 4, but torture is a skill, and it takes time to prepare and implement it. It cannot just be inflicted blindly at the last minute. It also takes time to have an effect.

What is the problem here? The more imminent the threat, the less likely torture or any other method is to be able to avert it. Yet imminence is a vague concept. Consequently, the absence of any analysis of imminence and a bare appeal to an ill-understood concept is problematic. The sorites problem suggests that this omission results in an unprincipled and arbitrary dividing line. Given this problem, real intelligence agents are unlikely to be able to restrict the use of torture to an "imminent" threat. There is no way for them to determine for certain which threats are imminent. There is no principled away to decide even with high degrees of probability.

Stipulating a guideline will not help. Assume we specify that "imminence" refers to any period from 0.1 seconds to a week, with anything beyond a week rendering torture impermissible. Such a guideline lacks flexibility and may prevent an interrogator from acting in time to prevent an attack – imagine that the torture team has worked for seven days and produced no results. Suppose further that the threat has not yet materialized and that the team members believe another couple of hours of torture will finally break the suspect. If they are right, the guidelines will prevent them from averting the threat. It is possible to formulate a rule according to which torture might be used, but it is not possible to formulate a rule governing the cases where interrogators might believe that they have to violate the rule. The sorites paradox, when applied to the concept of imminence, tells us that every rule we set concerning imminence must have its grey zones. The consequence is that setting a given time limit will be arbitrary and, if strictly adhered to, may prevent the achievement of intelligence goals.

The ticking-bomb hypothesis presupposes that a bomb has been set and is about to go off. Once a bomb has been planted, it is unlikely to tick for a long period of time, as this would increase the chance of discovery and disarmament. Political actors favour quick actions because these increase the chance of achieving desired goals. In the event that a given group seeks to attack another, it will try to minimize the chance of failure and to reduce the possibility of effective resistance by exploding the bomb as soon as is desirable after it has been set. But few intelligence officials would ever want the state of affairs to reach this point. At that stage interrogations are too late: torture could no longer make any difference. In reality, the challenge is to stop bomb attacks at the preparation stage, so "imminence" comes to include considerably long periods of time.

Lest this seem fanciful, in a discussion of the impact of the report by Israel's Landau Commission,* Eitan Felner (2006, 34–5) describes the ways the ticking-bomb hypothesis was extended beyond immediate or imminent threats: "However, from the moment that the Landau Commission stretched the concept of the ticking bomb to include cases where the danger to human life is not immediate, and sanctioned instead the use of force in cases of immediate need, the exceptional case of the 'ticking bomb' became the paradigm for almost every GSS [General Security Service] interrogation." Although this is a historical observation, the point I wish to make is that given the vagueness of imminence and the multiple purposes that torture serves, such extension of the hypothesis to cover scenarios where torture might be considered necessary for strategic purposes, rather than to prevent imminent harm, is inevitable. In most cases, effective torture will be used to try to prevent bombs during the planning stages. Hence it will have to be applied distinctly far in advance of the immediate danger. And once the bomb starts actually ticking, it will often be too late for torture to work, even on the dubious assumption that torture is effective.

Consequently, imminence will necessarily be interpreted liberally. It will not refer to actual bombs about to explode but will concern the detection of possible bombs – those that might be in the planning stages (but perhaps not) – and other security threats. In prosecuting a counter-insurgency war or in seeking to counter other threats, intelligence agents have the choice to interpret imminence either liberally or restrictively. Given a primary aim of protecting

---

* The Landau Commission's official title was the Commission of Inquiry into the Methods of Investigation of the General Security Service Regarding Hostile Terrorist Activities.

the public, a liberal interpretation will extend the threat more distantly into the future, whereas a restrictive interpretation of imminence will restrict it in some equally nonprincipled way. But there are costs for the interrogator whichever direction he or she goes: torture will be used more commonly as threats are interpreted liberally, and bombs will go off more commonly as imminence is conservatively applied. But either way, there is no basis for determining which interpretation is correct. The vagueness of "imminence" means that judgments about threats are also likely to vary both between cases and between intelligence agents. Kenneth Roth (2006, 197) emphasizes the problem: "the ticking-bomb scenario is a dangerously expansive metaphor capable of embracing anyone who might have knowledge not just of immediate attacks but also of attacks at unspecified times in the future." It is expansive not merely because of its conceptual vagueness but also because of the pressures under which intelligence agents are put to get actionable intelligence. It is expansive because of the fog of war, which renders it difficult for intelligence agents even to distinguish real from possible threats, let alone imminent from distant threats. The result is that in practice the threat can extend indefinitely far into the future.

The ticking-bomb hypothesis supposes that imminence restricts the use of torture only to those cases in which a threat is immediate. But vagueness considerations dictate logically and empirically that this is no limitation at all. The more we extend judgments of imminence beyond a couple of days, the more extensive and lengthier is the torture that the ticking-bomb hypothesis justifies. In the atmosphere of fear that accompanies violent political struggles, the liberal interpretation of imminence is likely to trump the cautious interpretation. If interrogators are put under any pressure at all to get results from their torture interrogations, they will be pushed to be liberal as well. Either way, torture cannot be used only in absolutely necessary cases because the vagueness of imminence makes it impossible to determine when torture is absolutely necessary. Since imminence is logically vague, interrogators cannot tell which cases are absolutely imminent anyway.

Threat

What is a threat? Just as with the concept of imminence, those who construct the ticking-bomb hypothesis typically provide no analysis of the nature of threats. In consequence, it is unclear precisely what they mean when they claim that a threat is imminent. The *Oxford English Dictionary* (1989) defines a *threat* as an "indication of impending evil." It is related to peril. *Peril* is "the position or condition of being imminently exposed to the chance of injury, loss, or destruction." Notice that in both cases, threat is intimately related to imminence.

The ticking-bomb hypothesis presupposes that there is a risk of evil, injury, loss, or destruction. It is artificial in that it presumes not the possibility of evil happening but its inevitability. The point of the ticking-bomb hypothesis is to establish that conditions exist where we are morally obligated to torture – for a simple cost-benefit analysis will determine, advocates say, that there is greater harm arising from refusing to torture the individual than that prevented through successful torture.

The same vagueness problems that burden imminence also obtain for threats. One can construct a sorites sequence ranging from an obvious and clear threat to something fully harmless and never be able to determine an appropriate line between the two. Threats, like imminence, admit of grey areas. Hence the same problems that arise with imminence also arise with the concept of a threat.

But the concept of a threat has an additional problematic feature, and this concerns modal questions of possibility and actuality. That is, does a threat need to be real? The *Oxford English Dictionary* definitions of *threat* and *peril* do not discuss whether threats need to be actual or potential, but a great deal hangs on this distinction. The ticking-bomb hypothesis stipulates the existence of a bomb. Ticking-bomb hypotheses do not consider possible bombs, and for good reason, since they are designed to generate a calculus showing that the harms connected to torturing the "fanatic" or "terrorist" are outweighed by the harms that would be suffered if the bomb were not disarmed. This calculus may work if the bomb is real, but it becomes increasingly implausible as the existence of the bomb fades into mere possibility. Indeed, there is an infinitely large number of possible bombs that could explode, but only a finite number of actual ones. If torture is permitted for every possible threat, a rather large number of people will be subjected to it, and most of those tortured will be tortured for the sake of unreal threats.

Since no defender of torture desires unnecessary torture, the ticking-bomb hypothesis needs to be constructed such as to eliminate this scenario. The actuality stipulation achieves this but at a remarkable cost: the complete artificiality of the notion of threat. Not only is the concept of threat conceptually vague, but in the ticking-bomb scenario it is also contrived. No intelligence agent works only with genuine bombs. Threats are always possible until they either occur, are eliminated, or turn out to be fanciful. Prior to resolution, no intelligence agent can determine for certain which of these threats are genuine. Many of the possible threats will be highly plausible yet false. There is no reason to believe that interrogators will be able to distinguish between those that are less plausible and any real threats. But if this is the case, and if interrogators are permitted to torture to prevent imminent threats, they will inevitably torture for more than just the actual cases. If interrogators torture for the possible cases, torture already exceeds the strictures of the ticking-bomb hypothesis.

Here, we need to be careful about the notion of possibility. We cannot mean logical possibility because that is far too inclusive. Every non-self-contradictory proposition is logically possible. If by "threat" we meant every logically possible threat, the number of threats against which we would have to take precautions would be infinite. This is impossible and fits no real-world situation. The same goes for physically possible threats. The number of physically possible bombs is not as large as those that are logically possible but is still far greater than any intelligence agency or nonstate opponent could deal with.

These two senses of possibility are in any case irrelevant to the torture debates because what is in play here is what one might call epistemic possibility. Here, the possibility has to be defined relative to a given interrogators best available judgments of the situation. Possibility is situational. A given interrogator will judge the probability of a threat based on his or her experience, background knowledge, and awareness of the current situation.

But the ticking-bomb hypothesis is not, all appearances to the contrary, situational. Indeed, it is logically general. It theorizes over all possible relevant exceptional circumstances and determines a unique answer for the appropriate behaviour for each one of these imaginable circumstances: torture. To be sure, it constructs a hypothetical situation and asks us to consider whether, in that context, we would have to support the use of torture. But there is no possible real-world referent for this situation, for threats are uncertain until they occur. The "real" threat envisioned in the ticking-bomb hypothesis is artificial precisely because it is treated as though it is known to be certain even though it has not happened. No real-world situation is like this. Nor could it be. Suffice it to say that a bomb may or may not be in place. Both are possible. But the bomb is a threat for interrogators as long as they have some reason to believe that it could exist. It becomes a serious and potentially imminent threat once they think it is probable that it has been set.

To believe that a threat exists involves some level of probability. We are talking about an epistemic state here, not an ontological one. The issue concerns what a real interrogator could plausibly know on the basis of a mass of information, at least some of which may be misleading and/or false and none of which he knows for certain to be true. Once we recognize that threats are always empirically and conceptually vague, we realize that the torture of the ignorant and innocent is built-in no matter how much we refine the ticking-bomb hypothesis. The interrogator could easily believe that a given individual knows the relevant information about a threat even though no such threat exists. The victim is tortured because of a belief in a threat, not because of its reality.

Necessity

Since defenders offer moral arguments for torture while conceding its evils, control and minimization of torture are crucial. In each case, torture should be used only when necessary and even then as a last resort. All other avenues should be explored first. Here, the statment that torture is necessary has to be considered in light of the logical possibilities first. It is required neither by logic nor by the laws of physics. Rather, the necessity here is also situational. It has to do with a hypothetical imperative to minimize harms. The idea is that an interrogator has a finite number of means available to him for avoiding the feared catastrophe and ought to explore the least evil means prior to using torture. To say that torture is necessary, then, means that all *perceived* available alternative means have been explored and have failed to work. If an interrogator does not work from the least harmful means first, he or she is not using lesser-evils reasoning and not working from any standard moral assumptions.

The absence of alternatives is stipulated. Ticking-bomb theorists assume that there are no alternatives available and then infer the necessity of torture. Yet in real interrogation situations there are always a variety of alternative interrogation strategies. The appropriate question here is not whether there are alternatives but which of the available alternatives is most likely to work.

Here, we should be aware of the skepticism voiced by many interrogators employed by the FBI, the US army, and other bodies about the value of torture as an interrogation tool. A number of professional interrogators are skeptical about the utility of torture. For example, there is no reliable and publicly available evidence of its effectiveness (Borum 2006, 8; Wahlquist 2006, xxi; Coulam 2006, 18–19). But even assuming that it offers some chance of success, it will still take a certain amount of time – time better spent using the other more reliable techniques. The *US Army Field Manual* expresses this reservation well: "Experience indicates that the use of force is not necessary to gain the cooperation of sources for interrogation. Therefore, the use of force is a poor technique, as it yields unreliable results, may damage subsequent collection efforts, and can induce the source to say whatever he thinks the interrogator wants to hear" (US Army, *Field Manual*, ch. 1).

The manual also stresses that interrogators have only about forty-eight hours to get actionable intelligence. Such intelligence is the kind of battlefield intelligence necessary, say, to prevent a surprise attack or to attack an opposing mobile high-value target. After that period, the opponent will have had time to move, to change the conditions of its action as a result of the capture of knowledgeable personnel, or to otherwise alter its behaviour in such a way as to render the sources information valueless.

In this context, assuming the authors of the *US Army Field Manual* are correct in their evaluation of the relative ineffectiveness of torture, and assuming they are correct that nonviolent approaches have been shown to be more effective, intelligence agents always have alternatives to torture. They might be wrong in their judgments about the effectiveness of specific techniques or they might execute a given option weakly, but they do have options. These options take time to implement, and each second spent in implementation is a tick against the clock of the perceived threat. This is especially the case given that the forty-eight-hour period is one in which the exploration of the alternative tactical methods will exhaust the available time before one is even in a position to begin the torture of an individual. Appendix H of the manual identifies at least fifteen different interrogation techniques. Whether the approach is simply a matter of carefully questioning a suspect or of using a variant on the "Mutt and Jeff" (otherwise known as "good cop, bad cop") approach, each one of these will take considerable time and expertise to implement.

This suggests, additionally, that imminence considerations show that torture could not be used as a last resort, for the sequential exploration of the direct approaches, whether "good cop, bad cop" or any of the other means of interrogation, is not compatible with the use of torture in the imminent timeframes under consideration. By the time the interrogator turns to torture as a last resort, the threat is so close that torture will not have time to work. Each failed interrogation method accelerates the imminence of a threat. So if torture is to be employed, either it will have to be employed in the absence of an imminent threat or it will have to be used as a technique of first resort.

Everyone in this debate concedes that torture is of dubious value and that its ability to yield truths in ticking-bomb-style situations, rather than information, is highly doubtful. Every sound, cry, emotional reaction, word, phrase, and sentence is information of some kind. It is all potentially of interest to an interrogator. Some of that information will simply be false; other bits of it will be true and completely irrelevant.

But if torture is of such dubious value and if there are always plausible alternatives, the existence of a threat does not entail torture. Since even defenders of torture concede that it is a crude and unreliable tool, even the existence of a catastrophic threat does not entail torture. Rather, an adequate security response to a public threat requires the better alternatives. Given that these alternatives are to be preferred, and also that competently exploring alternative interrogation technique takes time, deployment of nontorture alternatives will reduce the remaining time to the point where torture will not work either.

To eliminate alternatives to torture, ticking-bomb hypotheses exclude the real-world alternatives that are in fact always open to an interrogator. These options are not mere logical possibilities. They are historically developed alternatives to torture, which, in the opinion of at least some intelligence professionals, are more effective. Interrogator Steven Kleinman (2006, 135) remarks that both rapport building and coercive interrogation strategies are time-intensive.

Given the lack of knowledge of the efficacy of torture and existing psychological reservations arising from its tendency to generate resistance in torture subjects, it is likely to be counter-productive. Hence it is not a justifiable method. Yet the ticking-bomb hypotheses do not even consider the existing evidence for the ineffectuality of torture or its time-intensive nature precisely because such empirical considerations destroy the "no-alternative" or "last-resort" assumption that is built into the ticking-bomb scenarios.

In Dershowitz's (2002) hypothetical case, it is presumed that all of the alternatives have been explored and have failed. He does not explore the thought that mediocre interrogators might have overlooked or misapplied a functional method. He fails to explore the possibility that, in real-world situations, the interrogators may have already gotten the desired information yet failed to recognize it. In real cases, lack of interrogator imagination is a problem. Badly trained or untrained interrogators are more likely to reach for torture because they have no idea how effectively to get information. In practice, the absence of alternatives is quite plausibly the conclusion reached by an incompetent or malicious interrogator (a point supported by a number of experienced former interrogators, each of whom signed a declaration against torture affirming its counter-productivity and asserting that the techniques defined in the *US Army Field Manual* are sufficient for intelligence purposes (Bauer et al. 2006). In any case, the claim that there are no alternatives must always be empirically dubious.

The Epistemic State of the Interrogator

The ticking-bomb hypothesis also pays little or no attention to the epistemic state of the interrogator. Yet it does not take a great deal of thought to recognize that as levels of uncertainty about imminent threats increase, the likelihood of torturing the wrong individuals must also increase. Moreover, an incompetent or untrained interrogator is unlikely even to be aware of alternative interrogation methods, let alone to exercise good judgment in choice or application of these possibilities. In reflecting on arguments for torture, we need to consider as well what interrogators can be reasonably expected to know. Ticking-bomb hypotheses generally work from one of two assumptions. The strict case assumes knowledge on the part of the interrogator. The weak case assumes a "reasonable" belief. Both cases exist in the torture literature. The following analysis shows that the strict case corresponds to no possible interrogation situation and that insofar as we are able to approximate the epistemic state of real interrogators, we have to abandon the ticking-bomb hypothesis.

The distinction between knowledge and belief matters here because an appreciation of the infallibility of knowledge and the fallibility of belief is crucial to understanding why the strict case is at best a caricature. If we know something to be the case, that thing cannot be false. It is incoherent to state, for example, that "I know the Canadians won the hockey game last night" when the Canadians in fact lost. If I know that something is the case, this is because it is the case. If I believe that something is the case, my belief may be wrong. I may believe that the Canadians won last night but then learn that they drew or lost. Either way, beliefs are always fallible in a way that knowledge is not.

The strict and the weak cases are to be distinguished by their emphasis on the knowledge or belief of the interrogators. The strict case emphasizes that the interrogators know salient facts about the case other than the location of the ticking bomb and whether torture will be effective. The weak case emphasizes their reasonable belief and thus concedes the fallibility of their knowledge about every element of their situation.

The Strict Case. So what do interrogators in the strict case know? They know that the suspect is a bomber. They know that the suspect knows the location of the bomb. They know that there is a bomb and that the clock is ticking. They know that the threat is real and imminent. The strict case does not and need not suppose that the torture will be effective. The advantage of specifying knowledge is that the ticking-bomb scenario then does not have to worry about torturing the innocent and irrelevant. Only the knowledgeable "terrorist" is tortured. There are no possible third parties, and all potential messiness and accident are eliminated from consideration.

The question is: Can interrogators know that a suspect has planted a bomb yet not know its location? If they cannot locate the bomb in space and time at a given moment, the interrogation team cannot be certain that it exists. Team members may well have strong reasons to believe in the existence of a bomb. However, if they know it exists, that is either because they have already discovered it (in which case the torture of the "terrorist" is unnecessary) or because the bomb has already exploded (in which case torture interrogation is again unnecessary). The only reason they believe they have to torture their victim is because they do not know that a bomb has been set. Knowledge of the existence of the bomb presupposes the ability to prevent it and hence the irrelevance of torture.

One can complicate the hypothesis to try to avoid the objection. For example, suppose that the suspect has been captured immediately after setting the bomb. Imagine further that the bomb cannot be moved and that we do not have time to discover how to disarm it. Oddly enough, proximity does not change the uncertainty dilemma because the bomb could be a fake. The interrogation team still will not know that it is a bomb until it either explodes or is disarmed.

The same objection governs knowledge that a particular suspect is in fact the bomber. If interrogators know that he or she is the bomber, they must know the location of the bomb. If they are unaware of the location of the bomb, they may still have excellent reasons to believe that the individual is the bomber and may also have strong reasons to believe that there is a bomb, but they will not *know* it.

The perceived need to torture is due only to interrogator ignorance, not to interrogator knowledge. If the interrogators had the knowledge they required, they would not need to torture. That is, if they knew that the suspect was the bomber, they would know that he or she had planted a bomb. To know that a bomb has been planted, they would have to know its location. If they knew its location, they would have a team in place disarming it. If they were already disarming it, torture would be unjustified.

Those who defend torture believe that it can be used to establish knowledge. Perhaps it can, but we have no reliable evidence for this. And whether or not it can, the epistemic state of the interrogators is most certainly not one of knowledge. They do not and cannot know any of the components of the ticking-bomb hypothesis. If they knew all of the components, there would be no need and no argument for torture. Hence torture has to do with confirming suspicions. Torture is used because interrogators want to make their beliefs more reliable, not because they know.

The Weak, or "Reasonable," Case. The strict case has the advantage that it avoids a host of morally controversial consequences like the torture of the innocent and also that it reduces cases of torture only to those that are absolutely necessary. But it gains this to the detriment of coherence, for the knowledge presupposed to eliminate the possibility of torturing in error simultaneously eliminates the point of torturing. Consequently, it does not generate an argument for torture.

Of course, knowledge need not be presupposed. Torture defenders can substitute a belief-based account in its place and stress the reasonable behaviour of public officials. It is perfectly possible to tweak the scenario so that the interrogator is appropriately uncertain about each component of the ticking-bomb hypothesis.

Allhoff (2005b, 253) in particular insists upon reasonableness. This is unsurprising given the incoherence of the strict case. He supports interrogational torture alone and only where there is no alternative. The interrogators have to have a "reasonable expectation" that the suspect has the desired information, which expectation should be based on reliable intelligence. The interrogation team must further have a reasonable expectation that the information possessed by the suspect corresponds to an "immanent and significant threat," and additionally they must have a reasonable expectation that the knowledge possessed by the suspect can help to prevent the feared catastrophe (254). However, the absence of an analysis of reasonableness, likelihood, and intelligence judgment is disturbing, for the terms are sufficiently vague as to leave the reader wondering how an intelligence team might determine any of these. The previous considerations about the vagueness of threats and imminence, combined with fog-of-war issues, are not encouraging in this context, as they suggest that it will be impossible in principle both to define minimal levels of suffering and imminence and to identify cases of last resort that are supposed to constrain the actions of torturers.

However, the more the ticking-bomb hypothesis is constructed to account for such vagueness and uncertainty, the less it can generate the conclusion that torture will be justified, for increasing the levels of uncertainty about each constitutive element in the hypothesis entails a host of evils that Allhoff would find undesirable. For example, we know that in any real case torturers will vary in their character and abilities. Some torturers will be skilled and others incompetent. Some will be zealots and others sadists. Some will hate their work and others love it. All of these will impact how it is that torture is implemented in any given case. Fog of war entails the increased likelihood of the torture of ignorant sympathizers and innocent third parties, for much of the intelligence is false or irrelevant. Yet interrogators still have to evaluate and act upon it. They will not know that it is false. Furthermore, there will also be the inevitable counter-productive tortures arising either from successful suspect resistance, from torture of the ignorant, or from torture by the incompetent, all of which will increase the unjustified suffering. There will also be the problem of the failure to recognize good information when it does emerge. Once we accept the fallibility of the interrogator, a great deal of violence becomes inevitable. If we eliminate knowledge from the ticking-bomb hypothesis and replace it with belief, we inevitably build in a range of ills that the stricter model manages to avoid. The strict case does so in order to preserve the elegance of the cost-benefit calculations but thereby fails to fit empirical and political considerations. The weak case violates the cost-benefit calculations insofar as it *approximates* the empirical conditions under which torture can be employed. Certainly, it does not fit the one-many cost-benefit calculation that torture defenders employ to justify torture, and this is especially true when we remember that torture is never just the infliction of suffering on one person but always harms communities.

In real historical cases, torturers will get the truth and not know it. Hence they will torture pointlessly. Eric Lomax (1995, 136) describes the ignorance of his interrogators and his attempts to tell them the truth about the impossibility of constructing a transmitter radio given the limited materials available to him. "The two men sitting across the table from me simply did not know enough to judge what I was telling them, which was that the technical problems of making a transmitter were too great, and that no group of prisoners with the pathetic materials available to them could work a miracle." The problem is important. What counts as reasonable to either of these two torturers? The real world of intelligence and interrogation work will include mediocrity, finite resources, and fallible interrogators. No law or policy can avoid this. Real intelligence organizations have no choice but to work with finite resources and fallible interpreters. Once we recognize that they are trained to be suspicious and to doubt the truth of the information provided by a victim, we realize that even if a suspect does tell the truth, interrogators have a good chance of disbelieving or misunderstanding it. This is especially difficult if the interrogators do not speak the language of their victim, as in Mr Lomax's case. This of course increases the likelihood that the torture will be ineffective, prolonged, and irrelevant as well as ensures that it will spread beyond the minimal limits imagined in ticking-bomb experiments.

It is easy to do a cost-benefit analysis when we stipulate that one person suffers in order to avoid the suffering of a large set. The calculation becomes much more complicated when we are uncertain about whether there is a bomb. It becomes still worse when we recognize that interrogators do not know whether their victim is a bomber and equally do not know about the imminence of the threat? When we realize that torture inflicts suffering on whole communities, we can no longer construct a meaningful calculus at all. We do not know how many people will be harmed on either side and thus cannot assess the aggregate consequences of anything. Ticking-bomb hypotheses either presuppose an omniscient interrogator – which gets them the desired result of never torturing the innocent but thereby fails to engage any real-world practice – or they introduce the muddiness, complexity, and mediocrity of real-world torture interrogation and thereby lose the ability to construct the cost-benefit calculus that shows that torture is justifiable in the first place.

The Suspect/Source

That thousands are typically tortured in counter-insurgency campaigns and other war contexts is not an accident. Conceptual vagueness and the fog of war dictate this. As should be unsurprising, "terrorist," "fanatic," "suspect," and like terms are also conceptually vague. In every ticking-bomb hypothesis, there is always a "fanatic" or some other witch-hunt target. But the ticking-bomb hypothesis fails to recognize the vagueness problems here, for the identity of the subject of so much fear is unclear.

Historical cautions matter a great deal at this point. The French army in Algeria used an intelligence gathering technique called mass screening to develop organizational charts of the leadership of the Front de Libération Nationale (FLN) in Algiers. Mass screening is a technique whereby agents interrogate large numbers of a given target population in order to home in on desired objectives. The French successfully combined mass-screening interrogation with the use of torture and were eventually able to locate and eliminate the FLN leadership in the city.

Historical torturers are aware that torture is unlikely to work if applied only to a single individual. It is tactically ineffective unless used as a mass-interrogation technique, a point that McCoy discusses in some detail. French and American experience with torture, hard-won in many conflicts since the 1950s, leads to two clear conclusions. First, torture of the few yields little useful information. Second, torture of the many can produce results but at a prohibitively high political cost (McCoy 2006b, 196). One of the reasons mass screening can work is that in counter-insurgencies one will often have no idea even of where to start looking for the opposition. At the point when interrogators lack detailed information, the pool of possible suspects is the entire target population, for a given insurgent can exist only within a supportive population. This means that the surrounding population inevitably knows a great deal about the insurgents in its midst. In mass screening, the *US Army Field Manual* recommends taking advantage of hostile attitudes that will have developed toward insurgents among some of the population – because of recruiting strategies, enforced taxation, and other unpopular policies that the insurgent group will have to employ (US Army, *Field Manual*, ch. 9).

In the context of an army or other unit that employs torture, this means initially interrogating huge numbers of people to work down toward the list of those who are actually involved in the insurgency. This is quite a common method. Former British army officer Bruce Moore-King describes how he constructed the pool of possible suspects during the British counter-insurgency campaign in Rhodesia:

As years passed and the conflict escalated, the Grey's Scouts often found themselves in villages populated only by women, children, and old men. The usual suspects – young males – were all away with the guerrillas. Moore-King would then search for the village elder. The most efficient method of questioning, he says, was not to torture the elder, but to find the elder's grandson. Once the grandson was in hand, Moore-King would order a soldier to hold the child by the ankles and lower his head into a bucket of water. The boy would be brought up for air just before he drowned and would be set on the ground, where he would spew water, writhe in pain, and

weep from fear. The process would be repeated until the old
man talked. (Conroy 2000, 92)

Torture interrogations and bomb threats never happen in a
vacuum. They always take place in ongoing conditions of political
struggle. Recognizing this point helps us to understand why it is
that intelligence and army officers like Moore-King resort to the
use of torture. Their operational goals have to do with the prosecution of the political struggle. Given that those who commit
counter-state violence are unavailable, how else do intelligence
agents find out where they are? They torture close friends and
family members or relevant others whom they have reason to
believe possess the requisite information.

The problem here is not just a matter of torturing one person to
get at another, which was an important element of Moore-King's
practices, but also has to do with who you count as the enemy. As
indicated in chapter 1, torture is never just a matter of attacking
one individual but is always an assault on nests of social relationships. Family members are part of that nest. To the extent that they
protect someone whom the interrogators believe to be involved in
a political campaign, they are themselves members of that opposition. Torture is used to force them to yield information that they
will not release willingly.

The challenge, for those who employ ticking-bomb hypotheses,
is to show why family members are not an appropriate subject of
torture. Suppose that the only way to gather information about
perceived bomb threats is believed to be the torture of third-party
children; if the threat is imminent and the interrogator can envision
no other way to prevent it, the calculus in fact favours the torture
of innocent third parties.

Since the category of "suspect" is itself irredeemably vague and
plausibly includes not just the suicide bomber or other pawn who
plants a bomb but also a whole range of other individuals, the
interrogators must be tempted to extend the class of suspects. For
example, the leaders of an opposition organization count as "terrorists." Capturing them may help to prevent a given threat. Hence
a suspect whom agents believe to be one of the leaders of the oppositional group would count as an appropriate subject of torture. I
suppose the combat soldier might count as well. But what about
the supply people who provide housing, food, and clothing? What
about those who move messages back and forth – the couriers? All

of these individuals have real information that could be of value in preventing an attack. What about those who provide ideological support for the oppositional movement – journalists, academics, and others who defend the perceived justice of the opposition and condemn the injustice of the torturing group? And what about family members, friends, and others who provide moral and psychological support for the "terrorist" or at least are valuable levers that might be exploited to get crucial tactical or strategic information? All of these people are possible subjects for torture, provided that the interrogators believe they are appropriately knowledgeable about some threat and provided the torturers believe they have no alternatives. Historical actors, as we have seen, have drawn this conclusion and chosen to torture third parties. They do not do so because they desire to fail but because they believe it will allow them to achieve tactical or strategic goals. Torture defenders do not desire the torture of the innocent or third parties. But their arguments in fact entail such tortures. The only condition is that the cost-benefit calculation has to turn out in the right way.

No ticking-bomb hypothesis even begins to address these issues. Rather, the suspect is a given, an individual who has planted a bomb and who knows that he or she has done so (this avoids tortures of the innocent and cases where the bombers are unwitting dupes of other political agents). The interrogation team knows or is reasonably certain that the suspect has planted the bomb and that the threat is imminent. This introduces a further wrinkle that demands ethical reflection. Apart from designating the individual with the loaded term of "terrorist," the ticking-bomb hypothesis pays no attention to the kinds of suspects that an interrogator might encounter.

The *US Army Field Manual* (ch. 1) divides sources into three kinds: cooperative and friendly, neutral and nonpartisan, and hostile and antagonistic. Hostile sources are the most challenging. The suspect in the ticking-bomb hypothesis probably falls into this class since it is hard to imagine that a neutral and nonpartisan individual would knowingly plant a bomb. But vagueness considerations should give us pause since we are entitled to wonder who counts as neutral and nonpartisan. Depending on uncertainty levels and diminished trust of the neutral and even friendly sources, a temptation to torture could arise here as well.

In any event, the ticking-bomb hypothesis presumably envisions the torturing of hostile and antagonistic sources since the other two are more likely to be cooperative and thus more likely to be open to the alternative interrogation methods. But this is not made clear. Assuming that those being interrogated are hostile and antagonistic nonstate actors, the following problems emerge. The *US Army Field Manual* (ch. 9) notes that an important resistance method for insurgency leaders is to instruct their followers to remain silent for a given period of time. In consequence, this degrades the value of the information ultimately revealed to interrogators. This has consequences for imminence considerations because it shortens threat times for bomb planters. Those who plant bombs are hardly going to leave a great deal of time between planting the bomb and detonation. The longer lead time that they are able to provide, the greater is the amount of time that becomes available to a security force to find and disarm the bomb. Rational planning on the part of the bombers will take into account the possibility of capture and will take as many advance steps as possible to minimize the effectiveness of intelligence gathering even in the event of capture. But this means that the amount of time available to use interrogation methods to gather information is going to be relatively short – in the range of a couple of days in the estimation of the US army – for tactical threats like bombs. Consequently, it will be even more unlikely that there will be any time left over for torture once the more effective methods are explored.

Even the presence of a hostile source is not a reason to employ torture, at least not according to the field manual. On the contrary, the other methods are likely to prove more effective. The ineffectiveness of torture in comparison with the other methods does not just vanish because the source turns out to be hostile. The manual is quite clear that a captured individual experiences the first twenty-four hours in an enormous state of disorientation and is vulnerable to interrogation at that point. They are also often trained to expect brutality. Hence the authors believe that compassion and concern are a more viable alternative, especially given those expectations. This is especially important given that brutality and failure to abide by the Geneva Conventions are likely to foster sympathies for the opposition or to induce people to remain neutral when their support is required (US Army, *Field Manual*, ch. 9).

Nor do ticking-bomb hypotheses pay any attention to the kinds of knowledge that a source can have. For example, in a discussion of individual background and memory, the field manual discusses the speed of memory loss and asserts that "much of the information of value to the interrogator is information that the source is not even aware that he has" (US Army, *Field Manual*, ch. 6). Yet the ticking-bomb hypothesis presupposes that what is of value to the torturer is explicit, meaning that torture of the individual only for some explicit knowledge will not help. For example, a suspect might have just left a cell phone in a specific location and have no idea that the phone was a bomb or perhaps the transmitter for the bomb. This individual has planted a bomb and is completely unaware of the fact, so the knowledge the interrogators seek may be something that neither they nor the suspect knows. As a result, whatever information the suspect has might be discernible only through background evidence that the interrogators need to bring out through careful rapport building and questioning.

If the desired information is known tacitly rather than consciously, torturing the individual to get it takes on an entirely different cast because we are now talking about something deeply uncertain, something that may not exist at all. Yet if torture is legitimized and if the *US Army Field Manual* is right in stressing the problem of tacit knowledge, an interrogation will exceed the constraints that the ticking-bomb hypothesis constructs. If torture is permitted, trained torture interrogators will also torture with a view to discovering tacit knowledge. Forbidding the torturer to explore tacit possibilities can significantly diminish the possibilities of success.

In previous chapters I have pointed to a pernicious, tacit, individualist assumption underlying much protorture debate. It reemerges here in the interpretation of the suspect as an isolated individual and in the failure to acknowledge that intelligence work typically deals with groups or populations. A suspect refers to a pool of possible individuals with specific historical, political, familial, and ethnic relations. The individual of the ticking-bomb hypothesis rides roughshod over these complexities and could not possibly fit a historical individual.

Ultimately, we should recall one of Michael Taussig's (2004a, 40) warnings about words like "terrorist" and "fanatic":

Hated and feared, objects to be despised, yet also of awe, the reified essence of evil in the very being of their bodies, these figures of the Jew, the black, the Indian, and woman herself, are clearly objects of cultural construction, the leaden keel of evil and of mystery stabilizing the ship and course that is western history. With the cold war we add the communist. With the time bomb ticking inside the nuclear family, we add the feminists and the gays. The military and the New Right, like the conquerors of old, discover the evil they have imputed to these aliens, and mimic the savagery they have imputed.

We can add to this the stereotypical "Islamic terrorist." Such terms fit with witch hunts and other forms of hysteria but correspond to no flesh-and-blood historical individual. The choice of such terms alone is pernicious and quietly begs important questions of justice. For example, it illicitly allows theorists to ignore the unjust contexts in which political violence takes place and excludes the grievances that motivate the violence in the first place – such as exploitation, oppression, and inequality or unfair distribution of material resources. It is relatively easy to torture a terrorist or a fanatic, just as it was easy to burn a witch. It was relatively easy as well to construct a "rational" argument to justify torture and burning, and given the prevalence of the ticking-bomb hypothesis in popular consciousness, it remains relatively easy to do so in the context of "counter-terrorism." Terms like "terrorist" build in the idea that there is something intrinsically evil about such classes and that they therefore deserve the horrors inflicted on them. We are not torturing individuals, as the ticking-bomb hypotheses envision, but inflicting terrible suffering on whole classes whose boundaries are conceptually and empirically vague. Yet the ticking-bomb hypothesis deludes us into thinking otherwise and contributes to the legitimation of these horrors.

ADDITIONAL CRITICAL CONSIDERATIONS

By decomposing the ticking-bomb scenario into the above elements, I display the artificiality and unreality of the ticking-bomb hypotheses. They are artificial and fail to model any possible empirical practice. Intelligence-gathering policies are far more complicated than the elimination of ticking bombs. They serve a wide range of strategic and tactical purposes, only one of which is even recognized by the ticking-bomb hypothesis. As David Rieff (2002, 108) notes, the idea that torture would be employed solely to prevent a ticking bomb from detonating reveals the total failure to understand intelligence. Torture is a way to wage war and a way to conceive and counter an enemy. The logical and epistemic nonsense gets still worse when we realize, as Susan Marks (2004, 385) maintains, that such thinking divorces reflection on torture from the wider political context of coercive and oppressive relations.

This consideration becomes more important when we realize that there are significant differences between individual acts and institutional behaviour. The individualist assumption that I have already criticized emerges in part because of a failure to appreciate this distinction. The ticking-bomb hypothesis claims to model the behaviour of a single interrogator reacting to a catastrophic threat. But in all cases involving governments or nonstate resistance groups, we are talking about individuals who act in a public capacity as a representative of institutions and states. In other words, we are dealing with institutional problems. In criticizing the idea that the tortures at Abu Ghraib and elsewhere were a result of the behaviours of a few poorly trained individuals, Gregory Hooks and Clayton Mosher (2005, 1628) emphasize the systemic nature of the torture and other violence: "The problem is that the United States has developed and refined a callous and calculated method for extracting information and intimidating civilian populations. The decision about when and how to deploy violence is made on the basis of efficiency calculations, not human rights conventions."

Soldiers do not act independently of their institutions. They act in terms of established training practices and defined policies, often secret, which determine the frame of possible actions they may employ. Hence we are talking about policies, and although policies result in acts, the policies define classes of acts, not unique instances. A secretary of defence does not usually order a single torture. He or she constructs the policies that enable other persons across a chain of command to employ torture under the desired conditions.

What this means is that if a torture policy is constructed, it will have to be interpreted by a wide range of people. The interpretation will lead to practice variations that the policy maker will not anticipate and hence will not be able to control. When Dershowitz or the others claim to know what horrors would be unleashed by the use of torture in the ticking-bomb scenario, they do not seem to consider this inevitable lack of control.

Furthermore, if a torture policy is conceived at some advanced institutional level, it will have to be subjected to experiment, tested, and revised at lower levels. Torture policies will have to be improved over time in order to ensure effectiveness. But as the various histories of torture demonstrate, this can be accomplished only with multiple victims and research programs over time. As a program is implemented, for example, a failure to achieve results will lead to an extension of the use of torture in "fishing expeditions" that are either intended to discover information or deemed a necessary reaction to unexpected needs, as Juan Mendez (2006, 61) discusses.

The point of this chapter is that the ticking-bomb hypothesis is pseudo-consequentialist. It is not that the scenarios it imagines are unlikely but that they are empirically impossible. The hypothesis systematically and deliberately ignores the empirical circumstances under which torture is possible and takes place; it ignores the institutional nature of torture and its problems; it fails to understand the difference between the behaviour of individuals and the policies of institutions; it fails to account for the social nature of either the victims or torturers; it creates a demonizing myth of the "terrorist"; it refuses to introduce any real consequences of torture at all; it provides no analysis of the nature of torture; and it pays no attention to problems of conceptual or fog-of-war vagueness.

In consequence, Allhoff's ticking-bomb hypothesis shares the weaknesses of other such thought experiments. Effectively, the refusal to pay attention to the nature and structure of torture and the elimination of the historical and real consequences mean that his thought experiment, like those of Dershowitz and others, is not really about torture at all. "Torture" functions like an unbound variable of predicate logic, bearing no relation to possible empirical instantiations.

Allhoff (2005a, 260) distances himself deliberately from American use of torture at Abu Ghraib and remarks that he is not making any arguments for that. He is simply interested in testing whether a hypothetical case for torture can be constructed. He calls himself a "first order agnostic," suspending judgment on whether utilitarianism, deontology, or virtue ethics ought to be the theory by which we evaluate behaviour. He also stresses that "Many of those who discuss the morality of torture are concerned with whether torture would ever be permissible in the real world, even if it could be philosophically justified in principle. As a moral philosopher, the question of real-world justifiability is really not one on which I have much to say; I am more interested in the theoretical arguments that can be rendered on either side of the debate."

But this means that Allhoff is not discussing the tortures that worry absolutist opponents and that motivate its absolute prohibition in international law. Torture appears in these experiments as something relatively simple, yet it is structured, inherently institutional, and far more damaging, violent, and complicated than existing defences address. In any case, no human rights activist is interested only in the abstract world. What matters is the behaviour of governments and the arguments they use to justify their evils. The merely logically possible justifications for torture are and ought to be irrelevant.

Moreover, if he had wanted to develop a valid argument, he could have done so using formal symbols and the apparatus of symbolic logic. This at least would not lead people to think he is arguing for torture. My point here is that it is of course possible to construct a valid argument for torture, just as I constructed a valid argument for the influence of little green men from Mars on current politics. That is easy. But to say that you have constructed a valid theoretical argument for a position is – to use a cricket analogy – like being on the pitch without having any runs on the board. It does not mean that you have provided an argument for torture. To do that, you have to deal with the practice, and that involves empirical reference, knowledge of history, knowledge of practical ethics, and all of the other messy details.

To justify torture, theorists need to do a great deal more than construct a formally valid argument using separation of cases or any other valid argument form. To make the point further, I need only note that I can insert antitorture terms into a separation-of-cases structure and get a valid argument against torture. All this shows that validity will not get us far. We need it, but we had better be able to work with the empirical issues if we are going to discuss torture.

Such ahistorical and nonempirical ethical theorizing creates the moral illusion that torture is justifiable. Applied ethical problems cannot and should not be treated in this fashion. All that the ticking-bomb hypothesis does is create a structure in which we are compelled to concede that *if* that premise set is true, the conclusion must also be true. It does not tell us whether the premises are true, whether some might be false, whether the conclusion is true, or whether the conclusion is false.

This is why ticking-bomb arguments are question-begging. They do not even attempt to justify the truths of any antecedent premises and do not bother to justify their motivating intuitions. They are taken for granted, and the reader or listener is pushed to accept them uncritically.

The considerations I have developed also provide a clue as to how we can arrive at the position that Henry Shue wants in his classic paper but that he does not ultimately provide. His view is that torture should be absolutely prohibited in all cases but that in the theoretical case of the ticking bomb it might be justifiable. He escapes licensing torture even there by claiming that hard cases make bad law. However, it seems that the problem is not that the ticking bomb is a hard case but that it is not a genuine case at all. It belongs in the abstract realm of pure logical possibility and thus has nothing to do with the world in which human beings act. As an unreal possibility, it should have no influence on debates about torture.

In the best-case scenario, the ticking-bomb hypothesis contains an argument that is valid yet unsound. In this case, the reasoning can be fine, but at least some of the sentences from among the premise set and/or conclusion are untrue. But in this case, the ticking-bomb hypothesis is unsound and a vacuous logical experiment.

Why then are ticking-bomb thought experiments so popular? Why does it appear attractive? Politically, it appeals to liberals who are otherwise opposed to cruelty and the deliberate infliction of suffering. David Luban (2007, 252–3) suggests that ticking-bomb hypotheses are simply rhetorical moves designed to convince liberals that there are cases in which torture is morally required. The logical sleight of hand and the confusion of abstract and real possibility is one reason. It models a set of intuitions that, at first sight, seem plausible for being neither logically nor physically impossible. It is only because the intuitions are not subject to careful historical and conceptual scrutiny that they preserve their plausibility. But nobody would think it good to construct an argument on the basis of ignorant and unschooled intuitions.

For this reason, I reject even Felner's (2006, 42) argument that the ticking-bomb hypothesis should be left to the ethics classroom. Likewise, while M. Cherif Bassiouni's (2005, 259) remark that "nothing in recent torture practices at Abu Ghraib, Guantanamo Bay and Afghanistan conforms to the strictures of the ticking bomb hypothesis" is correct, we need to understand that there is no possible empirical correlate to the imagined situation. Consequently, the ticking-bomb hypothesis belongs on the list of bad arguments and therefore may have some role to play as a caution to students. But other than as an object lesson in how not to construct a moral argument, it does not really belong even there.

Hence the right answer to the question of what to do about the ticking bomb is "so what?!" It is a complex appeal to fear, but its sophistication does not make it sound.

We should be careful to recognize that arguments for torture do not stand or fall by ticking-bomb hypotheses. Not all authors use them. Consequently, the critique of the ticking-bomb hypothesis that I have developed here is not sufficient to refute all moral arguments for torture. However, once we realize how weak ticking-bomb hypotheses are, we can at least eliminate them from the debate and approach the ethics of torture with the respect that such a complex issue deserves. Hence elimination of the ticking bomb removes the apparently easy argument for torture and forces us to consider the real ugliness of torture. It is one way to avoid the sanitization process that is employed to make torture easier to accept.

3

Why Utilitarians
Must Oppose Torture

One will not approve the action of a queen who, under the pretext of saving the State, commits or even permits a crime. The crime is certain and the evil for the State is open to question. Moreover, this manner of giving sanction to crimes, if it were accepted, would be worse than a disruption of some one country, which is liable enough to happen in any case, and would perchance happen all the more by reason of such means chosen to prevent it.

Leibniz 1951, 138

Chapter 1 explored the nature of political torture as an attack on identity. Since identity is intersubjective, torture not only assaults the body of a discrete entity but also violates nested sets of social relations and the individuals embedded within. The harms of torture are complex and extend long into the future life of the victim. Moreover, the resulting damage is widespread, affecting relatives and close friends of the victim as well as entire communities. It is a myth to think that the harms of torture are suffered by the victim alone. Such a thought is far too simplistic and does not reflect the nature of torture or the circumstances in which it can be inflicted. Despite extensive medical and psychological research (Somnier et al. 1992, 66), the precise extent of the harms is still neither adequately mapped nor understood. Yet the research we do have offers a powerful demonstration of the complexity of the suffering caused by torture.

Chapter 1 also argued that torture is essentially terroristic and coercive. Whatever success it can have, if any, is due to the deliberate infliction of terror on the minds and bodies of individuals as well as to spin-off consequences and the awakening of terror and suffering in the individual's community. Any other purposes for which torture is used are incidental. Hence a classic distinction in the literature between interrogational and terroristic torture is untenable. Whether defenders of torture realize it, arguments for torture are necessarily arguments for terror.

This error arises because defences of torture never explore in detail the nature, structure, and real sequelae of torture. These issues are subtle and complicated, and they resist any simple consequentialist calculus. Chapter 1 noted as well the absence of any attention to questions of gender or race. As torture attacks identity, it will inevitably have a gender component, and where race is a relevant concern, torture will ineluctably assault that as well.

Hence I believe that existing defences of torture are consequentialist in name only. A consequentialist analysis that fails to closely examine the real consequences of a practice does not deserve the name. It is pseudo consequentialism. This is particularly prominent in the unsoundness of the ticking-bomb hypothesis. Commonly invoked to elicit favourable audience intuitions in support of the justifiability of torture, the arguments are in fact weak arguments from fear. The arguments are wholly artificial and fail to support the inference that torture is justifiable either in principle or in practice. I now begin a consequentialist defence of the absolute prohibition of torture.

UTILITARIANISM AND TORTURE

Utilitarianism is a deeply controversial moral theory. Some critics challenge that it misunderstands the nature of personal identity. Philosophers such as W.D. Ross (1988) believe that it fails to comprehend the moral status of special relationships and obligations. Some feminists believe that utilitarianism fails to appreciate the unique moral issues surrounding gender and identity. Other theorists believe that utilitarian theories fail to appreciate the centrality of autonomy, integrity, and community. (For detailed exploration of utilitarianism and its critics, see Sen and Williams 1982 and Smart and Williams 1973.)

I am going to withhold judgment on these rich meta-ethical debates and assume that a sophisticated and creative utilitarian can meet the objections. My strategy is to show that, on the assumption that utilitarianism is coherent, careful consideration of consequences entails that utilitarians must absolutely oppose torture. Here, the following comment is important: "Even an out-and-out utilitarian can support an absolute prohibition against institutionalised torture on the ground that no government in the world can be trusted not to abuse the power and to satisfy in practice the conditions he would impose" (Twining and Twining 1973, 348).

The reference to institutionalization is important. Indeed, it is the key to understanding many of the additional harmful consequences that I shall shortly describe. However, Twining could have put the point more powerfully. Although trust is a genuine and legitimate concern, the problem is not that there is a risk of abuse but that the abuse is inevitable. Once we consider what is entailed in establishing the institutions needed to torture effectively, we cannot avoid the conclusion that torturing introduces an enormous class of additional harms beyond those discussed in chapter 1.

INTRODUCTION TO UTILITARIANISM

A common error is to assume that utilitarianism and consequentialism are identical. They are not. Utilitarianism is a subset of consequentialist moral theories, but there are other consequentialist philosophies. Consequentialist moral theories assess value in terms of the public benefits and harms that a given action, rule, or policy brings about. As we will see in the next chapter, the problem of dirty hands is also a form of moral consequentialism. Yet its defenders reject utilitarianism.

There are many different forms of utilitarianism, and I cannot cover them all. However, there are only two variants present in the torture debates: act and rule utilitarianism. Act utilitarianism is the classical version of utilitarianism first developed by Jeremy Bentham. Rule utilitarianism is associated with John Stuart Mill and later philosophers.

Certain core concepts are shared by all utilitarians. For example, sentience is the basic value. Sentience is the capacity to experience pleasure and pain. Pleasure is good and pain is bad. In moral practice, according to utilitarians, we seek to maximize pleasure and/or to minimize pain. The criterion for being morally considerable is sentience alone. If a being can experience pleasure or pain, we are obligated to consider its interests. For utilitarians, any other criterion is morally arbitrary.

As a result, all utilitarian theories are universal and cosmopolitan. We owe moral consideration to all sentient beings and cannot exclude them from consideration without good reason. Utilitarians assert that as moral beings we are obligated to maximize happiness and minimize suffering. Those actions are good that maximize the happiness of the greatest number of beings possible and that minimize suffering. Utilitarians require us to consider the like interests of all those affected by our choices (Singer 1993, 21).

Individuals do not lose moral significance by virtue of group membership; they are morally considerable simply by virtue of their sentience. Exclusion of relevantly affected beings from consideration on grounds of gender, race, state membership, or cultural identity is similarly immoral because the criterion for considerability is not justifiably drawn by community membership but by physical and psychological capacity. Moral considerability is grounded in the physiology and psychology of the relevant beings, not in cultural membership.

The utilitarian position is not that you should never deliberately inflict harm. It is rather that whenever we act or construct laws, we should always act with a view to maximizing good and/or minimizing harm. Occasionally, we will have to deliberately inflict harm in order to maximize good consequences. It can turn out that the deliberate infliction of harm is occasionally necessary if we are to increase the overall wellbeing of a community. For example, punishment can be extremely harmful. It is the deliberate infliction of suffering on an individual. Thus, considered in itself, it is wrong to do. But for utilitarians, punishment can be justified provided that it reduces crime and enhances public security and wellbeing. Punishment creates incentives to obey laws and refrain from harming others. Therefore, it can be a good thing even though it has obviously harmful effects on those the society punishes.

Although utilitarians share a commitment to sentience and happiness maximization, different utilitarian theories can diverge considerably over how best to maximize good consequences. For instance, act utilitarians argue that we have to focus on specific happiness-maximizing actions rather than specifically on policies or laws. Morality is concerned with individual choice making. For an act utilitarian, obeying a law will generally be good, but there are occasions in which a failure to disobey the law will cause more harm. For example, there is a universal prohibition against theft.

Prohibitions against theft are important in ensuring citizens security against violation as well as in helping to guarantee them the possibility of pursuing a rich and meaningful life. However, an act utilitarian might argue that there are cases where theft is the right act to choose. In such cases obedience to law might invite a preventable greater harm. For example, suppose that a single individual is hording food in time of famine. He or she is legally entitled to that food and elects to keep it even though many will starve in consequence. Act utilitarians can morally support the theft provided that it results in greater overall happiness. So redistributing the food in that case may be the right thing to do, even though it is a theft.

Rule utilitarians argue that happiness is best maximized through the establishment of effective rules and laws. It might be the case that in specific instances deliberately breaking the law could prove beneficial. But if people generally break the law when they believe it is to the good, this threatens the legal institutions themselves. Consequently, the law should be obeyed even if law breaking might promise good consequences in specific instances. The general practice of upholding and following laws will provide greater benefits than any tendency to break the law whenever the good consequences are believed to be happiness-maximizing. So a rule utilitarian might reject the act-utilitarian inference to steal the food in the famine situation on the grounds that undermining the laws of the state is a greater harm than allowing the starving to get sufficient food.

I have no intention of finally resolving the dispute between act and rule utilitarians. It is a complex and fascinating debate in its own right. In the torture debates, rule utilitarians typically support the absolute prohibition against torture and act utilitarians treat it as prima facie valid. I next intend to discuss why they diverge on torture. The rest of the chapter will argue that a careful consideration of consequences means that act utilitarians must also absolutely oppose torture. The absolute prohibition of torture is a rare issue that the two utilitarian camps should equally support. Even if it is true that there are some rules and prohibitions that should be broken under relevant circumstances, it does not follow that all rules are derogable.

At stake here is the moral justification of state torture. Institutional and state behaviour is quite different from individual action and raises different moral considerations. State torture raises concerns about the consequences of institutional and collective behaviour that are quite different from those that arise from individual choices. I argue that state torture must be institutional and that institutionalized torture cannot be happiness-maximizing.

RULE-UTILITARIAN ARGUMENTS AGAINST TORTURE

Rule utilitarians argue that happiness is best secured by establishing stable laws and institutions. Violating these, even for the sake of a clear momentary good, will produce more harm than one might think. So the apparent plausibility of encouraging the violation of a rule for the sake of some good masks much greater difficulties. William Casebeer (2005, 262) provides a good example. Although he allows torture in principle, he suggests that utilitarians should never justify torture in practice. The problem is that standard act-utilitarian arguments for torture neglect to consider the institutional harms inflicted in practising torture:

> [M]ost consequentialist justifications for the permissibility of torture neglect to consider the institutional and character-based harm that we do to ourselves when we actually attempt to build a system for torture interrogation that the utilitarian would find praiseworthy. Perversely, consequentialist justifications for torture interrogation require well-trained torturers who know where and when to apply pain, but establishing the institutions required in order to sustain such well-honed practice is fraught with perils that the utilitarian would condemn, all things considered.

This problem of institutionalization is central. Social psychologist Jean-Maria Arrigo (2004) has written an exceptionally good essay devoted to the problem. One of her central points is that "the establishment of an official torture interrogation program produces long-term disfunctions in key institutions – notably health care, biomedical research, the police, the judiciary, and the military – due to institutional dynamics that are independent of the original moral rationale for torture" (544).

The problem is that effective torture requires harmful policies, institutions, and practices that entail far more than the infliction of violence on a torture victim on a discrete occasion. Casebeer is willing to countenance torture in principle while prohibiting it in practice. Arrigo is different in absolutely opposing torture. Although I believe that Casebeer's practical reservations are sound, I think that Arrigo has it right. The institutional requirements for torture make it impossible to satisfy the conditions under which utilitarians can justify torture. The problem is that because the decision to torture establishes harmful regularities, the act of torturing an individual inflicts far more harm than torture advocates recognize.

ACT-UTILITARIAN ARGUMENTS FOR TORTURE

I want to emphasize again that no utilitarian defender of torture thinks it is a good thing. The deliberate infliction of harm is always evil and generally to be avoided. The problem, utilitarian defenders believe, is that there are cases in which we have to choose between greater and lesser harms. The number of these cases is always believed to be small, but act-utilitarian defenders of torture assert that they exist. Jeremy Bentham has the following to say on the subject: "I have given the subject a very attentive consideration, and the result is that I am inclined to think there are a very few cases in which for a very particular purpose, Torture might be made use of with advantage" (Twining and Twining 1973, 308).*

The relevant conditions are the following:

1 We must have good proof that the prisoner is able to do what the torture requires.
2 Torture is only to be employed in cases where one can afford no delay. The cases must be urgent.
3 It must be done in cases where there is at least a great probability that not performing the torture will be unsuccessful. If time is available, then the compulsion should be less severe and thereby less unpopular.
4 Even in urgent cases, the benefits of torture must outweigh the harms.

---

* Twining presents this previously unpublished essay of Bentham's in a more extended discussion of the ethics of torture.

5 Torture should be limited by law to ensure that an individual is not being compelled to do something that is beyond his power to do.

6 In order to restrict wasteful torture, the tortures employed should be such as to be the most acute for the time period that the torture is applied, and in which the pain ends as soon as possible after the application of torture ends. (Bentham 1973, 313–14)

Utilitarians are committed to the belief that, if torture is to be justifiable, there must be a reasonable chance that it is effective. This is unsurprising, as an ineffective torture will not serve any public interest. Such torture inflicts harm while achieving no possible good. This imposes important constraints. For example, as Bentham's first point indicates, officials should not torture the ignorant, nor should they try to compel an individual to do something of which he or she is incapable. If we have captured an accomplice to a bomb plot but this individual knows no significant details, there is no point in torture to prevent the attack. This means that the suspect is not to be tortured unless there are strong intelligence grounds to believe that he or she has relevant information that can prevent the attack.

As we have seen in the discussion of the ticking-bomb hypothesis, urgency (or imminence) is another important limitation, for the more time that is available, the more alternatives are available to interrogators to follow up leads and choose less harmful means to prevent attacks and secure vital public interests. Since utilitarians prefer a priori the lesser suffering, torture is never to be chosen when genuine alternatives exist.

The fourth constraint noted by Bentham is particularly important, as Fritz Allhoff stresses (2005b, 254). An attack may be catastrophic and its prevention urgent, but the mere fact that the attack would be catastrophic is not a sufficient reason to torture someone. The interrogators must have reasonable grounds to believe that preventing the attack will bring about more benefits than harms. Suppose that the only way to torture to prevent the attack was through a mass-screening program: in such a case, the tens or hundreds or thousands of individuals who would be harmed to prevent an attack that would kill twenty are not justifiable – at least not to a utilitarian.

A striking feature of Bentham's discussion of torture is that he argues for pain maximization. This is quite different from more recent utilitarian defenders of torture like Allhoff (2005b, 255–6). The problem, for Bentham, is that judgments about severity of suffering are deeply uncertain. But since it is overwhelmingly important that torture be effective, officials need to err on the side of severity without destroying the torture victim. If they apply insufficient torture, they will fail to secure a vital public interest. Hence Bentham insists on inflicting the most acute suffering for the period of the torture.

Allhoff (2005b, 245) generally agrees with Bentham:

> The utilitarian argues that the right action is the one, out of those available to the agent, that maximizes total aggregate happiness. We could quite easily imagine a scenario wherein the disutility of torturing a captive (his pain, the discomfort of the torturer, expense, permanent negative effects to both, chance of negative events causally connected to torture, etc.) is outweighed, or even dramatically outweighed, by the utility of torture (information is provided that saves many lives and therefore garners all the associated utilities).

It can be the case that increasing aggregate happiness obligates us to deliberately inflict a certain amount of suffering. Punishment is a useful example. In itself an evil, punishment can be good only insofar as it contributes to public security and perhaps to the extent that it reforms a convicted individual. Similarly, although torture is generally prohibited, the threat of catastrophic events raises the possibility that it will be justified where it can prevent the catastrophe.

The conditions under which torture is justified are those outlined in the ticking-bomb hypothesis. Hence the basic act-utilitarian position in favour of torture is quite simple. We are justified in torturing an individual when we reasonably believe that torture is happiness-maximizing. For the most part, this will not be the case, but there are always exceptions to rules. Act utilitarians stress that we also have to be prepared to act on the exceptions. Not just that, but they think that blind rule worship will cause catastrophes if we are not sensitive to the cases where the rules can no longer usefully apply.

Although Bentham recognizes that torture is most effective when it breaks the spirit, he seems explicitly to consider only physical torture: "Torture, as I understand it, is where a person is made to suffer any violent pain of body in order to compel him to do something or desist from doing something which done or desisted from the penal application is immediately made to cease" (Twining and Twining 1973, 309).

He does not explore the psychological nature of torture and thus does not appreciate its assault on selfhood. Consequently, he does not recognize the details of the damage torture inflicts. While Allhoff's account also neglects to explore the specific details of physical and psychological torture, he does accept that there is a distinction – even though he defends both. All forms of torture are justifiable in principle, being subject only to the constraint that the amount of suffering be the minimum necessary to achieve the aim (Allhoff 2005b, 255–6).

Furthermore, Allhoff is aware of the considerable scientific advances that have taken place since Bentham wrote, and he takes as positive the possible employment of psychological and medical expertise to develop psychological profiles of suspects and to determine as precisely as possible the type and extent of pain that a given individual can endure. He seems to hope that new scientific expertise can allow us to more precisely map the amount of suffering, thus reducing it to only what is deemed necessary to break the suspect and thereby acquire the desired information.

PROBLEMS IN EVALUATING PAIN

There are considerable problems in evaluating the severity of pain, problems not addressed by defences of torture. If the sufferings experienced by the torture victim are to be balanced by the benefits to be gained for the society that the torture interrogator supposedly protects, we need to ask whether it is possible to balance the benefits against the suffering. If so, how is this to be done? By what standard do we assess that a certain amount of pain is inflicted upon a given individual? According to what criterion do we even quantify the suffering? The problem is that there is no available standard, and defenders of torture offer none. Allhoff (2005b, 255–6) acknowledges that there are epistemic burdens to pain calculations but does not explain the problems or show either that they are surmountable or how. He simply asserts that the problems should be resolvable. He provides no critical assessment of the strengths and weaknesses of psychological profiling and takes for granted that it can achieve the desired intelligence goals.

There is medical and anecdotal evidence to support the idea that we cannot do a calculus of suffering. Here, we should recall Susan Brison's (2002, 6–7) criticisms of Ross Harrison and utilitarianism. We should also consider Consuelo Rivera-Fuentes's (Rivera-Fuentes and Birke 2001, 660) anguished denial that any scientific language could capture "what I felt and remembered: anxiety, humiliation, powerlessness, my potty-training down the drain in a string of jerks and tears, degradation to the point of feeling like a 'speck in the universe,' no/body; I was just a set of 'basic functions' – as you call them – not working at all."

Given the specificity and uniqueness of individual suffering, the notion that one can put all the different forms of suffering on a scale and then add up utilities and disutilities is false. For example, the subjectivity of the experience of pain means that one individual might perceive as terrible the same suffering that another regards as comparatively mild. We cannot even calculate the pain involved in superheating a needle and jamming it under someone's fingernails. Aside from the fact that this may kill those with weak hearts or other conditions, the experience some people have in hospitals with needles suggests that this might be absolutely horrifying to one person yet stoically bearable to another depending on variations in individual psychology.

Finn Somnier and colleagues (1992, 67) discuss the complexities of torture-induced trauma and note that therapists dealing with torture do not yet understand the interactions between torture trauma and the victim's individual personality, age, gender, strength of political convictions, cultural background, coping strategies, and defence mechanisms. The experience of pain and suffering varies significantly depending on the physiology, psychology, gender, and culture of the given torture survivor. Utilitarian defenders of torture pay no attention to the complexities here and do not seriously consider the possibility that these will defeat any utility calculus. At the very least, they do not consider the possibility that the complexities will defeat the utility calculus as applied by a given interrogator at a given time. Since medical experts are dubious about the possibilities, there is no justification for the optimistic attitude adopted by defenders of torture. The same point goes for calculating values for the humiliation that is an essential element of state torture. Inge Lunde and Jorgen Ortmann (1992, 313) and Elaine Scarry (1985, 5, 7) note that humiliation is culturally defined as well. So enforced nakedness might be a comparatively minor experience for individuals from some cultures but, given the appropriate background belief system, might be experienced as intolerable by others.

Stephen Lukes (2005, 9) identifies a set of different continua according to which suffering can be ranked, each of which is quite distinct: a continuum of pain induced by physical force, a continuum of distress, a continuum of fear, a continuum of humiliation, and a continuum of offensiveness. All of these can cause profound mental and physical disruption of a given individual, but they assault different aspects of the mentality of an individual. Even if it is coherent to speak of quanta of physical suffering, working out the quanta of pain experienced by an individual stabbed by a red-hot needle will not identify the sum of one's suffering. It is not clear that the scales are commensurable and even less obvious that such suffering is even quantifiable. The suffering may be identifiable without being quantifiable.

In any case, the concept of minimum pain employed here is inadequate because, even if some rigorous scientific testing might be employed to determine the capacity of human beings to experience pain, the interrogation setting is nothing like a randomized clinical trial or other scientifically rigorous experiment. The interrogator will not know the specific pain capacities of any individual. These need to be discovered through torture. This discovery in turn will presumably require some combination of background experience, professional torturing judgment, and existing information (if any is available) about the source. What will break a specific individual is not knowable a priori.

Since defenders concede that torture is dubiously effective, an inability to calculate quanta of suffering entails a great likelihood that the violence will be either insufficient or excessive. Hence trial and error will have to be employed over time to home in on the methods that might actually break an individual. That the interrogator will have to explore multiple interrogation and torture options means that the idea that he or she will be able to apply "minimal" pain is nonsense. Not only is it impossible to know in advance how specific tortures will affect a given individual, but we have no scientifically respectable measures for different kinds of pain and suffering. To attempt to ensure that a torture vicitm suffers only the most "minimal" pain is to pursue some kind of perverse regulative ideal. In practice, effectiveness alone is likely to determine the choice of methods.

In any case, as Dinah Pokempner (2006, 161) notes, the concept of the torturer as a disengaged and rational scientist is a myth incompatible with the intimate nature of torture. Torture is an assault on identity and requires the torturer to engage closely with the victim:

> "[C]linical" torture, the idea that there is a cold science to imposing just the precise amount of pain necessary to extract the needed information, is a myth. However much the torturer wishes to see him or herself as professional and disengaged, torture is an intimate act that engages the torturer's own emotions and imagination. This may be why it is so difficult to control. Yet official torturers are not usually sadists or psychologically aberrational, as such persons would be susceptible to letting their proclivities get in the way of extracting reliable intelligence.

If Pokempner is correct, the idea that torturers construct anything like an objective utilitarian calculus is nonsense. Torturers cannot work out with any scientific or mathematical rigor the minimal amount of pain for a torture victim. They are trying to figure out how to break down the complicated identity of a discrete human being, a task that may demand considerable judgment and skill but that is anything but clinical or mathematical.

Hence the complexities of suffering push the concept of a pain calculus beyond any range ever contemplated by defenders of torture. They assert that a pain calculus can be constructed but never demonstrate its practical possibility. At the least, they make no attempt to show that they can construct a calculus in light of the psychological and medical evidence. Consequently, the invoked concept of minimum suffering is obscure and pragmatically vacuous. In turn, this means that one important element of the utilitarian calculation is irrevocably obscure. The torturer/interrogator cannot possibly have any precise idea of the quanta of suffering that will be inflicted on an individual. Although the calculation is supposed to balance suffering against public good, it is based on no clear idea how much suffering the torture actually inflicts.

While it may not be possible to quantify the suffering imposed through torture, it is possible to identify sequelae. But utilitarians can take the identification of harms, along with their knowledge of the inevitability of sets of these harms, as a reason to absolutely forbid torture.

NECESSARY AND POSSIBLE HARM

Utilitarians should pay careful attention to the distinction between necessary and possible harms. If we know that certain terrible events are inevitable, our fears are far more rational than in cases where the feared harm is within the bounds of mere possibility. A meteor might make it through the earth's atmosphere and strike me down as I walk, but the likelihood of this is so small that there is no point in fearing it. However, the fear of being hit by a car as I walk a street is sufficiently large that looking both ways every time I cross a road is sensible. Hence we teach children how to safely cross roads and thereby minimize the risk of injury or death. But we also know that possible dangers can become inevitable if the wrong conditions hold. We have to teach children of the dangers of tides and wave patterns because the excitement they feel at the sight of a pounding surf might tempt them to play with the waves. Yet getting caught by a strong tide in the North Atlantic will kill them, and quickly, if they are completely unaware of the dangers. A calculus that treated the dangers associated with a small meteor on a par with with those presented by an angry sea or the edge of a cliff would be weak, as any utilitarian should concede. What matters are either the harms that are inevitable unless some course of action is taken to avoid them or those that are reasonably likely.

In the context of torture, this point matters because everyone knows that torture inevitably causes harms to the torture victims and because, as I have already demonstrated, further medical and psychological consequences are both widespread and substantial. Although torture can be inflicted for the sake of getting information, its effectiveness for this purpose is highly disputed and has never been demonstrated. But it is extremely problematic to infer the justifiability of torture given the inevitability of its violent, widespread, and long-term social harms. If the harms are certain and the benefits highly dubious, on what grounds do torture defenders claim that the calculus speaks for torture? Torture defenders fail to consider that the distinction between necessary and possible harms provides a further reason to interpret the calculus as weighted against torture.

Suppose, then, that public officials contemplate the introduction of a torture policy. They know that the policies will inflict a great deal of harm on the victims. If the medical evidence about suffering is correct, they will not be able to know all or even many of the specific harms that will result. However, they do know that a great deal of harm is inevitable. If they are informed about torture at all, which we cannot assume, they will also know that considerable long-term harms are inevitable as well.

A utilitarian can and should build these harms into a calculus of those that are inevitably or probably inflicted by torture on an individual. But these harms are already far too complicated to be accounted for in any calculus employed by torture defenders. Such harms make it very difficult to defend the idea that preventing multiple deaths is obviously more beneficial than torturing a single individual. Given that the harms of torture are inevitably complicated and wide-ranging in cultural space and time, and given that they are also difficult, if not impossible, to quantify, a calculus that says the benefits of torture will outweigh any costs is difficult to imagine.

We may not know qualitatively how specific tortures impact torture victims. However, we can use the historical and medical evidence to identify classes of harms. Additionally, we also know that subsets of the harms must happen to any given torture victim. That is a certainty. What we do not know is that there is even any greater harm to others that might be prevented. As analysis of the ticking-bomb hypotheses demonstrates, intelligence is uncertain. Interrogators may believe in good faith that an attack is about to happen, but their intelligence could be wrong. Yet because they believe that a future catastrophe will take place, they torture to prevent an attack. In a case like this, there are no harmful consequences to balance against the harms that torturers will inflict. Yet somehow the utilitarian calculus still includes these future nonexistent harms. In the strict case of the ticking-bomb hypothesis, this is not a problem. The interrogators have perfect knowledge and thus do in fact know the costs and benefits. But in the reasonable case, they have imperfect knowledge and thus employ torture on the basis of belief.

A feared event may not happen at all. It lies within the space of logical possibility, but possibility and actuality are different things. The feared catastrophic explosion does not exist and may never exist. The problem of possibility and uncertainty, combined with the dubious intelligence value of torture, suggests a further reason why act utilitarians should reject torture. If we seriously accept that it is a bad method, we must also see that defenders are far too quick simply to conclude that it is still better than nothing at all. The wide ranging and inevitable harms more than outweigh the phantom possibilities that ticking-bomb cases and fears of catastrophe create.

The historical evidence from Algeria, Vietnam, and Northern Ireland suggests that isolated torture is unlikely to be effective. Where it may have produced useful intelligence, it was used as a mass-screening technique. Here, I have in mind the scale employed by the French in the Battle of Algiers, where they tortured and murdered thousands, most of whom were ignorant, to discover the order of battle of the Front de Libération Nationale (FLN), or the scale of the Phoenix Program employed by the United States in Vietnam to torture and assassinate Viet Kong leaders. But mass screening is used by many intelligence agencies to compensate for the practical impossibility of easily locating the real bomber from among a target population. If torture is used, it is difficult to imagine it would not be implemented as a component of such a program and thereby impose enormous suffering on a target population.

Here, the torture might produce tactically valuable results. But in these situations, there is not even the remotest hint that the torture is done to prevent a catastrophic event. It is employed as one among a large set of techniques intended to help win a war. In both cases, there is no utilitarian calculation at all. There are prudential calculations about the means necessary to achieve a perceived desirable tactical or strategic objective. But these have no immediate connection to maximizing the happiness of all beings relevantly affected by the torture. They have to do with the victory of one state over another state or set of nonstate actors. State interests are perfectly compatible with maximizing the casualties and suffering of another state or of an internal target population. There is nothing classically utilitarian about this because it excludes the suffering of the target population and third parties from significant consideration.

What I am arguing here is that there is not just a plurality of types of harms that do not fit easily onto the act-utilitarian scale employed by those who defend the use of torture; there is also a problem arising from the difference between the certainty that substantial harms will be inflicted on individuals and target populations and the equally substantial improbability of benefits. A utilitarian calculus that does not balance certain and highly probable harms against the merely possible benefits is not much of a calculus. Given the doubtful effectiveness of torture as an intelligence-gathering technique, the calculations are even more impoverished.

HARM TO TORTURERS

Torture's violence extends much further than the victims of torture and their friends and relatives. This is a point that defenders of torture sometimes acknowledge briefly, but they neither seriously consider it nor include it within their calculations. One additional class of harmed individuals is comprised of the torturers themselves. If, as utilitarian defenders concede, torture is always a prima facie wrong because of the suffering it inflicts on its victims, it is equally true that it is a wrong because of the suffering it inflicts on many torturers.

There is a great deal of evidence to support the claim that torture inflicts suffering on the interrogators as well as on the victims. One kind of harm to torturers has to do with the destruction of their character. This is a harm of which they may be unaware. However, just as military officials have to teach combat trainees to overcome their basic moral instincts and create a readiness, predisposition, and expertise to kill an enemy, so there is a similar requirement that training torturers should create a readiness, predisposition, and expertise in the infliction of suffering on victims. Edward Peters (1985, 184) describes how training torturers alters their personalities, ensures their acceptance of an ideological indoctrination that enables and predisposes them to use torture for the sake of state values, and employs a set of punishments and rewards intended to maximize the torturer's effectiveness. In the past, in the case of the dictatorship in Greece in the 1960s and early 1970s, this has involved the deliberate infliction of suffering on the trainees – their deliberate brutalization (Conroy 2000, 95) – but this is not required. Where such suffering is a part of the training methods, it must also be factored in as a wrong.

But whether or not the torturers are themselves brutalized, they still have to be trained to violate their most basic moral norms. Just as officials have to find ways to suppress the combat trainee's natural respect for the prohibition against deliberate killing, so they have to find ways to suppress the torture trainee's natural respect for the prohibition against deliberate infliction of suffering. In the case of torture, the brutality unfolds within a face-to-face encounter. Since the relationship between torturer and victim is intimate (Krog 2004, 375), there is no avoiding that torturers have to develop an expertise in emotionally violent relationships, a training that will inevitably violate basic moral norms of their community. John Perry (2005, 92) observes: "Torturers must develop a consciously manipulative emotional relationship with their victims, treating them as individuals without feeling empathy for them. And torturers need to master techniques for securing information quickly and skilfully without killing the victim. They must see each torture subject as part of an incomplete process in which the victim at best provides only some of the information needed to achieve the stated goal."

That the torturer's recognition of the victim's individuality is divorced from normal feelings of solidarity and empathy is important.* Since state torture is always an assault on individual identity, torturers attack the unique characteristics of the victims. They must identify suspects' cultural values and fears, as well as specific strengths and weaknesses, and then target vulnerabilities to break suspects down. Despite recognizing the individuality of suspects, torturers cannot possibly empathize with them – at least, any empathy that interrogators initially have must be suppressed in favour of the pertinent mission goals. But training individuals to suppress their

---

* One anonymous reviewer expressed some concern about my use of "empathy" here. The worry was that I incorrectly use "empathy" when the suppression of compassion should be my focus. Although I agree with the reviewer that empathy is an essential element of well-performed standard interrogations, torture interrogations are distinguished from normal interrogations in their suppression not merely of compassion but of empathy as well. Standard interrogations seek to build a rapport between the interrogator(s) and the source. But torture inevitably both creates a negative image of the source in the interrogator and increases the resistance of the source (Borum 2006, 25–6).

empathy is a dangerous exercise since a subset of the torturers will lose their capacity for empathy altogether. The social consequences of this in the future are considerable since individuals incapable of empathy will not function well in their respective communities. This causes various harms not only to them and to their friends and relatives but also to more distantly connected community members.

This, too, is not idle speculation. Frantz Fanon (2004, 447) observed two of his patients, both former torturers. One of them found it impossible to sleep and couldn't maintain satisfactory relations with his wife or relatives. He used to stuff his ears with his pillows to try to shut out the screams of his victims. Another started beating his children and then tied up and beat his wife before finally realizing that he had deteriorated so badly that he needed psychiatric treatment. Other torturers suffer from having done such wrongs and from the irresolvable conflict that arises from the incompatibility between the wrongness of torture and the fact that they have done it. The use of torture will thereby greatly damage and degrade moral norms and reduce their ability to determine human behaviour. Where characters are corrupted by torture, as is inevitable for a reasonable selection of cases, the damage is long-term and often permanent.

My point is not that torture turns every interrogator into a sadist. Whether this occurs is a difficult question. However, it necessarily reinforces and rewards the sadist, turns average characters into sadists, turns decent interrogators into average characters, and generally produces character decay. For exceptional individuals like Mr Nagase in Eric Lomax's autobiography, the damage had a different trajectory. He suffered terrible psychological harms for the rest of his life, even though he understood and worked ceaselessly to redress the harms in which he had participated and that had so savaged him. Character decay is a direct consequence of creating the disposition to torture and training torturers in their craft. This disposition does not just shut itself off the minute the crisis ends but has its own long-term impacts on the torturer and his or her community.

Mark Osiel (2001, 52) quotes an unnamed Argentine officer on the horrible impacts of participation in torture:

> At first, I'll be honest, it was hard to accustom ourselves to put up with torture ... We're like everyone else. The person who

likes war is crazy. We would all have preferred to fight in
uniform, a gentleman's fight ... It was horrible. The prisoner
was tied down, and I'd have to interrogate him. I felt
destroyed. When you think about the "enemy," it's
depersonalized. But it's not that way.

Notice the remark that torture was hard at first. It gets easier as
the activity is repeated. The inhibitions that prevent torture are
gradually removed through training and practice, producing a character perversion. Henri Alleg (1958, 82) also discusses the impact
that torture had on his interrogators:

> I looked at this youth with his sympathetic face, who could
> talk of the sessions of torture I had undergone as if they were a
> football match that he remembered and could congratulate me
> without spite as if I was a champion athlete. A few days later
> I saw him, shrivelled up and disfigured by hatred, hitting a
> Moslem who didn't go fast enough down the staircase. This
> "Centre de Tri" was not only a place of torture for Algerians,
> but a school of perversion for young Frenchmen.

State torture requires the development of routines and habits of
action that not only destroy the torture victims but also inflict terrible harms on the torturers. These routines repeat over time and
are inevitably nonexceptional. John Conroy (2000, 108) cites one
official on the problem that torture becomes routine even where it
is initiated to combat an emergency: "there was initially an urgency
to the torture, that it was done to save the lives of military personnel
who might be in danger of attack by revolutionaries, but that 'sub-
sequently the idea began to lose its force and changed into the
application of torture for its own sake, as part of a routine, and
also as an act of vengeance against the detainee.'" This is not just
a possibility; routinization is inevitable. Military and intelligence
officials must train their staff in habits, regulations, and policies.
They cannot predict all of the contingencies their staff are likely to
encounter and thus try as best as possible to develop reliable routines. If the torture trainee becomes disposed to inflict intimate suffering on an individual, as torture requires, this disposition is not
going to be constrained solely by some imagined policy restrictions
but must spill over into other practices and contexts as well.

Destruction of character is a serious enough matter in its own right, but the harms suffered by torturers extend well beyond this. Antje Krog (2004, 377) notes that they experience some of the symptoms commonly endured by their victims – for example, flashbacks and the inability to maintain a healthy family life. Osiel (2001, 53) also describes how several naval death squad members in Argentine were brought before a medical board and discharged because it was learned that they had begun to beat their wives. Not only that, but torturers are often ostracized from the ranks of their professional colleagues and, when exposed, experience alienation and social disdain. Furthermore, although they are often acting under higher orders, torturers are at risk of prosecution for their actions. This happens even though many torturers believe they are acting for the common good. In consequence, they feel they are persecuted for having done what they believed was the right thing.

Given that there is considerable evidence that torturers and their immediate communities suffer quite seriously, one would expect defenders of torture to take this more seriously and to carefully consider it. But, as mentioned, they do not. Knowing that harm occurs is not the same as appreciating either the nature of the harm or its extent. Without careful analysis, no utilitarian can claim to say that the suffering experienced by torturer and victim is outweighed by the supposed good benefits of the torture.

INSTITUTIONAL HARMS

Perry (2005, 75) also warns of the risk of the "contagion problem." This is the concern that torture practices used for one set of purposes may easily come to be applied for a wide range of other strategic and tactical goals. The problem then is the slippery-slope issue concerning how a state can prevent the spread of torture. As he remarks, the same argument that justifies the use of torture in one situation also justifies its employment for other purposes.

Here, we should recall the various purposes for which states use torture that I outlined in chapter 1. Recall that on the basis of this act-utilitarian analysis, torture can be justified if it is happiness-maximizing. That is, a public official may torture the suspect if he or she reasonably believes that the torture will prevent a catastrophe. But this reasoning justifies all of the possible uses of torture. To show this, we need only envision possible situations in which a given agent believes that the specific purpose is happiness-maximizing.

For example, Marcelo Suarez-Orozco (2004, 382–3) notes that Argentinian military officers justified the torture of children in front of their parents in terms of the necessity of combating urban terrorism. Those officers certainly claimed that they were acting for the greater good. It is possible that their justifications are lies or self-deceptions. However, there is nothing logically or historically incoherent about the idea that they may in some cases have been telling the truth. To appreciate Perry's point, we need to note only that their reasoning can be applied to support any state torture. Since nobody assumes that the agents involved are infallible, the utilitarian reasoning has to do with justifications offered according to the best evidence available to the given torturer. It is perfectly conceivable that a public official might honestly believe that the only way to get the desired information and to maximize happiness is through the deliberate torture of children in front of their parents. For the happiness calculus to generate this result, we need only the reasonable belief that the one way to prevent the feared result is to torture children. After all, what is the torture of one child compared with the suffering and deaths of many? On the basis of a simple act-utilitarian calculus, there is no possible a priori reason not to torture the child and, in principle, an obligation to do so.

I can construct similar arguments for the establishment of rape and torture camps, the deliberate spreading of terror, or *any* of the other purposes for which torture is used. Hence there is a logical slippage in the argument for the torture of "terrorists" to prevent bombs. The same argument that justifies the torture of the "terrorist" also justifies torture as a tactic to win a civil war and reimpose order. There are no a priori exclusions of torture practices in these simplified act-utilitarian calculations.

The contagion problem is a real worry, but a defender of torture might object that the solution is just a matter of adopting the right laws, policies, and constraints. If those can be developed, the risk of torture sliding out of control can be minimized. Aware of the institutional worries, Alan Dershowitz (2002, 147) suggests that we limit the use of torture by "acceptable principle" and that we insert "principled breaks." Yet he neither provides examples of such principled breaks nor shows how they will prevent the contagion.

Furthermore, the same emergency reasoning that justifies torture also justifies the violation of a principle to control torture. Such violations themselves may be necessary for the public official to react quickly and effectively.

Nonetheless, the contagion problem is not an a priori objection to torture. Defenders of torture consistently hold that torture is justifiable only if it can be controlled. They have to worry about contagion, but more argument is needed. We need to show that the contagion is inevitable. It is not the result of a failure of policy but is a built-in consequence of torture. Recall now the concept of a hypothetical imperative and suppose the following torture axiom: no state will deliberately torture badly. If it decides to torture, it will take the steps it believes are necessary to maximize its effectiveness. The choice of a given end commits the state to a selection of the means that it believes will maximize the achievement of its goals – for, as every utilitarian since Bentham has stressed, effectiveness matters. An ineffective torture is a useless evil. Consequently, it is not sufficient that we develop an argument in support of the use of torture; it matters just as much that we be able to torture well.

But how does a state torture well? We can take as axiomatic that those who torture wish to be effective; otherwise, they would be unlikely to achieve their goals. Even if their desire is sadistic pleasure, there are still more or less effective means for them to feel pleasure. In the arguments under consideration, sadism is irrelevant. What matters, defenders of torture claim, is that torture be an effective means of threat prevention. Since torture must be as effective as possible, any public official contemplating torture has to consider the requirements that have to be satisfied to best ensure its success. There is never any guarantee that torture will succeed. Nobody believes that. However, if one is careful, one might be able to increase the probabilities of success.

Perhaps this sounds like a virtue, but it is not. Consider what needs to be created if torture is to be as effective as possible. The first requirement is trained torturers, for if the interrogators are untrained, then they are unlikely to torture effectively. Interrogation is a difficult practice demanding fine judgment, and torture equally so. But if a torturer is untrained, he or she may use insufficient torture for the purpose. In this case, the interrogators will fail to break the suspect, and the feared catastrophe will not thereby be prevented. But it is just as great a danger that the interrogators will use too much force and either kill or psychologically destroy the individual. In this case, the suspect is no longer a valuable asset. If the goal of torture is threat prevention, a dead or destroyed suspect cannot help in averting it. Even if the interrogators are well trained, their use of torture is still likely to be ineffective. But it is more likely to be effective than the alternative.

So how does a state get trained torturers? What do torturers need in order to maximize their chances of success?

They need knowledge of alternative torture methods and their strengths or weaknesses. But to get this kind of knowledge a research program is required – for how do you tell whether a given technique is effective unless you test it against the available alternatives? This requires the employment of scientific resources, a conclusion that utilitarian Gary Jones (1980, 12) draws enthusiastically. He argues that to combat terrorism we need to consciously deploy the resources of modern science, psychology, and medicine. This is not simply a suggestion but, in fact, describes the recent history of torture. Alfred McCoy offers a detailed analysis of sixty years of horrific medical and psychological research. The current techniques used by governments worldwide are a consequence of many years of careful immoral scientific study. In his analysis of the roots of the Abu Ghraib scandal, McCoy (2006b, 6) demonstrates the involvement of a significant number of members of the scientific and medical communities in the creation of the torture techniques that then spread throughout Iraq, Guantanamo Bay, and the CIA archipelago. The problem is not merely historical. Steven Miles (2006, x) provides a considerable amount of evidence for the significant participation of medical and psychological personnel in existing torture practices in the above institutions. The consequence is violation of medical ethics codes and consequent corruption of medical and psychological practitioners.

Consider what scientifically rigorous research into torture requires: among other things, you need laboratory spaces, adequate financial resources, trained scientists and medical personnel, logistical staff, and research subjects. But since torture is ultimately about breaking people and destroying their identities, at some point the research requires unwilling subjects – for standard norms of biomedical ethical research give research subjects the option to withdraw from the study at any given time. Torture victims do not have such options. And thus to ultimately test any developed techniques, the state will have to find unwilling subjects and genuinely torture them.

As a matter of fact, the research into torture has historically used unwilling or incapacitated subjects. It has also experimented on prisoners of war, captured "terrorists," and similarly vulnerable individuals. According to McCoy (2006b, 27), the CIA conducted LSD experiments on twelve research subjects before subjecting thousands of unwitting US soldiers to the drug during Operation Bluebird. In Project Artichoke, the CIA tested dangerous levels of LSD on inmates of a drug-treatment facility in Kentucky. In addition, "Seeking unwitting subjects, the CIA injected not only North Korean prisoners, but also spiked drinks at a New York City party house, paid prostitutes to slip LSD to their customers for agency cameras at a San Francisco safe house, pumped hallucinogens into children at summer camp, attempted behaviour modification on inmates at California's Vacaville Prison, and collected powerful toxins from Amazon tribes. For 'terminal experiments' – those that were pushed to possibly fatal limits – agents trolled Europe for dubious defectors or double agents deemed 'expendable'" (29).

Nobody should be surprised at the use of science to test torture methods. There are no other reliable ways to determine how to break human beings. Science also helps to determine the relative strengths and weaknesses of torture methods. The presence of science in the recent history of torture is essential to that history and follows necessarily from the desire to torture well – for success in torture presupposes knowledge of psychology and physiology. Since state torture is an attack on personnel identity, the most effective strategies will emerge from careful scientific study of the mind. They will not emerge from ad hoc exploration of different techniques.

It is important to recognize that research takes a great deal of time and effort. Psychological experimentation cannot be done adequately within 24, 48, or 72 hours but takes years of concentrated effort. Hence it cannot be done under conditions of imminence. The knowledge has to be there in advance of any specific decision to torture an individual. Although much research is conducted in wartime, the most effective strategy for developing sound torture techniques, as with anything else, involves research in peacetime. All such work is done independently of any specific threat and has nothing to do with the emergency situation that utilitarian defenders of torture consider.

This is important because it means that the suffering imposed by torture can never be imposed only on "terrorists." The brutal history of torture shows that it is imposed on the vulnerable for the sake of gathering knowledge. The case of CIA agent Dan Mitrione, who brought in street people to carry out training sessions for torturers in Uruguay, is a good example, as torturers have to learn their trade somehow, and this requires victims. This knowledge can then be applied not only for preventing attacks but also for a wide range of strategic and tactical purposes. Intelligence gathering can be one of these purposes. Intelligence is gathered first and foremost to support state goals. Torture research serves state goals, and the prevention of specific threats is a contingent possible use for the resulting knowledge. Without this research – without deliberately imposing suffering on the vulnerable or unwitting (or both) – the interrogator will have little to no chance of effectively torturing.

If a society decides to dedicate resources to scientific research on torture, this means that elements of scientific careers, if not the entire professional development of specific scientists, will be organized around understanding and improving torture. But if torturing well entails devoting scientific funds, labs, and careers to torture, along with the suffering of the research subjects, this has to be included as a cost of torturing as well. At this point, the actual harms are getting staggeringly large.

Unfortunately, we do not know precisely how many victims have suffered as a consequence of all the legal and illegal research programs carried out in Canada, the US, the UK, Russia, Israel, Argentina, the Philippines, and other countries that have participated in various ways and to varying degrees in the research. But there have been many. Defenders of torture do not even mention all of this past and ongoing suffering as a consideration. But it is real, considerable, and an inevitable consequence of the state decision to torture. The science cannot be done without it. It is also naive to assume that the scientific research has stopped now, for no one assumes that the techniques have been perfected.

The consequences get worse once we start to consider ethics codes. All research on human subjects is now supposed to be governed by ethics codes designed to protect both the research subjects and the larger society from the potential damage that immoral research can impose. But research into torture cannot meet any of the existing norms governing research into human subjects. Those same scientific careers that benefit from violating professional codes also weaken the codes. Scientists cannot simultaneously respect a code and consistently break it.

Further bad consequences of torture emerge when we consider the impact of torture on scientific and medical practice. A mark of modern torture is the omnipresence of the doctor. Torturing well requires the presence of medical personnel for a host of good reasons. Doctors can help to ensure that suspects are fit enough to survive torture. I have already noted that killing the suspect does the interrogation no good at all. A trained medic can minimize the likelihood of death or complete psychological destruction by bringing his or her medical expertise to bear. There are many other purposes that doctors can serve. In addition to certifying the victim as fit for torture interrogation and monitoring his or her health during sessions, they can provide expert advice on possible weaknesses that the interrogators can then exploit. Medical personnel can design and refine torture devices and methods. Typically, medical personnel are also called upon to falsify medical records in order to conceal the evidence of torture.*

None of these practices can be reconciled with existing medical ethical norms. Consider the duty to do no harm. Torture by its nature deliberately inflicts suffering that is counter to any conceivable interest of the victim. Respect for autonomy is likewise incompatible here, for state torture is always inflicted on the unwilling, so neither norm can be respected. This creates an impossible situation for doctors because they can conform either to the norms of medical ethics or to those of the institution for which they work. But to conform to the one is to violate the other.

Michael Gross (2006, 1–2) resolves this conflict by arguing that military and intelligence physicians are governed by different norms in times of war and that these alternative norms override the standard ones of biomedical ethics. The point here is one of role morality. The doctor who works in a civilian hospital in peacetime is governed by the usual peacetime norms and principles. The military doctor or nurse in a state of emergency or war is governed by

---

* For an extended and detailed discussion of various ways that doctors contribute to torture, see British Medical Association 1992, *Journal of Medical Ethics* 1991, Human Rights Watch 1994, and Miles 2006.

considerations of military efficiency and duty to the state. As Gross is not a utilitarian, I will consider his arguments in detail in the next chapter. Suffice it to say at this point that the scientific and medical research, which requires the presence of medical personnel, takes place regardless of the presence of a state of emergency. If scientists are going to do the research, they undermine the peacetime norms as well. This is a terrible harm in its own right because the decision to do torture research imposes changes to the behaviour and character of various scientists as well as to scientific and medical institutions in both peacetime and war.

What this means is that the decision to torture well imposes a priori requirements that medical and scientific institutions be corrupted. They will have to operate at lower moral standards than we typically expect of them and have to deliberately violate autonomy, inflict harm, act unjustly, and otherwise act immorally. We need not conclude that all medical and scientific institutions are corrupted by the pursuit of such research. The point is that some are and that this is a worse situation for the victims, for the scientists themselves, and for the broader society than the alternative case of the absolute prohibition of torture.

Considerations of medical research generate additional real institutional harms, but there are many more. Suppose that the state wants to torture and that existing laws prohibit torture altogether. To torture well, the state must also provide legal support, and this will require profound changes to the legal structure of the state. If interrogators are going to torture, they will need some confidence that they will not suffer the consequences. If they are going to be punished, they are unlikely to torture. But if interrogators are not prepared to torture, the state will be unable to use torture to pursue its goals. Hence torturers have to be protected from punishment either by refusing to apply existing law to them or by changing the law to permit their activities.

As a result, it is no accident that the recent Military Commissions Act in the United States has successfully undermined the cornerstones of decent legal practice by permitting the following: secret detention; enforced disappearance; torture and other cruel, inhuman, and degrading treatment; denial and restriction of habeas corpus; indefinite detention without charge or trial; prolonged incommunicado detention; arbitrary detention; and unfair trial procedures. The state logically commits itself to undermining its own laws and its international treaty obligations when it implements a torture program (United States, *Military Commisions Act*).

A state that tortures to secure its goals must limit or abandon a host of legal protections. Among other things, it abandons the possibility of a fair legal apparatus for determining whether someone even legitimately should count as a member of the target population that a given public official believes to constitute a catastrophic threat to the state. Since the only thing that counts in determining the suspect's status as susceptible to torture is the judgment of the particular intelligence official, this means in principle that the class of torturable individuals comprises all living human beings. In practice, the decision to resort to torture is informed by the fears, beliefs, prejudices, machinations, political corruptions, and whatever influencing factors will drive the specific case at the time. The targeted suspects can include liberals, feminists, socialists, Jews, Arabs, or communists – all the usual oppressed classes. This means, in principle, almost anyone. The inability of General Iberico Saint-Jean of Argentina to distinguish the terrorist from the timid – noted in the Introduction – is particularly apposite here.

Not only are there institutional medical and legal problems, but we also should consider anew the moral problems surrounding the creation of categories such as "terrorist" or "fanatic." By defining a set of individuals as liable to torture, we create a habituation process, both within our public officials and in the larger popular mind. This habituation predisposes us to treat that entire set as less than human. Those comprising a given set are conceived to deserve their suffering simply by virtue of their assigned membership in the class. This means that both those who actually execute the torture and those of us who support it are rendered less sensitive to the suffering of others. All will have their moral compassion for others consequently reduced and their ability to identify with the victims diminished. The diminishment of the capacity for empathy is simultaneously one of the conditions for future imposition of enormous suffering. Empathy and compassion are barriers that inhibit us from harming others. If we lack that empathy and if we feel that others deserve the suffering that we inflict on them, we are that much more predisposed to harm them. No utilitarian could view such a non-empathic society as a good thing. Yet if a state tortures, this type of society will be an inevitable consequence.

Alternatively, we might choose to exempt torturers from the law. However, this generates a different set of problems. A law that is not applied is not much of a law. The United Nations Convention against Torture (UNCAT) is meant to apply to public officials. A conscious decision (whether or not publicly promulgated) not to apply the law amounts to a repudiation of the UNCAT. In this case, the law is on the books, but it might as well not be because the same activities against which antitorture activists strive will be supported – in principle, the entire range of them. In any event, this hardly encourages a respect for law. It also means that our public officials are now no longer subject to the law, which is an unpalatable case as well because in such circumstances these officials are now a substantial threat to us and to others. Here, we should pay careful attention to Major Adolfo Villegas of Argentina: "Always, when illegal procedures are used, the notion of what's criminal and what's not gets lost. Therefore, to take things that do not belong to the state, that belong to the prisoners, sometimes was thought of as a kind of war booty" (Marchak 1999, 295). What these considerations mean is that if a society wishes to torture well, it must build into its medical, legal, military, and intelligence institutions a predisposition to harm large sets of individuals. That this takes place is historically well substantiated. These are not hypothetical possibilities but real ones with historical instantiations. They replicate across quite different societies, and the pattern of their replication supports my claim that they are inevitable consequences of a state decision to employ torture.

The complicity of a community in torture is even more wide-ranging than this. Torturing well also requires the establishment of training bases and interrogation centres, with all the logistical support that this requires. For example, the state needs cooks, pay clerks, administrators, and maintenance staff in order to support the interrogation of the designated class of individuals. It also needs psychological profiling in order to best identify the character types who function as the best torturers. Weeding out incompetent interrogators and torturers is an important task in its own right. But how does a state determine who makes a good torturer? Here, it will need to do additional psychological research parallel and complementary to the work on torture itself. It will also have to create interviewers who can identify good torturers as well as policies that can govern all of these institutions and their practices (Wantchekon and Healy 1999, 607). This in turn means that a considerable bureaucratic effort will be required just to develop the policies governing torture. It is therefore no accident that the bureaucratic nature of torture is a recurrent theme in the historical and anecdotal literature on torture. The torture apparatus is and must be aimed at developing banal bureaucrats like the Nazi Adolf Eichmann.

Torturing entails a lot more than putting the screws to a single individual or group of individuals at a particular arbitrary moment. It is never a matter of an interrogator finding a red-hot needle and jamming it under a suspect's fingernails. Both training effective torturers and supporting and "improving" torture interrogation require a wide range of institutional, economic, legal, and social supports. To the extent that a given government or nonstate organization fails to provide these supports, it will fail to torture effectively.

This is also why it is senseless to focus moral attention primarily on the behaviour of specific individual interrogators and guards. State torture is always systemic and institutional. In a discussion of the abuses of prisoners at Guantanamo Bay and Abu Ghraib prison, Gregory Hooks and Clayton Mosher (2005, 1628) stress that the violence was a consequence of a highly rationalized system of interrogation involving a "callous and calculated method for extracting information and intimidating civilian populations." State torture is inevitably highly rationalized and callous. It is never a matter of discrete acts of torture inflicted on specific individuals, as the arguments for torture seem to envisage. It involves wide-ranging organizational forms that themselves presuppose considerable state planning.

Sophisticated utilitarians should also be aware that establishing systems that are themselves abusive makes excessive violence and loss of control likely. The so-called bad apples that sometimes get singled out for arrest and punishment in torture scandals do not act alone. They operate in an institutional environment that both orders them to mistreat prisoners and harms their character in ways that often explode into violence and that, rarely, emerge as scandal into public view. That torture training will create bad apples is just a further consequence that must be included in the utilitarian calculus since it is also a foreseeable consequence of a decision to torture.

The institutionalization problem creates a further public bind. Either public officials have to argue for torture institutions and defend them to their populations, or they have to create the institutions and operate them against the law and under a veil of secrecy. Whichever strategy they adopt has bad consequences. Assume that the public officials decide to publicly defend torture institutions. In this case, they further contribute to the normalization of torture within their society because they can reasonably expect that some of their citizens will come to support it. Thereby, they contribute to a public predisposition to believe in the justifiability of torture. But this increases public support for an evil practice and encourages its use by bringing public opinion into line with torture practices.

If the route of denial or silence about torture is chosen, public officials will institute routine and systematic illegality. Major Villegas's warning about illegality echoes here. He also notes that the choice to use illegal means commits public officials to choosing further illegal means to conceal the initial crimes: "This illegal methodology, even apart from the moral and legal problems, has the defect that when you use criminal procedures, normally you have to commit other crimes to cover up the first one. If you kidnap someone and submit them to interrogations with torture, later you have to cover up those previous crimes, and many times the way to cover them up is to kill the person" (Marchak 1999, 295).

This is an inevitable problem when one chooses to violate the law for the sake of the state. Historical actors draw this conclusion, as Major Villegas's remarks confirm. No utilitarian can accept the risk of routine and systematic illegality because the harms that this raises are extraordinary. Inconsistent legal principles or routine practices that conflict with existing law permit every course of action and cannot be action-guiding. If they fail to be action-guiding, torture is logically out of control.

As current events also indicate, if a government chooses to torture suspected opponents, it cannot try them for their alleged crimes. Of course, one could change the laws of the country to allow the consideration of evidence gathered under torture. But then the state just further wrecks its legal culture.

The prohibition against political torture contained in the UNCAT and other international legal conventions is aimed at the behaviour of public officials, not at the general public. Yet if a state chooses the route of illegality, the prohibitions do no work and might as well not exist. They then lack even symbolic significance for the actors for whom the status of the prohibitions matters most and, even more important, for their victims. If the public officials publicly defend torture and its institutions, they deny the international conventions altogether. In this case, the effects of torture are just as bad, and torture is defended as well.

Since utilitarians care about consequences, and since these are real harms as well, no utilitarian can afford to ignore the harms that either of these two paths will inevitably generate.

Sanford Kadish (1989, 356) warns that loosening the norms against torture will predispose a population to engage in cruel acts – a horrible mirroring of the brutalization inflicted on the torturer. What the institutionalization problem really raises is the problem of the evil community. Claudia Card (2002, 22) notes:

> To be potentially evil is to have more than the mere logical possibility of becoming evil and more than the mere capacity to experience the attraction of evil incentives or even to form evil intentions. It is to have something real (a persistent desire, habits of gross inattention) in one's character, in virtue of which one's evildoing would be no accident. To be human is not necessarily to have such desires or habits. But even though people are not all potentially evil, there may be families and communities whose practices really do have the potential to inculcate evil desires and habits among their many members.

In creating torture institutions and in defending these institutions as morally necessary, the institutionalization problem demonstrates the inevitable generation of nested evil habits and dispositions. These are created intentionally and necessarily, all with the view to maximizing the potential effectiveness of torture. A state that tortures must inculcate such desires and habits among certain of its members and must create dispositions to support the practices among wider elements of its community.

Utilitarians also have to worry about predictable unintended harms. It is not merely just-war theorists who have to worry about unforeseen consequences, for if they are foreseeable, utilitarians have to consider their possibility as well. For example, with certain actions and policies, we know that various evils result. We know that if a state drops bombs, innocent, neutral, and third parties will be killed and injured. The history of torture shows that the creation of torture policies also has predictable unintended consequences.

For instance, in the Argentinian case the torturers committed other violent acts such as murder, rape (where the rape was not part of the official torture itself), robbery, and witness and media intimidation. The nature of torture makes such additional violence inevitable, and history supports the view that it is neither controlled nor controllable.

This is a useful point at which to refute Richard Posner's outright denial that torture puts countries into a state of barbarism. Posner (2004, 294) claims that "The second objection is that recourse to torture so degrades a society that it should be forsworn even if the death of many innocents is an assured consequence. That is a proposition falsified by history. In very recent times the French (in Algeria), the United Kingdom (in its struggle with the Irish Republican Army), and Israel (in combating the intifada) have all used torture to extract information, yet none is a country that has 'sunk into barbarism.'" He provides absolutely no corroborating evidence for this assertion. For instance, he ignores that French army officers attempted a coup and set off bombs in France in an effort to, among other objectives, kill Jean Paul Sartre, Simone de Beauvoir, and president Charles de Gaulle. According to Darius Rejali (2007, 259), one supposedly successful case of torture in Algeria had the following effects:

> Under torture, Djamal revealed where the last FLN leader in Algiers lay hidden. But that wasn't so important; informants had identified this location months before. The important information Djamal revealed was that the French government had misled the military and was quietly negotiating a peace settlement with the civilian government. It deeply poisoned the military's relationship with the civilian government, a legacy that played no small part in the collapse of the Fourth Republic in May 1958 and in the attempted coup by some French military officers against President De Gaulle in April 1961.

There have been many attempted coups by former torturers in the Philippines and other countries. Moreover, Posner pays no attention to the turmoil that the United States has recently been experiencing over the use of torture in various parts of the CIA archipelago and likewise no attention to the degradation of political institutions in the Argentinian and other South and Central American cases. Each torturing nation undermines its culture in a wide range of historically demonstrable ways. Although the specific effects of the oppression and torture have played out differently in different countries, the use of torture inflicts enormous real historical harms and does push the countries toward barbarism.

It does not help that Posner neglects to explain what he means by barbarism or degradation. However, this discussion of institutional harm sheds some light on the problem because to the extent that countries have such institutions, they commit widespread violence and are not the moral beacons they claim to be. Perhaps he regards "barbarism" as an all-or-nothing affair and does not consider that countries can be more or less barbaric to the extent that they deliberately or tacitly mistreat whole classes of individuals, whether they be "terrorists," Arabs, African Americans or Canadians, Algerians, Jews, communists, Palestinians, or any other vulnerable set? If he thinks that a country is nonbarbaric because it does not torture its "own," he fails to recognize that this does not make the country any less barbaric. How a country handles other ethnic groups, nationalities, and minorities is an important clue to its moral character as well. If it treats these sets of people evilly, it does not have the pristine moral quality that supporters like Posner think.

SOCIAL HARMS

There are further problems. To this point I have explored subsets of the inevitable harms that arise for tortured individuals, for torturers, and for institutions of the torturing society. These are already considerable. But the problems get worse. The historical record also indicates a broad range of additional harms, all of which are unsurprising and inevitable consequences of torture.

For example, torture radicalizes the target population. Victory for the French in the battle of Algiers was pyrrhic since the use of torture and other dirty means further radicalized the Algerian opposition. As a consequence of dirty intelligence-gathering means employed on a massive scale, the French military was able to identify, isolate, and destroy the FLN leadership within the city. But this was done at a terrible cost in casualties, was nothing like the sanitized image of torture envisioned by those who defend its use, and ultimately served to further enrage opposition to the French presence in the country.

The "successful" French strategy involved the use of torture as a mass-screening tool. Since torture is unreliable when used singly and in isolation from a broad range of intelligence-gathering tactics, and since no real intelligence agent knows in advance the identity of the opposition, trial and error in interrogation is an essential element of information gathering. But this means that officials torture to zero in on the real targets, not that torture is used only as a last resort. And such mass screening exacerbates the number of victims and increases the harms inflicted on a society. In addition to the fact that torturing single individuals has widespread and long-lasting social effects, the necessity that multiple individuals be tortured, rather than just the "terrorists," means that the damage will be intense and deeply felt, directly affect many individuals and their many relatives, and generate hostility and rage against the tactics as well as the institutions and countries that practice them. This cannot be avoided.

The consequence of generating this rage is a further increase in dispositions to violence against the torturing state and its members, with a consequent increase in the number of attempts to bomb and otherwise damage the state. The desire for revenge emerges in the form of consequent further violence. In torturing to secure some desired goal, a state just creates the conditions for a great deal of further violence. This is hardly a strategy for reducing suffering and violence. Although torture is supposed to reduce or eliminate violence, the history suggests that it cannot do so.

Again, to refute Posner on barbarism, the British in Northern Ireland lit a terrible fuse by torturing Jim Auld, Paddy McClean, and others, contributing heavily to the subsequent explosion of anti-British violence in Northern Ireland with staggering costs in injuries, lives, economic dislocation, and political horror that are still being felt today. Furthermore, in the Middle East conflict, sixty years has been a rather large test tube with which to gauge the success of torture policies – at least if the point is to end conflict and reduce violence and suffering in Israel. The use of torture by Israel has hardly contributed to a reduction in Palestinian hostility or helped either state to reach a mutually acceptable resolution to their disputes. Such means do not reduce or eliminate conflicts. They can only contribute to them through an increase in hostility and rage in the target population.

The US Army Field Manual (ch. 9) also argues against torture because it will reduce opponent defections and serve as grist for an opposition propaganda mill. Both of these are easily foreseeable consequences of the use of torture. Likewise, torture policies reduce and destroy the possibility of dialogue with a political opposition. Any moderate voices within a group are likely to be silenced once torture practices become public knowledge – as will inevitably happen in the course of conflicts.

UTILITARIANS MUST OPPOSE TORTURE ABSOLUTELY

These consequences are not complete. Further possible harms include those mentioned by English ambassador Craig Murray, who warned of the dangers of using torture employed by allies like the Uzbek government because it generates confessions that "the Uzbek government wants us to believe" (Grey 2006, 171). The problem is that the intentions of one political actor do not necessarily agree with those of others, whether they are other governments, different agencies within a given state, or different individuals within a given agency. These problems point to additional unanticipated harmful consequences.

A utilitarian of any kind is bound to consider the consequences of any action. The action is good if it is happiness-maximizing and bad if it increases the suffering of all relevant beings affected by the action. The same point applies when a utilitarian considers the implementation of a policy. The basic question on torture is whether it is really conceivable that torture actions can be happiness-maximizing? The answer is clearly no. Consideration of the ranges of harmful consequences that I have begun here suggests that the choice to torture, when allied to the demand made by every utilitarian that the torture be effective, imposes sets of harms that are exceptionally violent to the tortured individual, to his or her family members, and to the wider community. Torture's violence also imposes considerable suffering on the torturers and their wider community both through psychological damage and through the enforcement of institutional changes that themselves threaten broader public wellbeing.

Many of these harms are logically inevitable, and others are highly probable. They follow from the nature of torture and from the state's desire to do it well. Once we consider what has to be in place in order to torture well, we realize that it presupposes an exceptionally complicated institutional and logistical apparatus –

the whole of which is organized around inflicting suffering and the destruction of individual identity. Where torture is used, it occurs in the context of the messy business of prosecuting wars and counter-insurgencies – none of which is even imagined by utilitarians who defend torture. If we want to deal with real consequences, rather than with cartoons, the utilitarian calculus has to consider the historical harms. Here, the calculus does not support a single case in which utility has been maximized through the use of torture. Given the certainty of the harms that I have explored, this is unsurprising. The certainty of widespread violence and suffering outweighs the merely possible fears that torture advocates use to defend it. Cases that can never possibly occur and that reflect no possible historical reality are hardly the kind of value to be inserted into a utilitarian moral calculus.

The harms are certain or highly probable, but the benefits of torture are highly unlikely at best. As we have seen, even defenders concede the dubious effectiveness of torture. If the situation used to defend torture is the impossible ticking-bomb hypothesis and if torture is generally conceded to be of doubtful effectiveness for the stated goal of acquiring true information, the utilitarian analysis must reject torture. Jean-Maria Arrigo (2004) is right. The utilitarian position speaks against torture under all circumstances and supports the nonderogability of the UNCAT and other international conventions against torture.

Torture cannot be practised solely in emergencies. The institutionalization problem demonstrates the emptiness of any belief that torture can be exceptional. It is impossible to torture well if torture is made the exception. It has to be a norm, researched, trained for, and practised in the absence of the emergency situations that supposedly are the only justifications for torture. This is why Allhoff (2005a, 2005b), Posner (2004), Oren Gross (2004), Dershowitz (1989, 2002, 2004), and others are simply wrong to think that torture can be restricted to conditions of dire emergency. If a government or state waits for such conditions, this just means that it will torture badly. If torture is to have any realistic chance of being effective, it must be practised and its practitioners must themselves study and learn it. This is why torture is far more violent than people realize. Arguments for political torture are not about single acts but about institutional reorganization for the sake of violence. Torture creates versions of Card's (2002) evil society.

ETHNOCENTRISM, TORTURE,
AND UTILITARIANISM

Although utilitarians are not always historically consistent about this, that sentience is a universal criterion for moral considerability means that we cannot exclude individuals from consideration simply because of group membership. If an entity is sentient, it is entitled to consideration. Yet torture is used in the course of political struggles between ethnic or economic groups, and the reasons for torture have nothing to do with utilitarian happiness maximization and pain reduction. State torture attacks identity. Individuals are tortured precisely because of their group membership. Their interests do not count because of gender, nationality, race, class, or similar categorization. They are tortured because they are part of the relevant oppositional group. No state-torture calculus considers the interests of all those affected by the actions. It chooses a much smaller group, and the sentience of the victim is the opportunity for violence, not a reason to withhold.

So not only is the utilitarian calculus that defends torture vastly oversimplified, but it also necessarily has racist, sexist, classist, religious, or other pernicious properties. Which specific properties emerge depends on the identity of the individual and on his or her political, ethnic, sexual, and economic background. The interests of the tortured are not considered equally with those of members of the torturing state. This violates the principle of equal consideration of interests, which no utilitarian should accept.

Simplistic utilitarian thinking fails to recognize also that there is a difference between the actions of individuals and those of governments. When public officials construct a torture policy or take a decision that torture will be one of the tactics employed by the government, they commit themselves and their states to a wide range of harms, a far more complicated web of violence than anything that defenders of torture articulate or even imagine. They certainly display no consideration of this problem in their writings.

I do not pretend that this list of harms is comprehensive. It is a start and identifies the broad classes of damage that torture policies inevitably inflict. Compared to the fictional benefits imagined by defenders of torture, these inevitable and real harms are fundamental and compel utilitarians to oppose torture. Hence the distinction between act, rule, and other utilitarians is a red-herring in the torture debate. All utilitarians must absolutely oppose torture.

4

Torture, Tragic Choices,
and Dirty Hands

By justice then do the just make men [*sic*] unjust, or in sum do the good
by virtue make men bad? Nay, it is impossible.

Plato 1978, 335d

In both present and future cultural space and time, torture imposes
widespread harms on torture victims and their communities, on the
torturers and their societies, and on the institutions of the torturing
state. Thus, while it takes some effort to construct a utilitarian
absolute opposition to torture, there is no great conceptual challenge. When we realize what it takes for a state to torture, we also
realize that torture will always violate utilitarian principles.

However, not all consequentialist arguments for torture are
utilitarian. There is an alternative moral position that legitimizes torture. This is the so-called problem of dirty hands, or tragic choices.
The idea is that there are circumstances in which public officials have
no alternative but to deliberately choose between evils. In such cases,
all options are bad, and the state agent is obligated to choose from
among the least bad options. Stephen Lukes (2005, 3) calls this the
hard question for liberal-democratic politics. Many theorists defend
torture through tragic-choice reasoning. The problem is that torture
contradicts the most fundamental principles of liberal-democratic
societies: their stress on transparency, accountability, and the inherent
dignity of the individual (13).

I do not dispute that we may sometimes face tragic choices; what
I reject is the claim that tragic choices ever entail torture. I will
argue that the dirty-hands dilemma has more violent consequences
than the utilitarian arguments for torture. The problem is that this
position lacks any universal constraining value and thus provides
no meaningful limits on violence. In part, this is because it restricts

itself to considerations of the obligations that public officials owe to their states. In the dirty-hands problem, moral obligations are defined parochially and are compatible with extraordinarily dispro- portionate violence inflicted on victims and opponents. This holds despite the commitment shared by all dirty-hands theorists to just- war principles like proportionality and military necessity.

Since I accept the plausibility of tragic-choice dilemmas, I will not argue against lesser-evils reasoning. Rather, my strategy is to demonstrate that virtue ethicists are also well served by an absolute prohibition against torture. Briefly, if we can demonstrate that a law, policy, or choice inevitably destroys virtue and creates vice, a virtue ethicist must oppose it. As I will show, torture is inevitably vice-creating and has no virtue-building properties. Since torture destroys virtue in torture victims, torturers, and torturing states and since it cannot create virtue, virtue ethicists must oppose it.

INTRODUCTION TO VIRTUE ETHICS

How are virtue ethics distinct from deontology or utilitarianism? As we have seen, deontology is the study of rights and obligations. It typically specifies the universal moral qualities possessed by human beings or citizens and then derives from these a set of rights. For Kant, for example, freedom and human dignity are the univer- sal qualities. Modern liberal democracies share this emphasis even if they diverge on interpretation. For liberal deontologists, a central question for political theory concerns how to order a society such as to maximize freedom and respect for persons. Utilitarianism also specifies a universal value – sentience – and defines the goodness and badness of actions, rules, and institutions in terms of their pleasure-maximizing properties.

Both traditions are cosmopolitan. They define moral values in terms of properties held by the entire class of beings. Both traditions deny that state, ethnic, or gender membership justifies the exclusion of an entity from equal moral consideration. To justify an action, the interests and rights of all relevantly affected beings must be considered. On these grounds, both deontologists and utilitarians generate absolute arguments against torture.

Virtue ethics are concerned with the cultivation of morally good dispositions and with the avoidance of the cultivation of vices. As such, they prioritize character; they explore who human beings are and ought to be. In virtue ethics, the challenge is to educate people in a manner that instils the right kinds of dispositions. If they have the right kinds of habits, they are morally likely to act well when they need to. Acts and consequences matter in virtue ethics, but they should derive from good moral education. The point is causal. If individuals are virtuous, then in consequence of their character they will act in ways that are beneficial for their communities. If they are vicious, then their character will produce harmful effects in their own lives and will damage the harmony and successful functioning of their communities.

Virtue ethics need not reject outright the insights of other moral traditions. However, they have one especially important distinguishing feature. They treat rights and principles as important but deny that they may be absolute. For many virtue ethicists, all principles can be overridden if the circumstances morally require. Thus the utility principle and the dignity principle hold prima facie. Rights are a good thing, until they conflict. Where rights conflict, rule worship will simply fail to resolve a tragic situation. Likewise, suffering and pleasure require consideration because a society in which people suffer too much is bad. But pleasure and pain are not ultimate moral goods. As a result, virtue ethicists can argue that other goods may trump them depending on the situation. Consequently, it may occasionally be necessary to deliberately inflict suffering in ways that increase rather than minimize aggregate suffering. In virtue ethics, pleasure and pain are two among many morally significant states and never primary. Also, some virtue ethicists (particularly the tragic-choice theorists that I explore in this chapter) prioritize the interests of their own state over those of others and therefore self-consciously diminish or exclude others from moral consideration.

ARISTOTLE ON VIRTUE AND THE GOOD

The central figure in virtue ethics is Aristotle. For Aristotle, (1984, 1095a 14–26), all actions are for the sake of happiness. It is the highest good at which things aim. But happiness is not to be confused with pleasure and pain. It is far more complicated. Happiness has to do with the realization of appropriately human ends and well-functioning communities. If happiness is the good, the virtues are those habits and dispositions that maximize community well-being, while the vices are those that undermine community cohesion.

Virtue ethicists do not disparage individual wellbeing but simply insist that the condition for individual flourishing is the existence of a well-organized community.

Every virtue has corresponding vices, one consisting of an excess of the virtue and the other consisting of a defect (Aristotle 1984, 1106a 25–32). For example, courage has both rashness and cowardice as excess and deficiency. The courageous individual is the person who, in the appropriate circumstances, is able to react well under stress in order to realize the relevant good. A cowardly person may be well aware of the needed action but may lack the moral strength to do what is necessary. The rash individual may also be aware of the needed action but may stupidly rush in before considering which of the available options is best. The consequence is that wisdom in action has to do with the choice of the mean between extreme possibilities. Agents have to recognize which choice must be made and then effectively implement it under potentially difficult conditions. In the case of courageous actions, the point is that both fear and decisive action are needed at the same time and have to be balanced in any choice of action.

Suppose, for example, that someone has fallen through the ice in a pond and is at risk of drowning. Rash individuals will charge out onto the ice as quickly as possible, without considering the available courses of action with their relevant costs and benefits. As a result, they may themselves fall through the ice and now create additional injury and death where originally there was only one problem. But those who react with fear are no better because they will be unable to act decisively either and will refuse to make any attempt at all given the potential cost of their lives. The courageous individual balances both fear and rashness in a considered action. This agent evaluates the risks and chooses the action best suited to resolve the situation and save the life of the victim. The courageous individual can save the drowning victim, but the others are unlikely to.

So virtues are dispositions to act well in requisite situations. Vices are dispositions that harm effective action and induce discord and damage community functioning. In moral and political action, those actions are good that aim at and choose the mean. Practical wisdom in morality and political action is the choice of the mean between opposing vices. The practically wise individual, whether in private or public political contexts, is able to deliberate well and choose actions and policies that are conducive to good communal life (Aristotle 1984, 1140a 24–31).

THE PROBLEM OF DIRTY HANDS

The dirty-hands dilemma is most famously invoked in Jean-Paul Sartre's (1989) play of the same name. The Communist leader Hoederer at one point remarks: "I have dirty hands up to the elbows. I've plunged them in filth and blood. Do you think I can govern innocently?" (218).

What is the problem? Here are some formulations:

> The problem of dirty hands "arises whenever, while doing the best thing in the circumstances, we know that we have done wrong." (Walzer 2004b, 208)

Max Weber (2004, 84) insists that:

> No ethic in the world can ignore the fact that in many cases the achievement of "good" ends is inseparable from the use of morally dubious or at least dangerous means and that we cannot escape the possibility or even probability of evil side effects.

Stephen de Wijze (1994, 29) describes dirty-hands dilemmas as special sorts of moral conflicts where an attitude is "justified, even obligatory, but also nonetheless somehow wrong." Although each theorist is concerned with the character of public figures, they concede that dirty-hands problems can occur in private life as well. As de Wijze notes,

> What is common to all cases of dirty hands is that actions involve the *justified* betrayal of persons, values or principles due to the immoral circumstances created by other persons (or organizations of persons) within which an agent finds herself. (30, original emphasis)

The dirty-hands dilemma is the problem of deliberate evildoing. It involves the idea that there are occasions when public officials are morally obligated to do evil. It is a form of tragic-choice or lesser-evils reasoning, in which, by the nature of the situation, all options are bad. The question then concerns how to choose the option that is least evil.

The dirty-hands dilemma is not a classically deontological problem. If we consider Kantian ethics, for example, it is always possible for us to act wrongly. But it is incoherent to say that we can be morally obliged to do something immoral. There is no formulizable categorical imperative here because such an obligation necessarily generates a contradiction and thus could never be a law for all rational beings. In doing evil, for whatever reason we can imagine, we treat individuals merely as means, not as ends in themselves. We allow consequential considerations to overwhelm our moral obligations.

Nor is the dirty-hands dilemma a problem in utilitarianism. Utilitarianism takes sentience as the primary value and defines evil in terms of pain and good in terms of pleasure. In utilitarianism, there is always a balancing of harms and benefits because we should always act such as to maximize the happiness of the greatest number of individuals affected by our actions. This may involve the infliction of suffering, as in punishment. Nonetheless, although pain is bad, the action itself is unconditionally good. If the person has committed the crime and if punishment is the best alternative for preventing future crime and suffering, punishement is simply the right course of action.

In both classical deontological and utilitarian traditions, morality is a matter of bivalence. Actions may inflict suffering, but this does not by itself make them wrong. If they are morally required, they are good no matter what. If they are forbidden, they are wrongs when performed. Both traditions would see morally obligatory wrongdoing as a contradiction in terms.

In the dirty-hands problem, however, the wrongs done for the sake of some desirable goal are objectively wrong. They are known in advance to be prohibited, and no good set of consequences will make the acts right. Furthermore, their performance is shameful. But dirty-hands theorists believe there are real circumstances in which an official has no good options. In politics circumstances occasionally arise in which all paths lead to terrible outcomes. When these situations occur, public officials do wrong no matter what choice they make.

We can appreciate the problem of dirty hands by contrasting it with a different kind of tragic-choice situation: that of triage decision making. In a triage situation the paramedic may have to withhold medical care from the dying because others who are more salvageable have a greater priority on time and available medical resources. Although omitting to aid the dying definitely harms them, on balance lesser-evils reasoning requires paramedics to save those they can. Paramedics do not do anything wrong in making these choices; in fact, they act correctly. Provided that they act correctly, no blame attaches to them for their choices.

A dirty-hands situation is quite different. In a triage situation paramedics may have to refuse to aid a dying person. But they may not murder the dying or deliberately increase their suffering, for doing so would be utterly unjustifiable. In dirty-hands situations public officials consciously inflict an evil or suffering that otherwise would not happen. Of course, they do not do so gratuitously. That would be an unjustified evil. They inflict evil deliberately because they can conceive no other way to avoid a perceived greater evil. Hence de Wijze (1994, 29) speaks of the justified betrayal of a friend, and Michael Walzer (2004b) defends a moral obligation to torture, provided an emergency situation is sufficiently extreme and imminent.

What distinguishes the dirty-hands problem from utilitarian consequentialism is that the harms done are treated as uncancelled wrongs. They are not sublated or eliminated because of the benefits achieved by the right action. For dirty-hands theorists, the actions remain wrong even though enormous good may have been achieved. Because the actions are wrong, dirty-hands theorists believe that each of us has a right not to be so treated. They think that rights are good general rules of behaviour. But they insist that every rule has built into it the conditions of its violation. Hence all rules and principles hold prima facie. The only exception is the general rule that public officials should always choose the lesser evil.

For most tragic-choice theorists, public officials are sometimes obliged to perform evil acts in order to fulfil their responsibilities to their states. The issue generally concerns the behaviour of public officials. If a private citizen kills someone deliberately, the act is murder and punishable by law. It is also prohibited morally. But acts that are forbidden for the private citizen are not necessarily prohibited for public officials. So the death penalty might be a wrong, and the public official might believe it to be a wrong, but a dirty-hands theorist is prepared to require a public figure to order an execution anyway if the circumstances dictate.

CHARACTERISTICS OF
THE DIRTY-HANDS POLITICIAN

It is crucial to recognize that dirty-hands politicians are conceived as moral characters. They are not sadistic or maliciously inclined. Nor do they mechanically obey orders. They experience the tragic-choice situation as a moral conflict. Furthermore, they know that the choice involves an act of deliberate evildoing and a violation of a genuine value. They also know that even though they have acted for the right reasons, they have nonetheless done something wrong and are blameworthy for having done so. That they may have saved many lives does not mitigate the suffering of the innocent or the guilt of betrayal. Those victimized by the wrongdoing are justified in criticizing those who have dirtied their hands, and the public official must accept such condemnation.

As a result, the dirty-hands individual is rare (Walzer 2004a, 45). A necessary condition for dirty hands is that the public figure experiences guilt for having committed an evil. But many people will perform the same actions without perceiving them to be wrong. Such individuals act immorally but are not dirty-hands figures because they lack the specific awareness of their guilt. Other individuals will be idealists who refuse to dirty their hands under any circumstances. Consequently, they will allow the greater evil to happen in order to keep their souls pure. And some other individuals will do the same things as the dirty-hands individual but will do so from opportunistic or sadistic dispositions.

According to de Wijze (1994, 27, 30) dirty-hands situations arise when (1) a conflict of values exists, (2) both sets of values are legitimate, (3) the public official is aware of the conflict, (4) he or she is aware that choosing one important value entails the sacrifice of the other, (5) he or she chooses to do evil because the alternative choices are even worse, or (6) he or she chooses the lesser evil on consequentialist grounds. Tragic-choice dilemmas can obtain for people who lack these values and intentions. But such people do not have dirty hands. This is not to say that they are morally superior but, quite to the contrary, that they are morally worse.

Naive idealists and cynical opportunists and sadists are equally undesirable. The problem with the former is that they will refuse to order the needed evil and thus will fail to meet their public obligations. In consequence, hundreds of innocent individuals may die. Jean Bethke Elshtain (2004, 82–3) remarks that as a result they would rightly be cursed by the parents, grandparents, siblings, relatives, and friends who lose loved ones. They are right to curse, in her view, because there is no unambiguously good course of action in a tragic-choice situation. There is a right choice to make. If the issue is torture to save lives, public officials are right to torture the "terrorist" because the evils that are prevented through the saving of lives more than counter-balance any evils done to the "terrorist." But that the choice is the right one under the circumstances does not make it any less evil. Hence, in her opinion, an idealist who refuses to torture under any circumstances is a worse person than the torturer who inflicts extreme suffering for the sake of saving the lives of others. Cynical opportunists and sadists are at least as reprehensible. They may torture or otherwise commit terrible evils for the sake of personal gain. In the former case, they might torture to further their own political prospects. In the latter case, they torture simply because they like it. Both types – the idealist and the opportunist or sadist – are unacceptable to tragic-choice theorists. The idealist denies the dilemma and permits terrible suffering to occur. The opportunist and sadist are amoral and desire the suffering.

If public officials lack the relevant moral feelings, they are not dirty-hands individuals. They may be rational calculators, sadists, or opportunists, but they are unaware of having done anything wrong. Naive idealists likewise fail to appreciate their wrongdoing. They could have stopped a terrible evil but consciously refused to do so. None of them has the right feeling of shame. For tragic-choice theorists, responsible public officials feel shame and guilt at having resorted to evil means. They may have acted correctly, but this in no way mitigates the evil, and they must be shamed by their actions.

Shame matters because dirty-hands theorists rightly fear that deliberate evildoing can spiral out of control. Shame ensures that the evildoing will not be repeated except when absolutely necessary. Possession of the requisite feelings of shame is proof of a disinclination to do evil except under tragic circumstances. Given that consequentialist reasoning trumps in tragic choice situations, if public officials lack a sense of shame, they lack the dispositions they need to restrict the use of torture and other violent means. They will do evil in contexts where it is not absolutely necessary. Shame and guilt are supposed to ensure that the public official lacks any desire to repeat a torture.

THE DIRTY-HANDS ARGUMENT FOR TORTURE

Given that the dirty-hands situation is one in which the only available choices have evil consequences, the right action is the one that is least evil. Officials must always act such as to minimize the evil consequences in tragic situations. It is unsurprising to find this view applied to torture. Walzer (2004b, 64–5) raises the issue in the following way:

> the capital is in the grip of a terrorist campaign, and the first decision the new leader faces is this: he is asked to authorize the torture of a captured rebel leader who knows or probably knows the location of a number of bombs hidden in apartment buildings around the city, set to go off within the next twenty-four hours. He orders the man tortured, convinced that he must do so for the sake of the people who might otherwise die in the explosions – even though he believes that torture is wrong, indeed abominable, not just sometimes, but always.

The details here are vague and have the artificial air of the ticking-bomb hypothesis. But the dirty-hands problem emerges in the final sentence – the public leader deliberately chooses an action that he believes to be always abominable and does so because he sees no other alternative but to torture the individual in order to prevent the explosions from going off. Furthermore, torture is a genuine evil and always wrong. De Wijze (1994, 28) notes that the point is not that the prohibition against torture ceases to hold but that, under the circumstances, it ceases to be action-guiding. Because there is a conflict of goods here, between the wellbeing of the people threatened by the bombs and the suffering the torture inflicts on the rebel, the leader must act; the only question concerns how to make the least evil choice. Walzer believes that the public official is morally obligated to ignore the prohibition against torture. Given the available alternatives, only torture offers the least evil possibilities. But authorizing the torture is an evil that will never be cancelled and that will irrevocably stain the character of the public figure.

Walzer (2004a, 46) stresses that these kinds of arguments hold only when the survival of the community is at stake – that is, only under conditions of supreme emergency. In most situations, even situations of emergency, these conditions do not hold. Nonetheless, under supreme emergency conditions, evil actions become necessary. So Walzer argues that the Second World War constituted just such an emergency for Churchill's government. Consequently, he was justified in refusing to evacuate Coventry in advance of a German air raid on the grounds that this would betray to the Germans that Britain had broken the Enigma Codes and thus seriously harm the war effort at a time when the nation's survival was in question. Similarly, while he rejects the late-war fire bombings of German and Japanese cities, Walzer supports early-war terror bombing in order to distract the Luftwaffe from attacking Royal Air Force bases and radar sites, thus taking pressure off a badly overstretched air force and allowing it to recover. In both cases, there was a deliberate choice either to kill or to allow the deaths of many thousands of people (Walzer 1977, 255). Given that he supports terror bombing and other forms of deliberate evildoing when the emergency is sufficiently extreme, it is unsurprising that he also supports torture for similar reasons. It is ominous to note, however, that torture does not require the existence of a supreme emergency for its justification. The constraints are much weaker and require only an existing terror campaign. In any event, the argument for torture is now straightforward: torture is sometimes morally obligatory because it can be the lesser evil in comparison to a range of bad alternatives.

CONSTRAINTS ON DELIBERATE EVILDOING

Because dirty-hands theorists are aware that there are terrible dangers associated with developing arguments for evil, they are deeply concerned to limit evildoing. I have already pointed out that character is the first constraint. Dirty-hands politicians have the right moral feelings and dispositions. So they know that the actions are evil and under normal circumstances should never be done. However, they also have sufficient practical wisdom to recognize the exceptional situations and to act decisively in resolving them.

Shame and guilt ensure the torture will not be repeated except when needed.

Additional limiting principles include popular opinion, proportionality, and military necessity. De Wijze (2003, 40) seeks additional limits in well-organized accountability procedures of democratic communities. Although public officials will occasionally be obligated to use dirty means like torture, legal and other procedures need to be established to ensure that they are held accountable and forced to defend themselves to the public. If public figures are aware that their actions will be scrutinized, they will be cautious in choosing evil. If they know that their evildoing carries a risk of public sanction, they will be similarly hesitant and torture only when they are genuinely convinced of the extremity and need of the situation.

Michael Gross (2006, 61) also argues that deliberate evildoing is bound by the principles of just-war theory. For example, any torture ordered must respect the just-war principle of proportionality. Gross also insists that military necessity is a further moral principle constraining the cases in which torture may be used. So, for example, you could never justifiably torture an individual for sadistic reasons. You could do so only for the sake of the goals mandated by a military mission. Also, you cannot subject an individual to torture that is excessive or disproportionate in relation to the specific military and intelligence needs.

CRITICISMS OF THE DIRTY-HANDS ARGUMENT FOR TORTURE

Further Reflections on Brutalization

I am going to argue that none of these proposals can do the work that torture defenders hope. I have already explored a range of the damage caused by torture in chapters 1 and 3 and thus will not repeat myself here. I now want to build on the remarks in chapter 3 about the brutalization of the torturer.

Recall that torture inevitably inculcates bad character in the torturer. Tragic-choice theorists at least partially recognize this problem. The image of character stain is a recurrent motif. Deliberate choice of evil shames and stains the agent. To stain personal character is to make an individual worse than he or she would otherwise be. Considered at the institutional, communal, and national levels, the institutional prerequisites for successful torture are culturally staining. They make the culture and its institutions worse than they would otherwise be and must push a torturing state toward barbarism.

I want to now extend these considerations by showing that torture destroys shame in the torturing individual, institution, and state.

It is clear from the historical evidence that torture has a corrupting effect both on individuals and on institutions. Torture brutalizes the interrogators. It creates in them dispositions to act in individually and socially harmful ways. It attacks the cultural norm to do no harm, perverting it into an imperative to harm. Although everyone agrees that torture brutalizes the torturer, defenders spend no time at all explaining just what this means. Lack of attention to the nature of brutalization and its sequelae is a serious weakness, especially since it is difficult to claim that character can survive brutalization if we have no clear idea what it is.

We have already seen that effective torture requires considerable skill, resources, and preparation. This means that the torturer has to develop violent habits if he or she is to become skilled in the destruction of human identity. But the more that states teach these habits and dispositions and the more that the torturers become accustomed to inflicting suffering, the less likely it is that they can feel shame and guilt. It is conceivable that individuals will feel shame if they torture once. But repetition of the actions must gradually reduce the shame. As intended, habituation destroys the inhibitions that prevent us from violating others. But if a state destroys the inhibitions of torturers to make them more effective in achieving its desired goals, it will also eliminate the shame. The shame is a consequence of the inhibitions against harming others, yet torture training must attack the inhibitions to maximize the possible effectiveness of torture. Damaging and destroying the intuitions will eliminate the shame as well.

We can strengthen these criticisms by considering possible character types and evaluating the possible ways that torture affects them. Suppose that the public officials are those imagined figures of rare strength and wisdom. They have the courage to take hard decisions and the wisdom to do so at the appropriate moment. Such public figures are still fallible and corruptible. Nothing in virtue ethics or in the tragic-choice situation undermines this fact. They must choose torture policies and contribute to the organization of the institutions that inflict the torture. They may or may not have to implement the torture themselves, but this makes no difference to the problem. The more they repeat an order to torture, the more accustomed they will become to doing it and the easier it will get.

How, then, do they preserve their repugnance over time and repetition? No tragic-choice theorist even tries to demonstrate that the dirty-hands individual can preserve character across repetitions. Nor do these theorists consider the possibility that in training others to torture, states must systematically root out precisely the dispositions that would control torture. Yet routinization carries exactly this inevitability: that torturing will cause torture interrogators to lose their repugnance and their shame. The situation is worse for public figures who order torture, for they do not experience the intimacy of the violence and thus operate at sufficient distance from the acts they have ordered and with insufficient knowledge of those acts to feel any shame at all.

The wise public official is comparatively rare, so assume we have an alternate comparatively rare type. Assume the public figures already have evil dispositions. Individuals like this lack the desirable moral dispositions and feel neither shame nor any other inhibiting emotion. Such people find torture rewarding and have an internal incentive to enhance and extend its use. Here, repetition will make them more sophisticated and capable of inflicting pain. Such individuals are also historically real and have been torturers. Hopefully, they are also comparatively rare, although this is not clear. Either way, they have incentives to overexploit torture, not restrict it.

The character most likely to be available is a zealous bureaucrat or an unimaginative order-follower. This individual is neither particularly wise nor stupid. He or she may be technically strong in torturing but may not be especially disposed toward evil actions. Furthermore, such individuals are obedient to their superiors and will pursue their obligations insofar as they understand them. They have no internal desire to inflict suffering. But they also lack the practical wisdom of the ideal dirty-hands character. Consequently, they are more likely to misjudge a situation and thus either to withhold torture when, on lesser-evils reasoning, they should apply it or to torture ineffectually when they do so choose. Such individuals are unlikely to appreciate the subtlety of the dirty-hands dilemma and will fail to understand that they may act wrongly in choosing a right action. The argument that an act is morally obligatory yet wrong will escape them. Instead, they will simply infer the correctness of their chosen actions and maintain a clean conscience.

In none of these cases can repetition preserve character. Even strong individuals must lose their repugnance given sufficient repetition. This is at least partly an empirical assertion, but it will be difficult to find a counter-example. Mediocre individuals are likely to pick up bad dispositions and habits and to become sadistic or otherwise violently disposed. Evil persons will have their evil dispositions rewarded. My point here is that shame cannot do the work that tragic-choice theorists envision because the conditions required to train and support torture must undermine and eliminate shame and other relevant virtues in the torturer.

The elimination of shame and other relevant moral dispositions is part of the problem with brutalization. Here, we have the systematic and deliberate destruction of the moral principles and values of the torturers and their institutions for the sake of effective torture interrogation. It is simply not possible that a torturer can become proficient without losing moral inhibitions against deliberate infliction of violence. If brutalization involves the loss of moral inhibitions, then brutalization of the torturer is inevitable.

An additional problem with the dirty-hands argument for torture is that, like the utilitarian defence of torture, it fails to appreciate the difference between the actions of individuals and those of institutions. Tragic-choice analysis always explores a choice made in a specific context. The choice has no institutional setting and, like the ticking-bomb hypothesis, strips away all the contextual details that are required to actually evaluate a choice. But government action is never primarily about choices. It concerns the development of institutions, policies, dispositions, and habits. These are intended to help public officials to apply policies in situations that planners cannot precisely foresee and thus must be prepared in advance of emergencies that may never happen. Consequently, violence and suffering inflicted on research and training subjects happens independently of any given emergency. If torture is to be a usable technique in an emergency, states must brutalize its interrogators and warp its institutions regardless of the appearance of any specific threat.

A further failure arises when we consider that public figures often order torture but typically do not implement it. This is particularly clear in Walzer's example, as he explicitly has the leader ordering the torture of the rebel. But it matters that other people have to carry out the torture. The problem here is that since practical political wisdom is rare, the qualities of the personnel who implement the orders are not likely to be optimal. States will choose the best personnel that they can get (according to their best fallible judgment). But they will have to take what they can get and will not be able to choose only the best personnel. Some of the top-notch individuals will be snapped up by other intelligence and military trades; others will simply refuse to torture when there are other jobs that are more valuable, more rewarding, and less violent. Consequently, the talent pool of simultaneously moral and talented torture interrogators will approach zero. As they are trained, the pool inevitably empties.

Insofar as they can, sensible public figures will pick the best candidates from a mixed group of people. However, since they have to train them in the dark arts of torture, they must take that entire set and train them to torture. That is, they must take a variously morally talented group of people and inculcate evil dispositions. Since few of these people, if any, can be of strong moral character, most of them cannot fit the dirty-hands model.

If the public official happens to be wise, he or she will organize the institution to minimize the evil effects as much as possible. But suppose what is more likely: that the public official is a normal bureaucrat. In this case, as with the consideration of individual character types, the situation instantly becomes a lot worse. The wise public figure will choose personnel who are as optimal as he or she can make them in the circumstances. But the average public figure will choose less optimal personnel, and the institutions will be less optimally organized. Such an individual simply has less wisdom to evaluate the harms and benefits or to judge the range of characters from which he has to choose and thus is far more likely to make errors of judgment.

In consequence, control of the torture environment will be less efficient than otherwise, and the inculcation of violent and cruel dispositions will likely be exacerbated. More errors are likely to be committed, and torture interrogations are less likely to achieve precisely desired results. Alternatively, the pertinent interrogator might be one of the "naive" purists whom tragic-choice theorists deride.

This individual may subvert orders and refuse to torture. He or she may also work to prevent subordinates from torturing. Either way, torture will be less than optimally successful.

The worst-case scenario assumes that some kind of sadist is in charge. This is especially bad if the sadistic official is also instrumentally rational and thereby good at achieving the goals that superiors set. Such sadists are by their nature disposed to enjoy the infliction of suffering and thus will see torture as a good. It is good, however, not just for the pleasure it gives them but also for the ways that it contributes to professional and political advancement and to the advancement of state goals. In this case, personnel and techniques may be selected precisely because of their violence intensifying qualities. This violence will be married to securing state goals. But the infliction of suffering will be deliberately increased, not minimized. A rational sadist has no interest in pain minimization, but he or she will wed the intensified infliction of suffering to state goals.

Strong moral characters and mundane, zealous rule-followers become brutalized by torture. Sadistic types are prebrutalized. Underlying this problem is what psychologist Ervin Staub (1989, 45), following Robert Jay Lifton, calls "psychic numbing": "When our emotions are overwhelmingly unpleasant or painful, we anaesthetize ourselves; soldiers become able to tolerate mangled bodies, and the capacity for horror becomes blunted. While this diminishes suffering, it also makes us insensitive to the suffering of others, especially when the other is defined as different."

The problem is that violence, like torture, cannot be conducted without such anaesthetization. This is one way to interpret Elaine Scarry's (1985, 29) claim that the pain of the victim is made invisible to the torturer. We "see" violence when we have the appropriate emotional and moral responses. Yet when we repetitively commit such violence ourselves or are repeatedly exposed to it, we survive the experience by blunting the emotions and gradually losing moral feeling. The emergence of such insensitivity is further evidence that the tragic-choice situation is incompatible with routine evils like torture. Since governments can institute torture only through routines, the prospects of resolving this worry are bleak indeed.

What this means is that shame and guilt cannot function as tragic-choice theorists envision. They cannot limit torture because state torture requires institutionalization. This in turn requires multiple and varied tortures and research programs conducted over substantial periods of time.

A reason for these weaknesses in tragic-choice treatments of torture is that virtue ethicists have been no more sensitive to its institutional harms than utilitarian defenders. Apart from a few brief allusions, there is no sophisticated exploration and hence a failure to recognize that institutionalization is incompatible with the preservation of shame and other inhibiting moral feelings. Given that torture makes individual and political character worse – as the historical, medical, psychological, and other evidence proves – it removes precisely those barriers that are supposed to limit torture.

These reflections are also historically supported. The Argentinean, Philippine, and Greek experiences with torture display many instances of the following problems: torturers developed predispositions to believe absolutely in their own rectitude and the cause for which they employed torture. Further, there is little evidence of shame but, in fact, the contrary: the development of a sense that the torture interrogators were part of an elite and privileged group. If shame was a factor, it made no difference to either the incidence or the violence of the torture. Its impact was felt only afterward, when the torturers were no longer involved and were seeking their own medical attention.

It is consequently no accident that Alicia Mabel Partnoy describes the following pressures experienced by her prison guards at the Escuelita torture facility: "The guards had weekly meetings and were constantly being pressured to dehumanize us. Their superiors told them that we did not love our families or our homeland and that we were killers without souls. They were pressured to punish our smiles, our sharing, and talking. Few of the guards resisted that pressure. Their attitudes changed and they became more repressive as time went on" (Stover 1985, 54).

Torture is not inevitable, but if public officials make decisions to torture, they will have to put such pressures on their staff, pressures that must dehumanize all of them. The mistake is to think that these effects are avoidable. Both the training and the environment are constructed to ensure that guards will act as desired. Those guards who somehow manage to resist the pressure get excluded from torture units, and hence they neither punish nor otherwise inflict torture.

We have to recognize that torturers will be incapable of fulfilling their roles if they are not systematically desensitized. They have to be trained both to know how to inflict terrible suffering on their victims and to suppress their own sense of the wrongness of their actions. If this is not trained into them, then they will prove ineffective. Yet desensitization has violent, long-term, harmful effects on the torturers, their families, and their communities. Eventually, they will have to reintegrate into their society, and they will not be able to just cast off their pasts without cost to themselves or others.

The Significance of the Milgram Experiments

Although character is supposed to limit deliberate evildoing, it will not be able to do so in the case of torture. Torture is necessarily character damaging. To torture at all, either torturers have to already possess a disposition to inflict suffering on others or they have to develop one. We should be skeptical that torture is compatible with character preservation, especially when we understand the institutional character of state torture.

This should already encourage tragic-choice theorists to abandon support for torture.

The Milgram experiments offer further empirical and psychological cause for doubt. One historical technique for training torturers is to systematically brutalize them. John Conroy (2000) focuses on the deliberate degradation and torture of trainees during the dictatorship in Greece. Brutalization of future torturers was a systematic means to destroy inhibition. But the Milgram experiments demonstrate that these are not essential and that psychological means alone can suffice to unleash extraordinary savagery.

In a famous sequence of experiments in 1963, psychologist Stanley Milgram explored the significance of obedience in communal living. The experiments were designed to study obedience as a psychological mechanism that links individual action to political purpose; obedience "is the dispositional cement that binds men to systems of authority" (Milgram 2004, 145). In the experiment, volunteers were assigned the role of "teachers." Unbeknownst to the volunteers, the learners were all actors. The teachers were then informed that their role was to punish the learners when they committed errors. After the initial explanation of roles, the learners were sent to cubicles that were out of sight of the volunteers. There was, however, voice communication between the volunteers and the learners.

The volunteers were informed, and believed, that they would be inflicting a series of increasingly severe electric shocks. Beginning with mild-intensity shocks, they were also informed that with each mistake they were to increase the intensity. As they did so, they received fake vocal responses from the learners. It began with mild responses, but at a certain point the learners would begin to scream in agony and demand that the teachers cease the experiment. When the learners went completely silent and gave no response to their teachers, the chief scientist told the teachers that a lack of response was to count as an error and that they should continue to increase the shock. Sixty-five per cent of them continued to do so. The volunteers were not compelled to do anything. They simply had the prodding of the chief experimenter and the explanation that their participation was essential for the experiment to succeed (Mook 2004, 336).

Gregory Mook (2004, 337) also remarks that Milgram experimented with what he called "psychological distance," which involved varying the intimacy with which the teacher engaged with the learner. In one case, the teacher was instructed to forcibly hold the hand of the learner to an electric shock pad. In another case, both the teacher and learner were actors, and a third party simply had to read out the instructions that the teacher was to follow and listen to the responses. In the former case, participation in the infliction of extreme shocks dropped to a rate of 30 per cent, and in the latter case, where there was greater psychological distance and less immediate responsibility for the suffering, participation rose to more than 90 per cent.

The case of torture is much more complex. Since the relationship between torturer and victim is one of immediacy, psychological distance matters. That Walzer's (2004b) public leader is extremely distant from those who actually inflict the torture is particularly dubious in this context because the Milgram results suggest that this increases the inclination to inflict terrible suffering. Obviously, an increase in such an inclination gives tragic-choice theorists little hope that shame will limit the actions of a government leader. For the actual interrogators, given that humans are much more averse to inflicting harm as psychological distance declines, additional work has to be done to dispose them to torture. This may require considerable training and rewards. Additionally, the training will have to be coercive and psychologically violent.

But this should lead us to ask what kinds of characters are most likely to torture. They must have a different character from human beings who will refuse to torture if the psychological distance gets too close. These individuals will not be the naive absolutists who oppose torture under any circumstances. But they will also not be those who have strong intuitions about the wrongness of torture. If their intuitions were strong, they would not be able to overcome their psychological proximity to their victims and thus would still possess their sense of the wrongness of torture. The dirty-hands interrogator is supposed to fit this latter intuitive type, yet this expectation is inconsistent with the circumstances. Torture training must damage the inhibition and transform the character of the torturer. The nature of torture alone guarantees that the torturer will not be the virtuous individual that dirty-hands theorists envision. Rather, the torturer is more likely to be a banal and unimaginative zealot or a sadist. The zealot could be your low- to mid-level career-oriented officer or could be found among low-level enlisted personnel and/or noncommissioned officers. In either case, the distinguishing features of the zealot are a predisposition simply to obey orders and a lack of moral imagination. The sadist, of course, pursues the suffering of others for its own sake. In either event, the constraining virtues envisioned in tragic-choice theory are absent.

In a discussion of evil and the roots of genocide, Staub (1989, xi) discusses a further dimension of the habituation problem: "It was clear to me that devaluation and loss of responsibility alone will not directly lead to genocide. Instead, an evolution must occur. Limited mistreatment of the victims changes the perpetrators and prepares them for extreme destructiveness. This was first suggested to me when in my laboratory children whom we involved in prosocial acts became more willing to help others. Research indicates that adults are also changed by their own prior actions."

Our prior actions influence the kinds of persons we become. Prior actions determine our character. Given that prosocial acts are enhanced through good treatment of individuals, the choice of anti-social and harmful acts will change the perpetrators of violence and make them worse. So committing one act of torture will alter torturers for the worse and make them more inclined to repeat those tortures as well as to inflict worse and alternative kinds of suffering in the future. There is no reason to believe they can preserve their character. The tragic-choice view of the torturer seems to hold that we can speak of a virtuous torturer. But these considerations suggest that the concept is incoherent.

The Likely Character Type of the Torturer

Leonard Wantchekon and Andrew Healy (1999, 598) offer additional reasons to think that the torturer will not fit the dirty-hands model. They remark that "obedience probably would be greater for torture than was the case in Milgram's ... fourth experiment. The torturer is most likely taught to hate the victim to create more of a sense that the victim deserves the pain. Greater rewards and higher punishments (e.g. in terms of job advancement) also exist for the torturer than Milgram's teacher."

The Milgram experiments were conducted in a highly neutral setting, where the volunteers had none of the prejudices, fears, and violent predispositions that characterize historical torturers. The research subjects did not see the learners as terrorists and hence did not see the actors as deserving suffering. Consequently, they had none of the beliefs that would cause them to deliberately exceed the orders of the experimental authority. But where a group of people believes that another group deserves to suffer, they have an additional internal incentive to inflict suffering. In the Milgram experiments, the participants inflicted shocks on the basis of authority alone. They were not influenced by racial, gender, or ethnic prejudice. Nor were they bombarded with mass ongoing propaganda aimed at dehumanizing their victims. But in real torture these factors are omnipresent. Staub (1990, 52–3) argues that ingroup-outgroup attitudes and devaluation play a ubiquitous and necessary role in creating the conditions for torture. In his study of the members of Reserve Police Battalion 101, a unit that conducted many massacres in Eastern Europe during the Second World War, Christopher Browning (1998, 184–6) particularly emphasizes the important role played by dehumanizing racist, sexist, and similar categories. Likewise, ambition and careerism encouraged the reservists to exceed one another in murder. Moreover, Milgram's dispositions to obedience were also married to tendencies toward group conformity. In combination, these are sufficient to get ordinary people to inflict terrible violence.

The Milgram experiments indicate that violent suffering can be inflicted by ordinary people under minimally coercive circumstances. But the violence that states inflict involves far more explicit systems of coercion and rewards. Establishing the institutions that will allow torture to be effective inevitably involves reinforcing and entrenching norms and practices that will badly damage character.

However, the problem becomes still worse if we ask what kind of character a state should choose if it decides to torture. Wantchekon and Healy (1999, 601) imagine a game whose characters are the state, the torturer, and the victim. In the event that the state decides to torture, it has to select torturers who are maximally likely to realize its desired goals. In turn, it has to provide incentives and payoffs to the torturers in order to reward them for the tasks they have to perform. Similarly, it has to provide disincentives for bad performances. The torturers are rewarded for successful tortures and threatened with punishment in the event that they refuse.

This puts the torturers into a competition in which each individual strives to outperform any peers. If they do well in torturing, they get rewarded for their performance; and if they underperform, they incur penalties. The competitors seek to maximize their rewards and to minimize any harms resulting from bad performance. The incentives have nothing to do with minimizing suffering; they concern success in achieving state goals. The competitive structure is not one that will minimize either the number of cases of suffering or the amount of violence inflicted. Because effectiveness in the realization of state goals is the aim of torture, the amount, type, and quality of torture will be contingent on goal realization, not on incentives to minimize the suffering inflicted on the victims.

This is an especially important point. Wantchekon and Healy describe three kinds of torturer: the professional interrogator, the zealot, and the sadist. The professional torturer corresponds roughly to the dirty-hands character envisioned by the tragic-choice theorist, as does the sadist. The zealot corresponds to an obedient individual – a type inclined to follow authority. They argue that it is not in a torturing state's interest to select either the professional or the sadist. The professional will refuse to torture in at least some cases where the state finds it desirable, and the sadist will torture in those cases where the state does not desire it. The character type that maximally guarantees pursuit of state goals through torture is the zealot, for this is precisely the personality type predisposed to obey authority without reflecting on or questioning the given orders (Wantchekon and Healy 1999, 607). Furthermore, Janice T. Gibson (1990, 78, 83) maintains that states will employ screening characteristics to exclude sadists and maximally ensure that torturers are normal character types.

Not only is the structure of the torture game such as to generate a zealot, but we should also ask who joins torture units. Staub (1989, 69) identifies a further problem in the issue of self-selection. While many people who inadvertently end up in torture interrogation units will evolve into habitually violent types, those who knowingly volunteer have predispositions to violence. Underlying these predispositions are a wide range of political, gender, racial, or other prejudices.

But if these analyses are correct, we have additional reason to believe that the dirty-hands argument for torture does not model any possible torture reality. No virtuous person will volunteer for a torture unit. There is no moral reward in that, only the inevitable prospect of character loss. Virtuous individuals know this and steer well clear of torture interrogation. If they are unlucky enough to inadvertently fall into such units, they find ways to get out of them. There are rewards for ambitious zealots and sadists, but for anyone who genuinely believes that torture is wrong, and who genuinely feels its shamefulness, there is no possible merit in involvement in torture. Furthermore, states will select torturers by defining character types that are most likely to serve state goals, not seek a priori to pick out the virtuous. Those in the candidate pool will have some interest that will lead them to volunteer, or they will be drafted into it. Either way, they do not fit the tragic-choice model.

It is no advantage to locate the dirty-hands figure at the policy level, as Walzer's (2004b) political leader does. This means that such public figures operate at arms length from the violence and are thus vulnerable to the problem of psychological distance. Because they are not intimately faced with the violence, they are less aware of the costs of their policies and in turn are more likely to order torture. Quite literally, they do not understand the consequences of their orders and thus cannot appreciate the harms that they inflict. In this case, whatever character traits they possess are still not going to limit torture.

Consequentialism and Evil Character

A further problem is that consequentialism trumps character. In the tragic-choice situation, consequences determine what is to be done. Hence, for tragic-choice theorists, they are normatively prior to questions of character. Suppose, for instance, that a state is confronted with a catastrophic emergency but lacks a virtuous torture interrogator. Since such individuals are affirmed to be rare, this is more than a possibility. It is the likely case. Would the tragic-choice theorist refuse to permit the torture because of the absence of the dirty-hands interrogator? The answer is no. This just creates a new dirty-hands dilemma. The policy maker must either choose to train and reward a sadistic torturer or allow the feared threat to materialize. If it is a lesser evil to hire the sadistic torturer, the problem of dirty hands requires that public officials do this.

In a discussion of the qualities required for a successful torturer, Antje Krog (2004, 375) treats the case of Captain Jeffrey Benzien. Benzien was a police officer in South Africa during the late apartheid era. She notes that the excellent torturer has to have the most intimate knowledge of the human psyche and that Benzien was a connoisseur. Further, such individuals must have a remarkable talent for emotional manipulation of their victims. They do not fit the dirty-hands model.

Krog (2004, 377) cites psychologist Ria Kotze on Benzien: "Benzien was a victim of his inhumane working conditions, Kotze says. He was a good cop at murder and robbery. But he was so good that he was moved to Security where he had to create these torture methods to fulfill the expectations about him. This destroyed his own sense of self."

He may have begun as a decent character, perhaps might have been the kind of individual tragic-choice theorists envision. Who knows? But he certainly did not finish up that way. This is someone whose character was completely wrecked by his activities. Would the tragic-choice theorist insist that the suspect not be tortured because the only available interrogator is Captain Benzien? No, for that would be a naive moral absolutism analogous to that of which dirty-hands theorists accuse absolutists. The problem of dirty hands cannot claim that the state should torture only if it has virtuous torturers. Since the class of virtuous torturers must be effectively empty, the result would be that we should never torture in any circumstances. But this is not the view held by most tragic-choice theorists.

Tragic-choice theorists place priority on the preservation of the state and on the resolution of its emergencies. But this means that if the state chooses to torture, it will do so regardless of the character of its agents. If Wantchekon and Healy (1999) are right, virtuous torturers are not even desirable for a state, let alone either necessary or sufficient for responding to the threat. The state will try to weed them out. So the state is most likely to have ordinary and mundane zealots as torturers. If it chooses to use torture strategies as elements of its strategy for overcoming its perceived emergencies, torturers must suffer various forms of character damage. In virtue of their mediocrity, the state will prove all the more incapable of controlling specific unanticipated damage and violence arising from its brutalization of these individuals and their brutalization of torture victims. This is also historically well supported. Witness again the behaviour of Argentinian soldiers, sailors, and policeman during the dirty war: in addition to planned torture, also widespread were robberies, sexual violence, and beatings beyond those inflicted in the torture chambers. The so-called bad apples of Abu Ghraib are another example.

This is a reason to think that worries about sadism are a red-herring. Tragic-choice theorists are uneasy about sadists because they believe these will inevitably intensify violence and employ torture where it is not absolutely needed. But assume that the state has only sadists available and believes itself confronted with a terrible emergency. Suppose further that the best interrogator available also happens to be the worst sadist in the interrogator pool. Given that he or she is so talented, the consequentialist reasoning that justifies torture also justifies the sadistic torturer. To refuse to employ sadistic torturers simply because they are sadists is also an instance of the naive concern for moral purity.

This raises the possibility that the tragic-choice problem may be irrelevant in the torture debate. Since the greatest evil lies in a supreme emergency that threatens the future survival of the state, those who defend torture can hardly hold out for the appearance of a morally good character. It also points to a further structural problem. Consequentialist arguments for torture are logically independent of the question of the ideal character type for a torturer. From the perspective of the state, consideration of consequences is also prior to that of character and trumps the latter when conflicts happen.

Although character matters a great deal morally, it cannot do the work in the torture debates that tragic-choice theorists think. It cannot limit or constrain torture and is only degraded by it. Since virtue ethicists are so deeply concerned about individual and communal character, and since character cannot constrain torture, virtue ethicists have to prevent torture before it begins. Consequently, they too should absolutely oppose torture.

Emergency, Necessity, and the Limit Problem

There are additional reasons to worry about the impact of tragic-choice reasoning on torture. The limit problem is central. It arises from the concern that lesser-evils reasoning can license an ever-increasing scale of deliberate infliction of savagery and suffering. It raises the question of whether there is an upper limit to justified evildoing. The problem is that lesser-evils reasoning has been and continues to be used to justify every historical act imaginable. It was offered as a defence of terror bombing in the Second World War and later. The Argentinean Junta and certain clerics justified terror and torture during the dirty war on just-war theoretical grounds (Marchak 1999, 236).

In a talk given to a Conference of Latin American Armies, General Videla argued that as many people must die as is necessary to guarantee the country's security (Marchak 1999, 151). Colonel Roberto Roualdes announced that the war would be successful if five out of every hundred people they killed turned out to be subversives (Osiel 2001, 54). The vagueness here is quite terrible, as it excludes any upper limit to evildoing other than state survival. Political necessity is itself dangerously vague and vulnerable to sorites worries. Furthermore, we have already explored the hopelessness of categories like "terrorist" and "subversive." Hence we should not be surprised to find Colonel Lorenzo remarking: "Well, I thought, and I still think, that there were – that it was necessary to destroy the guerrillas. That we had the bad luck to be forced to fulfill our military role in a war that no military wants, a war with very strong civil connotations, a war against brothers, a war with an undefined front, with an undefined enemy, in which it was very difficult to maintain the clarity and moderation of ideas" (Marchak 1999, 276–7).

The emphasis here is on vagueness and on the tremendous difficulties in identifying the opposition. This makes the "clarity and moderation of ideas" difficult to maintain. It should be no surprise that the opposition included everyone from the opponent who actually fired a rifle to the academic, psychologist, political scientist, philosopher, feminist, social worker, liberation theological priest, or for that matter, the protesting school children who just wanted their bus fees to be kept cheap.

Also, just as important – given the willingness to arrest and torture and kill one hundred people to get the five "subversives" – practical moral limits do not seem to be functioning at all. Given that the dirty war killed somewhere between eleven and thirty thousand people and tortured significantly more, and given that many of those who prosecuted the dirty war honestly believed that they were in a state of emergency, the question arises of whether the dirty-hands problem limits anything at all.

Tragic-choice theorists are perfectly capable of criticizing past actions that have already happened. They can condemn a past wrong on the grounds that it was not committed for the sake of the public good or that it was done for sadistic or ignoble motives. Alternatively, they might criticize a public figure for culpable ignorance if he or she makes what is deemed the wrong choice under circumstances in which he or she should reasonably have known better. Yet if public figures honestly believe that a state of emergency exists, and if they believe that there is no alternative but to commit torture or to allow a half-million children to starve in order to impose a set of sanctions, we must take seriously Eitan Felner's (2006, 35) conclusion that necessity alone dictates the course of action to be chosen, a necessity that is itself a vague matter of contextual political judgment. This is no limit at all.

In this context, tragic-choice theorists apparently think that the greatest possible evil is the destruction of the state and that all actions are permissible in principle to prevent this. As Felner (2006, 35) argues, this reasoning is perfectly compatible with any possible torture, including electric shock, removal of bodily organs, and sexual assaults. As long as the methods are perceived to be necessary and less evil than available alternatives, lesser-evils reasoning commits public officials to inflict them. This holds even though the amount of violence suffered by the target population might vastly outweigh that suffered by the larger community.

Reflection on the epistemic situation of the public official raises even greater cause for concern. Officials have to judge the existence of a state of emergency, and they can be wrong. They may have false information or misinterpret good information. Once they believe an emergency situation exists, tragic-choice reasoning begins and motivates violence. If we judge tragic-choice reasoning from a subjective point of view, every case is justified – for all torture is goal-oriented and is chosen only because interrogators believe that it is the most effective strategy for their purposes. That this judgment may be mistaken makes no difference.

Presumably, tragic-choice theorists will be uncomfortable with a subjective interpretation for exactly these reasons. If so, we need to consider the grounds for any criticism. Since subjective intentions are not sufficient grounds, they will have to be found in ex post facto communal evaluations of official behaviour. Unfortunately, this is not a happy alternative.

Lesser-evils reasoning creates the contextual prior obligation to torture and then afterward to submit oneself to public judgment. The situation is *not* tilted against torture; it is inclined toward it and motivates all state torture, even the most sadistic kinds.

How, then, do we avoid the conclusion that every instance of state-sponsored torture will turn out to be supported by the dirty-hands position? As we have seen, historical actors invoke tragic-choice reasoning in support of the dirty war and other cases where state torture is pursued. We cannot assume that they are lying simply because they are fascists or Nazis or members of some other tyrannical state. States always torture in the pursuit of perceived state interests. States do not torture for the sake of sadism, even though state agents may become sadists or satisfy sadistic inclinations in performing their tasks. At the least, this raises the worry that the number of individuals who act for the wrong moral reasons may start to look vanishingly small, especially if we take seriously Kai Nielsen's (1996, 2) remarks that the values of moral judgments are all situational. Not only are they situational, but officials make the judgments under conditions of partial and often complete uncertainty.

If this is the case, every possible purpose for torture can be justified by the dirty-hands problem. Every single one of those that I listed in chapter 1 – from the mythical interrogational form of torture through to the establishment of the torture and rape camps in Bosnia – has a possible supporting dirty-hands argument. All we need to do is fill in some relevant details – for example, sexism and racism, underpaid soldiers, low morale in a terrible civil conflict, and awareness of the need to control their behaviour and to allow them to let off steam, all in the absence of other imagined ways to solve the morale problems. Given the choice between boosting morale and having the army dissolve, some military officials will reach the conclusion that these systematic and exceptionally violent tortures are the lesser evil. In the absence of an absolute prohibition or some other inviolable general principle, it is not possible for the dirty-hands problem to exclude these cases, for they are deemed less evil in comparison to imaginable alternatives.

I want to emphasize that tragic-choice theorists clearly oppose the more extreme tortures. However, they have no clear argument to support their uneasiness. Elshtain (2004, 85) asserts that the more violent forms of torture are unacceptable and that interrogators cannot torture the innocent. However, she does not argue this and avoids confronting the possibility that her lesser-evils reasoning entails the most violent evils as well. As a just-war theorist, Walzer (1977) is also committed to noncombatant immunity and to respect for moral norms in war, but the problem remains. The state of emergency leads him to support terror bombings that kill thousands of people. If lesser-evils reasoning supports terror bombing, it cannot avoid supporting in principle any kind of torture that it is honestly believed to be less evil than the alternatives. He can criticize decisions on a case-by-case basis after the fact, but he cannot rule out any act a priori, no matter how heinous it might seem. Thus he cannot rule out in advance any of the evils that have ever happened. He can do so only contextually unless he affirms that some class of actions is prohibited without exception.

Torture Is a Violence Intensifier

Lesser-evils reasoning presupposes that torture can be violence-minimizing. But the murkiness of lesser-evil calculations should make us hesitate to treat torture as a lesser evil. In addition to the violence that I have already mapped, another failure in current lesser-evils debates is that the tragic-choice position considers the problem only from the standpoint of a single individual. What happens when we assume that all relevant public officials are in a competitive game in which they all share the same dirty-hands assumptions? In considering the violence of torture, it is insufficient to consider the standpoint of a tragic-choice individual. We also must take into account the character and behaviour of every other individual in the competition.

If one individual chooses a dirty means, the other players are forced to choose whether to employ the same tactics. Torture is used because public officials believe they gain a tactical advantage in some coercive struggle. If only some of the other players choose to use the tactics, the team that refuses fights at a disadvantage. We see these worries in practice when armies fighting counter-insurgencies feel disadvantaged if they are bound by rules that their opponents may not abide by.

It is incoherent to claim that a strategy choice is evil-minimizing if it locks competitors into choosing the same evils. It appears to reduce suffering only because it is considered from the standpoint of a single decision maker. Considered from the standpoint of a competitive game, which political struggles in some respects always are, policies like torture have predictable and inevitable tit-for-tat consequences. This is one of the reasons why some military personnel oppose torture. Whatever tactical gains it may have are counterbalanced by the fact that opponents will now employ the same tactics against the torturing state and its citizens. Tragic-choice theorists also need to recognize that since a choice to torture locks other states and/or nonstate actors into employing torture as well, a violence spiral is the result. If such actions commit the other competitors in the game to using the same tactics, which include minimally the opposition groups whose members are the subjects of possible torture, it is simply false to think that, in choosing to torture, public figures institute violence-minimizing practices. Virtue ethicists typically stress social complexity and relations both within and between communities. This makes it particularly unfortunate that dirty-hands theorists focus solely on an oversimplified situation and fail to consider intrastate relations and extrastate harms.

Some tragic-choice theorists are ambivalent about obligatory evildoing. Weber (2004, 92) makes a remarkable and curious statement at the end of his essay "Politics as a Vocation." Having defended the notions that responsible political figures have an obligation to refuse to act on altruistic grounds and that public officials are occasionally obligated to act in violent ways, Weber asserts that no law determines whether a public figure should follow an ethic of responsibility or an ethic of conviction. Many later tragic-choice theorists take it as a given that state obligations and responsibilities trump cosmopolitan values and altruism, but Weber disagrees.

Instead, Weber (2004, 92) invokes Luther's famous maxim "Here I stand, I cannot do otherwise," and he does so admiringly, indicating that it is at least not so clear that it is wrong in advance to abandon public responsibilities in favour of pure moral convictions. The constraint is that these decisions should be taken on the grounds of a political maturity that makes possible the public figure's awareness that the choice has consequences of its own. Such an individual is neither naive nor narcissistically concerned with his or her moral purity. It is possible for such individuals to do the right thing and refuse to commit evils, even though others might judge those evils to be lesser in comparison to the alternatives. Unfortunately, the discussion is tantalizingly brief. However, if Weber is right, tragic choices do not entail torture.

Similarly, Bernard Williams (1981, 60) claims that certain politicians have the moral cunning to be able to anticipate and avoid moral dilemmas. If this is true, we can reject the premise that tragic-choice dilemmas are inevitable and, with it, the thought that there are times when public officials have no choice but to dirty their hands. This raises the possibility that those who end up in tragic dilemmas may in fact be politically unimaginative. Such individuals are the morally unimpressive and mundane zealots of Wantchekon and Healy's (1999) model, not the dirty-hands individual of Walzer and de Wijze.

If Williams is right, the real virtuous individual will be the person who finds ways to avoid torturing, not the one who chooses it because he or she is too unimaginative to identify preferable alternatives. Mediocrity is a much more likely explanation, I believe, for the occurrence of torture. There is nothing odd about the thought that torture happens only because political figures and public officials appreciate neither the extent nor the magnitude of the violence that torture inflicts and lack the imagination to develop superior alternatives.

Given that the dirty-hands argument is about how the admirable public figure acts and given that moral cunning is a property of admirable moral figures, the dirty-hands argument for torture becomes even less convincing. Virtuous individuals judge how to avoid situations in which torture comes to be perceived as necessary. More important, they have a broader view of the social impacts of torture policies and refuse to create institutions that necessarily inflict so much damage on their societies and on others.

What about Public Opinion?

If individual feeling cannot do the job, perhaps public opinion can act as a limit. This is de Wijze's (2003, 37) suggestion. Discussing the problem that dirty-hands situations present for democracies, he states: "What is more, the 'dirty hands' problem has an additional dimension in democratic societies since legitimate policies and actions in this form of governance require public discussion and consent (at least to some significant degree). Consequently, in practicing deceit, for example, politicians actively prevent a public forum and collective decision-making process, thereby inflicting significant harm on the democratic process itself and the fiduciary relationship at its core."

For de Wijze, the challenge is to find ways for democracies to limit deliberate evildoing since it risks a spiralling series of harms. If public officials violate civil rights or lie, this inevitably damages citizen trust in their political system. If it becomes known that public officials are lying, citizens have difficulty rationally determining when they are telling the truth. Deceit undermines the possibility of identifying their honest claims. Public figures may also break laws for the sake of the public good. Given that they are supposed to represent the laws and desires of their communities and are supposed to be honest, dirty-hands situations threaten public trust in political leadership.

To limit this problem, de Wijze (2003, 40) suggests that public officials in a democratic society must first be duty-bound to publicly account for their actions retrospectively. As an example, he suggests that politicians be given a licence to deceive when it is necessary to achieve some laudable goal but that they are obligated afterward to publicly explain their actions. In the event that their reasons turn out to be weak, they must face public censure. He also proposes establishing secret oversight committees whose job would be to review the use of deception and to approve the decision to lie in advance of a politician's choice to do so.

De Wijze acknowledges difficulties with both proposals. If we give public figures an advance licence to deceive, they will damage others in doing so, and democratic procedures will play no constraining role. If they act wrongly, public evaluation will come too late for the victims. The oversight committees offer the advantage of avoiding the retrospective character of after-the-fact justifications of acts, but they bring their own problems. For example, emergency conditions may demand a response before a committee can meet to deal with it. This creates a further tragic-choice dilemma over whether to follow procedure and thereby fail to meet the emergency. There are also problems in ensuring that a committee is independent, critical, and balanced. In any event, the creation of such a committee merely raises the possibility of tragic-choice dilemmas in which public officials have to choose between their responsibilities to the committee and their belief that an evil must be chosen immediately.

I do not believe public accountability can make any difference in limiting state torture. Institutionalization and habituation are the central problems. State torture must be routine rather than exceptional. It requires the range of institutions that I have outlined over the preceding chapters. But institutionalization also works to undermine the hope that public opinion could condemn "wrongful" torture.

State torture never happens in a vacuum but always takes place during a violent political struggle. In chapter 3 I briefly mentioned that institutionalization problems require the normalization of torture in the mind of the public. When states prosecute these struggles, they use propaganda against their own communities to ensure public support for state violence. The consequence is that the public is taught to believe in the legitimacy of state violence and to believe that the victims of this violence either deserve it or have been accidentally targeted. In the case of torture, only the "deserving" may be targeted. This makes it inevitable that torture will be aimed at a designated hostile target population. This population must be seen to deserve their suffering. But this creates an inevitable public bias against the victims of torture and disposes the home population to believe the dominant narrative of its state. Consequently, through propaganda the public is brought to believe that the victims are the legitimate objects of violence.

The consequence is ostracism, denigration, and demonization of the victims and their communities. For example, Hector Timerman (2006, 75) notes the ostracism of his family because of his father's imprisonment and designation as a subversive. He describes how public opinion seems inclined to trust the attitudes, policies, and decisions of government unless some kind of graphic evidence to the contrary emerges. For example, in a discussion of the anti-Semitism of the Argentine government, he remarks that "Nobody wanted to believe that the Argentine dictatorship was anti-Semitic" (73). Nor are populations generally prepared to believe that their governments are simply acting in evil ways or that they themselves are complicit in evil actions. Provided that the torture is restricted to the appropriate target class and does not become sufficiently widespread as to threaten the dominant classes, public opinion is trained to support violence. Given that a state needs to be as effective as possible, sustained efforts to create public predispositions are inevitable. If a state is not unified and thus lacks public support for its actions, the likelihood of defeat increases.

Propaganda reduces the capacity of public opinion to work as a critical limit on official evildoing. This is exacerbated if the public believes itself to be in a state of emergency because under such conditions it is far more likely to uncritically accept propaganda at face value. Furthermore, states typically deny that they torture and take advantage of semantic vagueness to conceal the worst violence from their citizens. Given the successful systematic manipulation and deception, no public can critically evaluate torturers. The home population is conditioned to accept the violence of its own state, and the conditions for critical judgment simply do not exist.

Racist, sexist, and other propaganda exacerbates this problem by feeding on existing prejudices or creating new ones. In both cases, the propaganda is consciously designed to create and designate a despised class of people. The inculcation of prejudice also unifies the home population and generates support for state violence. These dispositions do not vanish over night. Racism, sexism, religious hatred, and other prejudices last lifetimes and longer. Insofar as a state creates such dispositions, its prejudiced citizens are not going to hold state torturers accountable. The only people likely to call for accountability will be the few courageous individuals who reject state torture.

A further compounding problem is that in the context of wars and states of emergency, whether real or "perceived," public opinion tends to be desensitized and brutalized by past and ongoing acts of violence that the state has either suffered or inflicted. The cries for revenge in England during the blitz and afterward were very loud, and public figures listened, unleashing terror bombing on Germany and Japan. Indeed, the state makes its population complicit in its violence by extracting public support. If citizens believe that the violence is necessary for their own survival, they will not criticize even the most egregious violence.

Because of public complicity, there is a terrible temptation to rewrite and reconstruct public memory in a way that defines the torture of the survivors and victims out of existence altogether. Hector Timerman (2006, 78) describes a painful personal experience:

> Recently, the writer and literature professor Tomas Eloy
> Martinez wrote an op-ed piece about my father in a respected
> Argentine paper. In it he said that my father "never apologized
> for his denunciation of radical journalists who worked for him
> during interrogation by the chief of police, Ramon Camps."
> Martinez used the term "interrogations" instead of "torture
> sessions," dismissing my father's testimony of those episodes.
> He builds up his theory of what happened entirely on the
> writings of the torturer. Not only did my father have to endure
> unspeakable pain, but now his surviving sons have to see how
> the torturer's version is accepted as true. Many years after the
> physical pain has ended, the moral consequences of torture still
> exist, and we are still responding to the torturer's accusations.

If public opinion is supposed to constrain torture and hold officials accountable, stories like this are not encouraging. According to Timerman, Martinez trusts the government version of the story. He uses euphemistic language that distracts the reader from considering the specific tortures inflicted on Jacopo Timerman. He also tacitly blames Jacopo for betrayals that happen under terrible duress. To make matters worse, public failure to acknowledge the evil inflicts additional long-term suffering on torture survivors, their relatives, and their friends.

These considerations help to explain why it is historically rare for torturers to be called to account. The vast majority of those responsible for torture are never confronted with their actions and are in fact protected by their governments. In the rare cases where governments have systematically attempted to come to grips with a vicious past, as in Argentina and South Africa, this has happened because of a complete transformation of the political system (Conroy 2000, 244). That is, it has happened in part because the existing power brokers have lost their hold and can no longer protect themselves. Moreover, when torturers are called to account, it is the most minor functionaries, along with perhaps a few low- to mid-level officers, who are singled out. The number of political leaders held responsible for their torture is negligible.

This is also no accident. Juan Mendez (2006, 56–7) describes torturer immunity in democratic contexts. Although there have been some successes and although he believes that torture has been lessened, he notes:

> They are also relatively immune from prosecution for torture, because prosecutors and judges believe the practice is so pervasive that it may be unfair to isolate a few cases. Judicial officials may also look the other way because the whole framework of criminal justice is heavily dependent on the police for even its meagre successes in fighting crime. Impunity for torture may have begun in the dictatorial era, but it remains constant in the democratic era, despite a few valiant efforts and some signal successes in recent times. It must be recognized, however, that cases of torture do receive media attention in the democratic era, and that the exercise of free expression has yielded some useful instruments in fighting against torture. In that respect, it is highly probable that torture is now less intense and probably less systematic than during the military dictatorships. But it is still widely used, especially if the victim belongs to the poorer and marginalized classes, where cruel and inhuman treatment is less likely to arouse sentiments of solidarity or scandalize public opinion.

At any rate, the problem of dirty hands supports impunity and thus conflicts with accountability. Torture involves chains of evil choices that occasion not just the lesser evil of choosing to torture over risking the feared catastrophic attack but also the subsequent choice of whether to hold people responsible or to risk some other evils. Consider the possibility that decision makers believe that the costs of enforcing accountability are higher than those of providing impunity to current and former torturers. Genuine risks have accompanied the attempts to prosecute torturers in Argentina and the Philippines. In both cases, there were considerable concerns about a coup against the existing government. Alternatively, consider the Argentine military's fears of uncontrollable revenge on the part of its victims after the end of the dirty war. Kay Warren (2000, 227) describes how these fears of reprisals against military personnel were one motivation for withholding information and resisting public trials. If we use unconstrained dirty-hands reasoning, the costs of a possible coup are arguably worse than those involved in holding the torturers accountable. Hence there is a lesser-evils argument for impunity as well, and states will not hold torturers accountable.

Given that state torture is always institutional, calling it an isolated choice is simply false. State torture is policy-driven, routine, and logistically supported. But institutionalized torture creates networks of complicity, within which individuals develop vested interests in not being held to account. Mendez could have added that the problem is not just that it is unfair for a judiciary to isolate on a few cases but that the broad range of personnel involved all have strong incentives to avoid public review, especially if a review would mean loss of status, loss of livelihood, shaming, imprisonment, and other possible reprisals.

Since states typically have an Official Secrets Act and given that intelligence officials are bound by such acts, states have an interest in prohibiting disclosure even if a particular interrogator wants his or her story told. This prohibition is easily conceivable, for interrogators have information that, if public, could damage state interests.

These considerations suggest that effective states cannot permit their officials to be held accountable. This would damage other interests that public officials believe to be vital. Tragic-choice reasoning will support this as well and thus speaks against public accountability, not for it.

That few torturers are ever held accountable suggests that state officials draw exactly the conclusions I have sketched. Consequently, the desire for public accountability is naive – an ideal that will happen only if the state loses. Even then, there will be considerable forces dedicated to controlling public memory afterward and ensuring that the perpetrators – other than the most public ones – are not held to account. State interest suggests that this is not simply a fear but is rather inevitable. States will not permit accountability for torturers unless they have no other alternative.

Can Proportionality Limit Torture?

Tragic-choice theorists often resort to the principles of just-war theory for the limits on deliberate evildoing. Michael Gross (2006) argues that in choosing to torture, the actions have to be reasonably chosen and that the torture inflicted must be proportionate to the desired goal. Additionally, de Wijze (2003, 41) insists that any use of torture must satisfy a proportionality test that ensures actions are not "in excess of what is needed to achieve the desirable goal."

While de Wijze does not defend the viability of proportionality, Gross (2006, 61) treats it in some detail, and his analysis is worth exploring. He asserts that proportionality is intended to "limit but not eliminate excessive harm." In a more extended discussion, he adds:

> Proportionality limits *excessive* harm and draws on humanitarian concern for aggregate human life. An act violates the principle of utility when it produces more harm than it seeks to avoid, but is disproportionate if securing an important goal incurs considerable human cost. "Excessive" cost is not synonymous with "unnecessary" cost. The cost one pays in non-combatant lives to secure a particular military objective may be necessary for a mission to succeed, yet may remain disproportionate if *too high*. Assessing proportionality is difficult because the benefits and costs of military action are not commensurable. (Original emphasis)

Gross needs to be more careful here. If the costs and benefits are not commensurable, the assessment of the proportionality of cost to benefit cannot be performed at all. The reason lies in the definition of commensurability itself: the *Oxford Dictionary of Philosophy* (1989) says that "Two things are commensurable if they can be ordered by some single measure." If they are incommensurable, they cannot be so ordered. And if they cannot be so ordered, he cannot say that a given strategy is either proportionate or disproportionate. If this is the consequence, it would also be impossible to maintain that proportionality limits excessive harm because incommensurability conflicts with any judgment of proportionality. If they are genuinely incommensurable, public officials cannot determine whether they are excessive. Gross's final sentence may be true, but if so, assessments of proportionality are impossible. This suggests that the costs and benefits cannot be calculated to support torture. Hence invocation of incommensurability is not a wise strategy for justifying torture.

If we choose to avoid the problems associated with incommensurability, the problems do not get any better. In saying this, I want to emphasize that it is unfortunate but unsurprising that Gross offers no definition of "excessive" harm or "considerable human cost." It is unsurprising because these tragic-choice decisions are situational and have no prior rules or criteria by which to evaluate them. They are the practical judgments of specific military, intelligence, or other public officials made in specific contexts.

This means that proportionality judgments rely on the character of the officials who reach the decisions. But as we have seen, torture has terrible effects on the character of interrogators. It removes their shame and other inhibiting dispositions. Given that it undermines their sense of the wrongness and shamefulness of torture, character will not help the official to proportionately judge evil. Furthermore, since practical wisdom is rare and since states are likely to select against virtuous interrogators and in favour of zealots, the judgments of proportionality rendered by these zealots are not going to be maximally virtuous or wise. They are likely to be something far worse.

The problems are more severe when we realize that public officials may be in no position at all to calculate the lesser evil. Michael Ignatieff (2004, 13) warns:

> Sometimes we can accurately predict this hazard but more
> often we cannot. Choosing a lesser evil to ward off a greater
> one may bring the greater one to pass nonetheless. When
> escalating a military conflict, for example, a commander may
> choose the lowest possible increase in the gradient of force out
> of a desire to minimize harms and to secure a military objective
> at the lowest possible cost. But this may only redouble an
> opponent's willingness to resist, with the unintended result that
> the conflict costs more lives, possibly to both sides, than a
> short, sharp escalation would have done. Bad consequences are
> not always predictable, and so, in choosing the lesser evil
> course, we may have to take a shot in the dark, knowing,
> unfortunately, that good intentions cannot exempt us from
> blame when bad consequences result.

It is bad enough that there are different kinds of torturer and that the virtuous character is not one of them. It is also terrible that state torture is routine and thus inevitably character-destroying, which makes people bad. Situational uncertainty plays on already bad conditions to further exacerbate the infliction of suffering and to guarantee that interrogators will make bad decisions. But it gets worse once we realize that public officials often have to act under conditions of unpredictability, where a lesser-evils decision in fact produces a greater evil. Choice of proportionate means under conditions of great uncertainty borders on the impossible and offers no hope that the infliction of evil is going to be limited.

Gross also insists that proportionality judgments be reasonable. "Reasonableness" is a notoriously tricky word here, for what counts as reasonable to one person will mean something wholly different to someone with a different moral character. This is especially true if the situations are as tense as those emergencies he imagines. The problem is that it is difficult to define reasonableness in a state of emergency. All actions become reasonable as long as they work. It is common to hear the remark that necessity knows no law, that in genuine states of emergency people will do whatever it takes to survive, and that therefore they may be excused for doing things that are otherwise impermissible. Resorting to cannibalism is wrong, but if the food supplies run out and rescue has not arrived, nobody should be surprised if survivors turn to cannibalism. But to say that necessity knows no law is to believe that there are no upper limits and that everything is permissible.

Proportionality calculations become both impossible and irrelevant as a given individual or community approaches a state of necessity. The consequence is that proportionality does not build in a principled upper limit to the kinds of actions that a public official might order. Consequently, there is no theoretical upper limit to the amount or quality of suffering that may be ordered either. Given that, at various times, terror bombing, the deliberate starvation of millions, invasion and destabilization of whole countries, and destruction of industry and infrastructure have all been defended as proportionate responses to emergencies, proportionality is not an attractive way to limit torture.

To this point, I have analyzed proportionality as a judgment of the perpetrator. Certainly, this seems to be Michael Gross's (2006, 31) standpoint, as the judgments are made at the time by planners, policy makers, and field commanders. They have various means available for dealing with a crisis situation and choose from among the available means the one that appears likely to resolve the situation most effectively and least harmfully. These judgments are difficult and require considerable situational wisdom. Since the virtuous official will not torture, those who do so must lack the character to enforce any significant limits.

Another alternative is to seek proportionality judgments within the home community. Here, we can consider the problem either from the point of view of a government that currently justifies torture or from the perspective of the same community after cessation of a crisis. So an action is proportionate or disproportionate if a community judges accordingly. This fares no better than public accountability. Indeed, it is just a different formulation of the same issue and subject to all the same prejudice problems that beset accountability.

Not only will the government assert its own present rectitude, but after a crisis the community is not going to judge actions to be disproportionate unless it loses. Even then it is not likely to do so. As mentioned, a heavily propagandized and possibly brutalized population is not likely to reject actions conducted on its behalf and thus is not capable of fairly applying a proportionality test. If emergency conditions are sufficiently grave, judgments of proportionality become sufficiently vague as to suggest that they will become arbitrary. This does not suggest that postcrisis community judgments of proportionality are going to help to constrain torture. In any event, these judgments are too late to help past victims and will not prevent future tortures. The same lesser-evils reasoning will drive public officials to commit the same horrors in the future, all the while judging their actions to be proportionate under the circumstances. Consequently, proportionality judgments are futile for protecting future victims of torture.

Doubts about proportionality increase when we realize that torture defenders provide no discussion of how proportionality ought to be applied in cases of torture. As Paul Gilbert (2005, 100) states, it is unclear even what counts as proportionate and disproportionate. We are given no clues about how the judgments are to work or how evaluations of proportionality are to be conducted. Consequently, we have literally no reason to believe that proportionality judgments will in fact limit torture. Without a mechanism to show that it can and will have the effect that torture defenders envision, proportionality is hopeless. Defenders of torture simply assert that it limits harm. But they provide no argument for this.

Proportionality becomes still more irrelevant when we include the institutionalization problem. Since the conditions for state torture transcend its use both in war and in emergencies, proportionality will always be breached. Hence just-war theorists like Walzer and Gross should oppose torture as well. Otherwise, they fall victim to a problem that Brian Orend (2000, 132) identifies: that of either collapsing just-war theory into a raw unprincipled consequentialism or incoherently believing it possible to commit human rights violations while advocating international human rights.

Military Necessity

Michael Gross (2006, 15–16) also argues that military necessity and proportionality are complementary principles. It is difficult to tease out the precise significance of military necessity, but he does remark that it "attributes primacy to reason of state" and that it is an overriding consideration in wartime (17). He also remarks that it functions in concert with the principle of proportionality to limit excessive harm: "Necessity, together with the need to avoid excessive harm, limits the ends and means of armed conflict" (31). Furthermore, military necessity is defined in relation to the "good ends" that nations seek in prosecuting their wars (58). He does not explore these "good ends" and their properties, so it is difficult to know what he means here. However, Gross believes military necessity to be a moral principle, one that does "know law" and thus does not have the exceptionally violent, chaotic, and unpredictable character that many theorists think.

Military necessity will no more constrain the use of torture than will proportionality. It is all very well to define military necessity as a moral principle dealing with a nation's use of violent means to pursue its morally justified ends when no other means are available. But to say that military necessity functions as a limiting principle is simply wrong. Consistent with others who defend torture, he emphasizes that it should be employed only in conditions of dire emergency when no other alternatives are available. He acknowledges its shamefulness as well.

But he does not consider that, except for moments of madness, every military choice is made because commanders believe it to be the most efficient means from among the available alternatives. They do not choose their actions because they think they are unnecessary. If they believe that other alternatives are more effective, they select the alternatives. As with the principle of proportionality, he does not consider the problem of judgment. Military necessity is not a fact out there in the world like gravity. Robert Holmes (1989, 172) notes that even Hitler used military necessity arguments to justify extermination policies. That he had a rather twisted racist ideology and view of history does not alter this fact. Claims of military necessity are judgments of historical actors made under specific circumstances and thus are dependent on the prejudices and character of the officials who make them. Every historical state-sanctioned choice to torture has been made because the given officials have believed it the right choice in the circumstances. Wasteful tactical choices simply harm a state's ability to achieve its goals, so the state will never deliberately choose ineffective tactics.

Talal Asad (1997, 299) argues the point powerfully, noting that proportionality and military necessity are both judged in terms of the ends that a given state has. As the ends become more extreme and as the situation in which a state finds itself intensifies, the actions the state judges to be necessary become more extreme as well. Any measure that is intended as a contribution to that aim, no matter how much suffering it creates, may be justified in terms of "military necessity." Proportionality is not a mathematical concept and therefore cannot be calculated. This holds as well for necessity. It is a matter of practical wisdom, and, as we have seen, torturers are not going to judge this morally. Neither proportionality nor military necessity builds in principled upper limits to state violence. Consequently, the judgments are quite compatible with the worst historical violence that has ever been inflicted – with the explosion of an atom bomb and genocide. The only possible constraint must reside with the individual commanders who judge the situations and believe their actions to be necessary.

In any case, proportionality and necessity judgments cannot morally include all the violence conducted in support of torture – for example, the psychological and physiological research, the use of victims in nonemergency situations, and all the other considerable institutional violence. As we have seen, all this violence has to be inflicted in order to permit torture in any given state situation.

If proportionality is supposed to justify such widespread violence, then it justifies everything.

The only way to build in limits is to invoke some form of absolutism. Thomas Nagel (1979, 58) describes a limited absolutism. The only way to avoid justifying massacres or other atrocities is to define impermissible classes of actions and refuse to commit them. Here, we need to be careful in our account of absolutism. As Nagel points out, absolutism is not opposed to consideration of consequences; it sets limits to consequentialist reasoning. The problem with the dirty-hands dilemma is that since tragic-choice theorists place consequences above limits, all things become possible. If we refuse to set limits to military necessity, it will prove impossible either in principle or in practice to rule out anything. This is especially pressing given that there is no wise use of torture. The violence that torture inflicts certainly should make people hesitate to think that it has a wise use. It has the appearance of being potentially wise only because of simplistic cost-benefit calculations.

I will leave Nagel (1979, 59) the last word on military necessity and state interest:

> Someone unfamiliar with the events of this century might imagine that utility arguments, or arguments of national interest, would suffice to deter measures of this sort. But it has become evident that such considerations are insufficient to prevent the adoption and employment of enormous antipopulation weapons once their use is considered a moral possibility. The same is true of the piecemeal wiping out of rural civilian populations in airborne anti-guerrilla warfare. Once the door is opened to calculations of utility and national interest, the usual speculations about the future of freedom, peace, and economic prosperity can be brought to bear to ease the conscience of those responsible for a certain number of charred babies.

Such speculations serve the same purpose in the case of numbers of torture victims. It makes no difference that dirty-hands individuals have a conscience. Torture destroys the virtue of torturers and consequently wrecks the conscience. It makes them unjust and bad. By torturing, interrogators become unjust.

CONCLUSIONS

Virtue Ethics Entail the Exceptionless Prohibition of Torture

To finish, I want to emphasize once again that I do not deny tragic choices. What I am arguing is that tragic choices neither justify nor excuse torture. Torture can introduce only vicious spirals of complicated harms. Tragic-choice theorists only support torture because they fail to appreciate the nature of torture, its institutional character, and the complex harmful consequences.

Torture has terrible costs, has no discernible morally acceptable benefits, and most important for virtue ethicists, inevitably inculcates bad habits and thus produces bad character. This production is harmful not simply to the victims of torture and their relatives and friends but also to the torturers and their communities. No virtue ethicist can tolerate this. To claim that it is ever a lesser evil to deliberately and conscientiously introduce such widespread and uncontrollable evil into a community is incompatible with virtue ethics. Hence even if tragic choice theorists can countenance some deliberate evildoing, they cannot justify or excuse torture.

Virtue ethicists can also defend absolute prohibitions, provided they can show that the relevant classes of action are destructive of virtue by their nature. In cases like torture, such practices can contribute only to the harm of a community and can push it only toward barbarism. They can never push it away. It is a fundamental error to assume that virtue ethics and an absolute conception of rights are a priori incompatible. It may be that certain rights have to be overridden for the sake of some community interest, but it does not follow thereby that all are nonderogable.

The Prohibition of Torture and Moral Risk

Ignatieff (2006, 23) accepts the reality of tragic-choice reasoning yet maintains that the levels of moral risk involved in torture are so considerable that they demand an absolute prohibition. The suffering, violence, and perversion involved is extreme and its occurrence inevitable. Hence tragic-choice theorists also have to oppose it. Absolutism also has its costs. All moral and political paths are strewn with risk, and none of them are without cost, but the costs of torture are so horrific that it should never be employed, even as the "exception."

Torture, Violence Intensification, and Barbarism

The extent of the suffering necessarily inflicted just to make a state ready to torture effectively is so extreme that it is not clear what catastrophe would override the harm that states do in preparing and inflicting torture. As noted, insofar as torture policies commit opponent state and nonstate actors to use similar means, it locks both the torturing state and its opposition into a game of spiralling violence. Here, we should be wary of one of Hobbes's (1985, 186) warnings: that in time of war and violence, industry and culture collapse and are destroyed. Institutionalizing torture, far from mitigating violence, actually pushes us further in the direction of the state of war and violence. By itself, it may not be sufficient to wholly wreck a culture, but its occurrence is one of the proofs that the culture is declining rather than improving.

One final thought is perhaps relevant here. Torturing countries have done, and continue to do, a host of terrible and shameful things. But the only people who seem to feel ashamed of the behaviour of these countries are the critics who oppose torture in the first place. There is disturbingly little evidence anywhere that shame plays anything like the constraining role in state torture that tragic-choice theorists envision. Given that the choice to torture involves the deliberate inculcation of evil habits both in the public officials who plan and organize its use and in those who have to carry it out, we should not be surprised by this. Few real people, if any, can consistently do evil and continue to be ashamed by it. The subtlety of this move away from shame is beyond any of us.

It is impossible to torture and be moral. Hence the tragic-choice theorists should also resist the conclusion that torture is justifiable and that public leaders ought to order torture. Even given the reality of tragic choices, virtue-ethical considerations demand its absolute prohibition.

5

On Neither Excusing
nor Justifying Torture

Legal arguments for torture typically rely on the ticking-bomb hypothesis, tragic-choice reasoning, and utilitarian arguments. Chapters 2 through 4 demonstrate the invalidity of these general arguments for torture. I now build on those insights to demonstrate the inadequacy of a number of specifically legal arguments for torture. The debate typically centres on whether state torture should be excused after the fact or whether it is justifiable before the fact. In the event that torture is held to be justifiable, the arguments concern whether to legalize it. Miriam Gur-Arye (2004) accepts the prohibition against torture but believes that it is sometimes justifiable. When interrogators use torture, they should be able to raise the defence of self-defence. Alan Dershowitz (2004, 65) argues that public officials occasionally find it necessary to torture to save lives and that on some of those occasions a democratic public will support them. To ensure they can do those acts that they are publicly obliged to do, torture should be legalized, and careful controls should be put in place to ensure that torture does not proliferate. Oren Gross (2004) argues that the absolute ban on torture is sound but accepts that there are rare circumstances available according to which public officials will justifiably resort to torture. In those circumstances, they should disobey the law and act. Following this, they should submit their behaviour for public judgment. In this chapter I argue that each of these positions is misconceived.

CAN TORTURE BE EXCUSED?

One possible avenue for defending torturers is to argue that torture is excusable in principle. In this case, if the circumstances are so extreme that a public official has no alternative, he or she ought to torture. In the event that torture is judged to be necessary, the official should be excused. Alternatively, Miryam Gur-Arye (2004) maintains that interrogators should be able to take advantage of a self-defence strategy. In this case, the interrogators act correctly under the circumstances to prevent harm to third parties.

The distinction between excuse and justification is important. For Gur-Arye (2004, 188), an excuse negates the culpability of an actor for his or her wrongful conduct, whereas a justification negates the wrongfulness of the conduct. Hugo Adam Bedau (1997, 14) distinguishes excuse from justification in the following way:

> One *excuses* oneself from blame for the harm one has done to another by conceding that it was wrong to cause the harm, but that nevertheless in the circumstances it couldn't be helped and that therefore one can't really be blamed for it. Thus, if one cannot help but strike out to save one's own life, circumstances preventing any deliberation and reflection, then one ought to be excused by the law. One *justifies* oneself for causing harm to another by showing that one did it deliberately and after due reflection, because in the circumstances it was the right (or best) thing to do. (Original emphasis)

Gerald Dworkin (2006, 158) suggests that "We make excuses when we admit that we caused some harm but maintain that the action was not fully voluntary; we were drunk or negligent or too tired to pay attention. We say we were justified when we admit that we caused harm but claim that in the circumstances it was self-defense, or he had it coming to him, or we had the right to do it."

We excuse a wrongful act when it is inadvertent or unavoidable. The wrong is genuine, but it happens only because of factors that were partially or wholly beyond the control of an agent. In an excuse, the action done remains wrong and is wrong under the circumstances. Justifications, such as self-defence, occur when an action is performed that is prima facie wrong but that, in some given set of circumstances, is the right thing to do. It is crucial to recognize that both justifications and excuses of wrongdoing are circumstantial. The acts are wrong, but under certain circumstances we can nonetheless either excuse or justify them. Recognizing the significance of this point is crucial for understanding why torture cannot be either excused or justified.

State torture is incompatible with the definition of an excuse. As we have seen, state torture is inevitably institutional. As such, it is never a case of a unique exceptional response to an unanticipated emergency – and cannot be such a response if governments hope to succeed with it. Torturing states recognize this point. They do not spend such large sums of money on torture because they think they can do it ad hoc and unplanned. It makes no sense to excuse actions that are planned long in advance of the actual choice to act. It makes no sense to excuse torture when so much work, suffering, research, planning, and preparation are required in advance of the situations in which torture can be employed. The exercise of state torture is simply incompatible with circumstantial choice making.

There are other reasons for forbidding an excuse defence. Under the circumstances, public officials have a group of alternatives and believe that torture is the one most likely to be effective. One of these alternatives is the choice not to torture. They do not know that this will fail. They believe it will. They are not literally compelled to torture. Dershowitz (1989, 195) suggests an additional objection to excusing torture. As a state-of-nature defence, it has no principled upper limit to the actions it permits. In the state of nature anything goes that might achieve the specific desired end. Allowing a necessity defence is a low standard for sacrificing the interests of others and therefore is not an option.

TORTURE AS "SELF-DEFENCE"

Nonetheless, both Gur-Arye and Dershowitz believe that torture can be justified. Gur-Arye (2004, 192) accepts ticking-bomb justifications even though she is aware that the conditions under which interrogations are executed are far murkier than classic ticking-bomb scenarios envision. Consequently, she believes that torture interrogators should be entitled to a self-defence justification. Thus this is a legitimation strategy. There are circumstances in which public officials should torture, and these are defined by the defence of self-defence.

A virtue of the self-defence option, she believes, is that it forces interrogators to torture only the perpetrators and prohibits torture of the innocent. She is deeply concerned that we not justify the torture of the innocent. Both utilitarian reasoning and tragic-choice reasoning are prone to a terrible slippage in their ability to allow the torture and murder of innocent third parties. Necessity permits everything if the situation is sufficiently extreme. A self-defence justification can prevent the torture of the innocent, she believes, because we can defend ourselves only against the individual(s) who unlawfully plan and prepare the attack. In self-defence, individuals repel an assault with sometimes deadly force, but logically they can defend themselves only against an attacker. Hence innocents cannot be violated in self-defence. We can use violent force only against the perpetrator (Gur-Arye 2004, 193–4). The perpetrator, in turn, has options. In the face of torture, he or she can opt to release the information that will allow the defusing of a bomb or other threat.

Self-defence will not work either. It will not protect the innocent. The problem is that interrogators are never going to know that the suspect is a perpetrator. They will believe this. Due to fog of war and conceptual uncertainty, they will find it difficult to accurately identify the perpetrators but will face the same pressures to torture. This means that innocents are inevitably going to be tortured. Although torture is supposed to avoid harming the innocent, a self-defence option cannot achieve this goal. The problem here is that of collateral damage. Public officials may well point to the unavoid-ability of killing and harming innocents in prosecuting a war or resolving a crisis and thus claim that they were acting in self-defence. The innocent were simply unlucky enough to get in the way. The interrogator did not intend to torture an innocent participant; he just happened to mistake the identity of the guilty. There are more principled objections to self-defence as a justification as well.

The self-defence model is also circumstantial in its reasoning and does not comprehend the institutional character of state torture. No court would allow a defence of self-defence if an individual plans a torture long in advance of carrying it out. Nor would it be impressed by this defence given that torture puts together an interrogation team with supporting medical staff, scientific research, training bases, and all the other apparatus needed. That is not self-defence but carefully planned aggression. It is something quite different from the choice of an evil to mitigate a crisis. Torture is carried out in multiple and specific circumstances, but state torture is not circum-stantial; it is institutional and regular rather than exceptional.

LEGALIZATION:
ALAN DERSHOWITZ AND TORTURE WARRANTS

Although Alan Dershowitz (2004, 275) is emphatic that torture is normatively wrong, he believes there are occasions when public officials are going to torture regardless of the presence of laws prohibiting the practice. He also thinks that in some of those contexts, the public will praise their behaviour. In those contexts, the practice will be justifiable.

Since torture is going to happen regardless of prohibition, and since in at least some cases a democratic public will approve of it, Dershowitz's (2002, 153) concern is not the elimination of torture but its control. He seeks to restrict its use to the minimum number of possible cases. Furthermore, since torture sometimes works (he claims), we cannot assert that it is always ineffective. As we have already seen, he believes that torture can be effective at procuring information necessary to save lives. The primary question is how to minimize the use and severity of torture only to those cases and those methods and degrees necessary to prevent a tragedy. For Dershowitz, only interrogational torture may be used, and the tortures used may only be nonlethal. His argument is quite simple: "The simple cost-benefit analysis for employing such nonlethal torture seems overwhelming: it is surely better to inflict nonlethal pain on one guilty terrorist who is illegally withholding information needed to prevent an act of terrorism than to permit a large number of victims to die. Pain is a lesser and more remediable harm than death; and the lives of a thousand innocent individuals should be valued more than the bodily integrity of one guilty person" (141).

As I have already shown, interrogational torture is incoherent. Furthermore, the violence of torture is far more extensive then this simple calculus suggests. It is also odd to refer to a "guilty" "terrorist" given that in the situations he imagines there cannot be a finding of guilt by any recognized and independent legal authority. The same goes for the idea that a state or nonstate actor might be acting illegally as well. This cannot be determined without fair procedures that consider the interests of the suspect.

Dershowitz (2002, 145–6) mentions the institutionalization problem. He concedes that this allows rule utilitarians to generate a prohibition against torture. But it is striking that he merely lists a few dangers and fails to analyze them. Knowing that there are dangers is different from appreciating the nature of the threats they pose. Consequently, he fails to appreciate the point that state torture is incompatible with the problem of dirty hands. He treats the institutionalization problems as one of inductive risk. That is, he is concerned that if we start allowing torture in one case, we risk extending it to other cases. Since he regards it as an inductive problem rather than as an inevitable consequence of torturing, he mistakenly thinks that it is possible to work out the right policy set to limit the damage.

Following the Landau Commission, Dershowitz (2002, 150) imagines four general legal positions on torture:

1 to allow security services to operate outside the law
2 the way of the hypocrite, in which the citizens of a state tolerate the occurrence of the torture that is done in their name while pronouncing it illegal
3 to follow the "truthful road of the rule of law" and insure that the law provides the proper framework for the actions of state security services
4 to forego torture and allow preventable terrorist attacks to occur

In Dershowitz's view the absolute road is hopeless. By refusing ever to torture, public officials abandon their responsibility to avoid preventable tragedies. Deliberate evildoing is occasionally the only way to ensure that preventable tragedies do not occur. The way of hypocrisy is also untenable because it allows torture to proliferate beyond any possible control. Since under this strategy torture happens outside of any public supervision, no democratic state can control it. Furthermore, Dershowitz believes that the way of the hypocrite is unfair to the interrogators. They are acting for the sake of the public good. If hypocrisy is chosen, then they may be punished for acting well. Finally, democracies presuppose transparency and accountability. But actions that happen secretly and outside of any public scrutiny are incompatible with accountability. If the actions are done for the sake of the public good, the public ought to have an opportunity to evaluate their worth (Dershowitz 2004, 273). This same reason applies to the option of simply allowing state agents to operate outside the law. To put them in such a shadow zone is literally to allow anything to happen since their actions are now exempt from law in advance.

Hence, for Dershowitz, legalization is the correct option. In democracies soldiers, police officers, intelligence officials, and presidents should only ever act legally. They should never violate the laws of their country, and if they do, this should only ever happen according to values of which the public approves (Dershowitz 2004,

264). Furthermore, an action should be public, and the test of the appropriateness of an action in a democracy is that it should be able to survive public scrutiny (Dershowitz 2002, 152). Consequently, if torture is going to happen, and if there are cases when a public will approve its use, then torture should be codified and supported in existing law (153). Hence he proposes a system of torture warrants on the analogy with the Foreign Intelligence Surveillance Act (FISA) courts. The idea is that public officials will be able to apply to a judge for a warrant to torture an individual when they believe it necessary to prevent a catastrophe.

He believes that this will create a double-check. The first control is the interrogator. In the course of intelligence gathering, he or she determines that torture is necessary. Having exhausted all available options and failed to extract the necessary information, the interrogator applies for a warrant and provides the judge with the reasons why torture is necessary. The judge evaluates those reasons and either permits the torture to go ahead – thus giving the interrogator a warrant to torture – or forbids the torture. Hence the judge functions as a second check to determine the appropriateness of torture (Dershowitz 2002, 158).

The warrant system is supposed to enable interrogators to legally torture in order to prevent a catastrophe. Thus it avoids punishing them for doing those things that, given their public obligations, they ought to perform. Hence a torture-warrant procedure is fair to the interrogators. Furthermore, as legal documents, the torture warrants will be available for public scrutiny at some point after the crisis has been averted and thus will allow public debate about specific cases. This, in turn, will encourage critical reflection and minimize torture, for interrogators who act without a warrant will be subject to criminal sanction.

Before considering the precise details of the torture-warrant proposal and its various internal weaknesses, I want to emphasize some problems.

First, Dershowitz pays no attention to the nature and structure of torture. He contents himself with references to the definition contained in the United Nations Convention against Torture (UNCAT). The few historical references he does make are to disputed newspaper articles. There is no evidence that he has either read survivor stories or considered the psychological or medical literature concerning its specific harms and how these extend across the space and time of the given target community to which any torture victims belong. It is particularly disturbing, therefore, to see his reaction to the comments of a survivor of torture:

> The conference began with an emotional speech – replete with candles – delivered by a victim of torture who described how innocent people are tortured to death by brutal regimes around the world. The intended message of this introduction was that torture of the kind experienced by the speaker is bad – as if that were a controversial proposition. It was calculated to make it difficult, if not impossible, to conduct a rational discussion about ways of limiting and regulating the use of nonlethal torture in the context of terrorism prevention. (Dershowitz 2004, 265)

It is fascinating to see Dershowitz dismiss this victim's speech as an illegitimate appeal to pity and a fallacious distraction from a debate about the justifiability of torture. It is unclear why survivor narratives and artistic treatments of torture experiences do not count in a rational argument about torture. He certainly does not consider the possibility that they might be important and valuable resources for rational reflection. In any event, he treats the harms as obvious and fails to recognize that knowing torture to be harmful is different from knowing how it is harmful. Knowing that torture causes terrible suffering does not help us to appreciate the specific details of its violence. To appreciate the harms, we have to listen to and appreciate survivor stories and art, among other things. Otherwise, we do not understand the harm. Failure to do this undermines the rationality and sensitivity of the debate by excluding morally relevant considerations.

Second, he relies on the ticking-bomb hypothesis even though it is demonstrable nonsense. In combination, these weaknesses lead him to create a false dilemma in which the public official balances the pain experienced by the nonlethally tortured suspect against the deaths, injuries, and property losses suffered by numerous innocent third parties.

Third, the historical cases he provides are highly disputable. As I noted in the Introduction, there is evidence that the information needed to foil Abdul Hakim Murad's bomb plot was discovered on his computer within minutes of his capture by the Philippine security forces in 1995. His torture probably had nothing to do with preventing a specific threat but served other political goals. Alternatively, he contradicts fact by extrapolating from cases where torture was not used (and hence was unnecessary) to hypothetical cases in which it is deemed necessary – disguised variants of the ticking-bomb hypothesis.

Fourth, he examines the specific choices and acts of public officials and pays no serious attention to the policy-based and institutional character of state torture. He fails to analyze the problem that institutionalization is an a priori structural property of state torture. Consequently, he does not consider what institutionalization requires: all the personnel, logistics, communications, training bases, advanced preparation, and practice that will give torturers the chance to achieve state goals. Since legal transformations are also part of this, he fails to recognize that the warrant proposal is just part of the harm sequence. Consequently, he treats an evil (the legitimation of state torture through a torture-warrant procedure) as a good because he falsely believes that warrant procedures will minimize harms. As a result, he fails to recognize that torture warrants are part of the routine of torture and are just one additional contribution to their institutional entrenchment.

As part of a routine, these warrants are incompatible with exceptional-circumstances reasoning. Once we accept that states must always attempt to torture well, we recognize that torture has to happen independently of the circumstances that Dershowitz envisions. Just as fighter pilots have to train with their aircraft if they wish to hit a target in some war, so a torturer will have to train if his or her practices are going to have any chance (however limited) at success. The difference is that at least the fighter pilot's training can be in principle victimless; the same is not possible for the torturer. At some point, torturers have to practice on victims if they are going to be any good. The spread of state torture is not merely a risk but is in fact inevitable once the state decides that torture serves a state interest.

Dershowitz's failure to carefully examine institutional costs also means that he fails to recognize the specific torture-related costs that are imposed on the interrogators and the society that tortures. Indeed, Dershowitz does not fully appreciate the impact of legalization. He concedes only that it marks a "symbolic" setback for the struggle against torture. However, the problem is not about symbols but concerns the systematic, deliberate, and extensive infliction of substantial harm on entire classes of individuals and their social relations.

In affirming that public officials are going to torture, Dershowitz presupposes their reasonability and does not consider that they might, as a group, fail to appreciate the wider costs of torture and thus overemphasize its doubtful benefits. Given that torture is an extremely complicated problem, there is nothing incoherent or implausible in supposing that officials who torture fail to appreciate their own violence. Here, whether they are acting from "honest" or "evil" motives is irrelevant, for they will justify the infliction of suffering on the basis of unsound cost-benefit calculations.

Finally, the claim that torture is inevitable is an undefended empirical assertion. It takes as a given that we cannot eliminate this kind of state violence. If we accept this premise, it will of course be impossible to end torture. But this is neither a logical nor a physical truth. No support for this proposed truth will be found on the short arm of chromosome 6 or in any other bit of genetic coding. It is a contingent truth and becomes necessary only because specific states make choices to torture. The argument that since "torture is inevitable ... we should control it" has terrible consequences. For instance, during the antislavery debates at the end of the eighteenth century, slavery was widespread and the forces arrayed against the abolitionists were powerful and well funded. To reason by logical analogy, there was no point to the abolition movement against slavery because so many nonslaves believed that slavery was natural and inevitable. Yet decades of hard work did manage to eliminate one form of slavery. The abolitionists succeeded by arguing for an absolute ban against slavery, not by arguing that slaves deserve better treatment. According to Dershowitz's line of reasoning, since people at the time believed slavery to be inevitable, the right conclusion was to regulate it rather than to abolish it. Recognizing the noninevitability and the contingency of unjust practices is crucial. There is nothing invalid about acknowledging that many, if not most, states currently practise torture in various ways and simultaneously inferring that torture can be eliminated. If the inference turns out to be unsound, it is because states refuse to heed good moral and prudential advice.

If regulation is supposed to control and limit torture, the history of state torture is not encouraging. John Langbein (2004, 93) argues that European countries worked at the problem for half a millennium before finally concluding that torture cannot be controlled. Hence they chose to ban it. Edward Peters (1985) reaches the same conclusions in his seminal history of the subject. Initially, torture is restricted to a small class, and then it becomes extended to increasingly larger groups of people. If warrants are supposed to regulate and minimize torture, history gives us no reason for confidence.

There are also internal problems with torture warrants as well as the question of whether a state can secure the control for which Dershowitz hopes. The first problem is that tragic-choice situations and lesser-evils reasoning create the conditions for the obligatory violation of torture warrants. We need only imagine conditions under which the interrogator believes that the time needed to get a warrant conflicts with the immediacy of the threat. In a case like this, the public official now merely has a new tragic-choice problem: whether to obey the law and seek a warrant or to break the law and prevent the catastrophe. This means that in such circumstances the torture warrant will have no force and will not do its intended job. The same arguments that Dershowitz uses to support a warrant procedure also support the violation of the warrant whenever the needs of the situation dictate. In consequence, there are now two justifications for torture: the legal route and the illegal route. Both of these can be inferred from lesser-evils reasoning. The consequence is that torture warrants will also increase the acceptability of torture in the public mind while failing to minimize torture. There is no reason to believe that torture warrants will have any appreciable limiting effect.

Suppose further that a judge is willing to issue a torture warrant and that he also issues a statement permitting a limited set of tortures. Assume that the techniques are tried and fail. Now we have an additional dilemma, as there are other torture techniques that could be tried. Since the prescribed techniques have failed, the temptation will be to explore alternative possibilities as well. Tragic-choice reasoning, applied to the case of state torture, creates violence spirals as alternatives fail. Once torture is allowed, torturers will be tempted by a much wider range of possibilities than can be caught by any limited permissible set. What makes matters worse is that tragic-choice considerations dictate that the torturers explore these further options.

Furthermore, we need to ask how rigorous the warrant procedure should be. Does Dershowitz want it to be a safeguard or a rubber stamp? Presumably, it should be a safeguard, as it is supposed to minimize both the degree and the occurrence of torture while maximally ensuring that torture occurs only in the cases where it is necessary. But the more rigorous a state makes its court procedure, the more time it will take to issue a warrant (Oren Gross 2004, 1537; Scarry 2004, 286), so imminence and legal rigor are not compatible. To make a warrant system rigorous, we might allow a representative of the suspect to dispute the evidence given in the warrant. Perhaps a lawyer or ombudsmen or some other official could be tasked to prove that the individual should not be tortured. If some such strategy were to be adopted, adequate preparation time would be needed to ensure that interrogator, defender, and judge can fairly and neutrally consider the evidence. But the more time the warrant system takes, the less useful it will be for the purposes that torture defenders envision. In any event, measures like this increasingly transform a warrant procedure into some form of trial.

The warrant system is intended to provide a double-check on torture. But how is this supposed to happen? The interrogator provides the judge with a set of evidence that he or she already believes suffices to require torture. The judge is not in a position to determine the adequacy of the evidence because there is no critic there to carefully examine and reject it. All of the evidence and all of the arguments for the need to torture come from the interrogator. There is nobody to provide counter-arguments or counter-evidence, and there is nobody to defend the interests of the suspect. There are various steps that could be taken to increase the rigor of any warrant system, but the greater the rigor, the more time the court will have to take in order to decide any given issue, and the less the warrant system will be able to prevent attacks. If the court is a rubber stamp, it will permit a quick response to an emergency and thus will not serve as the second check. In that case, it is an irrelevant fifth wheel. Either it will not help to avoid the tragedy or it will fail to control and minimize torture.

According to Oren Gross, matters get worse when we recognize that fears of a catastrophe or other public emergency create predispositions in court officials to believe and support interrogators. They are likely to defer even though a thoroughgoing analysis would reject the warrant. Gross (2004, 1540–1) also remarks that the warrant system ties the courts and the judiciary to the deliberate commission of evil acts. This has negative consequences both in delegitimizing the courts and in legitimizing torture. Likewise, he warns that a warrant system will underdeter interrogators. If they believe that ratification for torture will be forthcoming, they will not fear refusal. Consequently, they will be more inclined to torture. Conditions of what Gross calls "low acoustic separation create substantial risks of undesirable behaviour on the part of officials, further undermining the ability of the torture warrant to secure its aim" (1532).

John Kleinig (2005, 623) identifies a further important objection. The necessity defence can be used only to support exceptional acts; it cannot be used to create policy. Not only are the torture warrants an advance policy, but it follows that state torture must be as well. It is not just that the necessity defence cannot be used to justify torture warrants; it cannot be used to justify any torture at all. One final empirical remark is useful. Kleinig also cautions that the specific history of torture warrants does not encourage us to expect that they will be effective. As noted, Dershowitz models the warrant system on the FISA courts. But Kleinig and Gross both observe that the FISA courts have almost never turned down a wiretapping warrant. There is at least as little reason to think that a torture warrant court would be any more rigorous (Oren Gross 2004, 1548; Kleinig 2005, 626). There is no reason to think that a torture court will provide any check on torture. Hence Andrew Moher's hope that a regulated system of torture will curb underground torture to a very significant degree is no hope at all. It will just legitimize most of the torture and still guarantee the persistence of underground torture.

We should consider one final warning about Dershowitz's torture warrants. In an extremely important critical analysis of the UNCAT definition of torture, Bob Brecher (2007, 5) notes that "if torture warrants were made a lawful sanction in certain cases of withholding information – then it would no longer count as torture, since it was 'inherent in ... lawful sanction!" The problem is that the UNCAT definition excludes from classification as torture those actions that are a part of the lawful sanction of states. Since the warrant procedure is a lawful state process, the consequence would be that no state torture conducted by warrant-using states could count as torture. Provided that the state has such a warrant system, and provided that all acts of torture are inflicted under a warrant, none of them would then count as being in violation of the UNCAT. This would render the Convention against Torture meaningless.

OFFICIAL DISOBEDIENCE

In my view this is one of the most interesting and sophisticated of the legal treatments of torture. Oren Gross explicitly acknowledges a substantial set of the harms and concedes that these suffice to make necessary an unqualified support for an absolute prohibition against torture. Thus Oren Gross (2004, 1492) argues that torture is never legally either permissible or excusable. Nonetheless, in concert with many others, he concedes that preventive interrogational torture may be necessary in extreme circumstances (1520). However, rather than arguing for codifying an excuse or legal defence, public officials ought to take the more courageous stand and torture – if they believe it to be absolutely necessary – in full knowledge that they may be punished. If they believe the situation to be this bad, and also believe that there is no alternative, they should torture and be willing to suffer the negative consequences. If they fail to secure public support for their actions, they must accept any punishment. As Gross conceives it, public officials must be prepared to leave the legal order and seek ex post ratification from their society. The society must then make a decision to excuse or punish.

Gross (2004) believes that the official-disobedience model offers the following safeguards:

- It provides a strong incentive for officials to follow the rules unless they genuinely think that the catastrophe is so pressing that they must act extralegally (1522).
- It forces public officials to violate the law at their peril (1529) and face significant burdens for torturing (1534). If they believe the stakes are high enough to merit an illegal action, they may take it and hope the public sees things their way. Gross believes that the risk of a negative public judgment is considerable, for it is at least possible that the public will evaluate the acceptability of the actions in a calm and rational manner and judge the act to have been wrong (1530).
- It preserves a commitment among public officials to abide by the law (1532).

- That the actions remain illegal ensures that the laws constrain public officials, especially in countries that have well-entrenched and well-internalized moral and legal norms (1527).
- It stresses that the harms not only impact the individual public agent but also expose the torturing government to significant international consequences and costs. For agents, this includes the possibility of civil or criminal prosecution in other countries. For the governments that torture, it involves loss of reputation and harmful consequences to its own citizens from revenge takers (1549).
- It preserves a commitment to the absolute prohibition against torture and thus supports the UNCAT's nonderogability clause.
- It does not override the laws against torture (1522).
- This provides a range of options for dealing with public officials in the event that they judge the actions to have been correct under the circumstances. For example, the society may decide not to bring charges, it may use jury nullification where charges are brought, it may pardon or otherwise grant clemency to the public official, or the government of the society may indemnify the state agents who are found guilty and liable for torture (1523).
- It stresses an ethics of responsibility for public figures. The country and its citizens are enabled to take responsibility for their actions (1526).

These seem to be significant safeguards that, Gross hopes, can prevent the proliferation of torture. Although he comes as close to an absolute prohibition against torture as one can without strictly forbidding it, there are problems sufficiently deep to undermine the official-disobedience model as well.

First, Gross accepts interrogational torture, even though this is a fiction. Torture even in those cases must terrorize many and cause the harms that I outline in chapters 1 and 3. Second, Gross concedes the harms that torture inflicts on torturers and torturing societies and acknowledges its destructive effects on political and legal institutions. Unfortunately, he neglects to analyze them in any detail. Here, the devil really is in the details. He does not consider how deeply rooted are the corruption problems and does not recognize that the harms are still worse than he envisions. Third, Gross provides no analysis of the institutional problems and thus fails to recognize the implications of a state desire to torture. The official-disobedience model would not allow training and research into torture, nor would it encourage medical participation or any of the other prerequisites for state torture. But this means that officially disobedient torturers would be maximally likely to fail because they would not know what they were doing.

Gross (2004, 1496) is also aware of, and partially accepts, the rule-utilitarian case against torture. However, he is ultimately willing to permit torture in principle by charging rule utilitarianism with rule worship. But the problem has nothing to do with a cold-hearted refusal to save the lives of people. Rather, the problem is that torture is never an exceptional act.

Rule worship can be a worry in some moral situations – especially where rights, moral norms, and laws conflict in some way. However, it is not a problem in the case of state torture because of its specific institutional complexities. If it were possible for torture to be an isolated act carried out only in some isolated circumstance, the charge of rule worship might hold. But the same considerations that explain why torture should not be excused also suggest the failure of the official-disobedience model. To have any chance of effectiveness at all, torture must be established as a rule, not as an isolated act in exceptional circumstances.

Given his clear rejection of torture, Gross cannot desire torture-research programs or torture-training institutes. Likewise, he cannot support the subversion of medical-ethical norms to allow doctors and nurses to aid in successful torture. But if this is the case, Gross also has to reject the official-disobedience model because it is incompatible with torture.

Gross (2004, 1510) identifies a number of institutional fears, but he treats them as inductive problems. He thinks that states can inadvertently lose control following an initial decision to torture in controlled circumstances. Downhill spirals then take place because of inadequate supervision and the emergence of uncontrolled cases of torture. He does not consider that the routinization and proliferation of torture is a logical consequence of various institutional precommitments.

Gross (2004, 1511) is also aware of the problem of designating a target population for possible torture and the consequent risk of imposing far too high a cost on that group. But it is a mistake to think that this is a consequence of a loss of control. It is not a risk but is inevitable. Torture attacks identity, and identity is social.

When states torture, they attack not individuals but groups and communities. To be sure, the tortures are visited on the bodies of individuals, but state torture is one tactic in a coercive assault on some community. Not only does it assault the communities by specifically targeting the mind and body of specific individuals, but because these individuals have families, friends, cousins, neighbours, and acquaintances, the harm also spreads out across these entire groups in complicated ways. This spreading is intrinsic to torture and cannot be avoided. As these are structural properties of state torture, the official-disobedience model fails because it does not understand the nature of the violence.

In addition, the later sections of chapter 4 explore some empirical grounds for doubt that legal sanction will have the constraining effect hoped for by Gross. Recall that the historical record does not suggest that a traumatized public will impose the desired critical constraints on public officials – at least not in the case of regimes that survive the conflicts in which they torture. A calling to account of public officials has happened in South Africa through the Truth and Reconciliation Commission and is happening to some extent in Argentina. But in both cases, entire regimes were replaced. In the case of victorious states, there is little reason to believe that officials will ever be censured. Perhaps this may take place decades or centuries later, but it is too late for the victims of torture and, moreover, will not prevent future tortures.

The central problem is that an ex post ratification for an act of torture is incompatible with the institutional nature of state torture. This is true of all excuse-and-justification strategies. Perhaps we can forgive or justify isolated acts of evildoing, but we cannot excuse or legitimate routines. Hence if torture advocates are to argue in favour of torture, they must confront the structures of state torture, not deal with abstract and nonempirical fantasies.

Conclusion

What these reflections demonstrate first is that the default position on torture is sound. Everyone agrees, and is correct in believing, that torture is evil. But there is no ceteris paribus clause. It is not just that we should refrain from torturing unless some extreme circumstance dictates otherwise but that we should never torture at all. Every theorist accepts at least a prima facie deontological prohibition of torture. They disagree simply about whether that prohibition holds under all possible circumstances. As we have seen, protorture theorists envision states of emergency where the right not to be tortured must be overridden. Here, the idea is that torture might be justifiable, permissible, or excusable when there is no other way to prevent a catastrophe. In such situations, to hold to the dictates of justice would create an even worse evil. On this point, even fierce opponents of torture are occasionally tempted to waiver.

In any event, some act utilitarians argue that, in cases like this, the greatest-happiness principle (along with a simple cost-benefit analysis) demonstrates that public officials are morally obligated to torture. The suffering of one individual is outweighed, they believe, by the suffering of all those who will be killed by the preventable attack. Some virtue ethicists add to these consequential considerations the specific obligations owed by officials to their states. Since they occupy public roles that specifically require them to act for the sake of state security, and since these roles sometimes compel them to do evil things knowingly because the alternative is yet worse, they occasionally have to get their hands dirty. They have no moral alternative but to torture an individual and thus must get some blood on their hands.

There are also a few rare rights-based arguments for torture. These maintain that public officials are obligated to torture where the violation of the rights of one individual is necessary to protect the rights of others. This argument takes two forms: (1) the rights are equal in importance, and it is simply a numerical calculation of the consequences of rights violation for the tortured individual versus the consequences for those deemed likely to be violated by this individual's actions; or (2) it involves a hierarchy of rights in which the right to life is held to be prior to the right not to be tortured (Allhoff 2005b). Steven Kershner (2005, 225) argues that in certain cases torture does not violate a natural right and consequently does not wrong the tortured individual. In either event, these arguments maintain that torture can be morally obligatory.

There are several reasons why these additional arguments require no separate treatment. Notably, the arguments are consequentialist despite their invocation of the language of rights. The purpose of the torture, according to both Allhoff and Kershner, is to acquire information to prevent an emergency, and it is this that generates the justification of torture. A suspect is classified as a "terrorist" and thereby loses his or her right not to be tortured. What justifies the torture is not an act already performed but imminent violence. In the case of state torture, there is no determination that a given individual has sacrificed his or her right not to be tortured, and there are none of the fairness procedures that would normally be in place to protect someone's rights. In state torture, legal protections cannot exist because they are incompatible with the imminence condition of the arguments used to defend torture. The deontological tradition is fundamentally concerned with issues of fairness and justice, neither of which is possible in state torture. This tradition certainly cannot come into consideration in the only cases for which torture advocates are arguing: the states of emergency where an attack threatens massive loss of life as well as the destruction of limb and property. State torture, whether employed against internal dissidents or against external opposition, is consequentialist. It has to do with perceived preservation of national security or with perceived preservation of the laws, rights, and structure of the state. But preservation is a consequentialist, rather than deontological, concept.

Since everyone accepts that torture is evil, and since everyone agrees that all human beings have a prima facie right not to be tortured, the debate has to be handled on consequentialist grounds. We need to show that careful consideration of consequences supports the absolute prohibition against torture.

Torture defenders pay no attention to the nature and structure of torture. They work with the definition in the United Nations Convention against Torture (UNCAT) and argue that it is possible to defend the violation of the right not to be tortured. They seem to think that knowledge of the convention definition is either necessary or sufficient for understanding torture. It is neither. It is a valuable operational definition that helps us to identify specific instances of torture. But understanding torture requires far more complicated analysis. Failure to examine the properties, harms, and purposes of torture confuses their consequentialist defence of torture. Torture cannot be handled within the confines of philosophy, of law, or of the two combined together. If that is all that we work with, we will generate some terrible arguments. To properly appreciate this kind of violence, relevant work in a wide range of disciplines has to be considered. To understand and engage in adequate moral reflection, attention to feminist, antiracist, and similar literature is important. Likewise, we must pay careful attention to history, psychology, medicine, sociology, economics, politics, literature, art, and sculpture.

Here, the absolute opponents of torture are on much stronger conceptual and empirical ground than are the defenders. If you compare the bibliographies of texts produced by both camps, the differences in concern for torture's real historical consequences are striking. There is a complete absence of attention to the historical realities of torture in the writings of torture defenders. They pay no attention to either psychological or medical literature and none to survivor narratives. The rare references to historical events are cherry-picked from the statements of government agencies that have an interest in depicting the successes of their own torture programs. Alternatively, they are also based on newspaper accounts rather than on rigorous historical and political analysis of state torture. Either this is the case or the references are stripped of their historical context in some way and thereby falsified. However you read them, protorture arguments are not paradigms of careful psychological, medical, sociological, political, or historical analysis.

The antitorture literature, on the contrary, is deeply concerned with the empirical impacts of torture and is full of careful analysis of the nature of individual suffering, the impact of torture on the

larger community to which torture survivors belong, and the transgenerational trauma inflicted on the relatives, children, and grand-
children of survivors, on those who die under torture, and on the
community as a whole. It is the antitorture literature that studies
the medical and psychological costs to torturers of their participation in torture and the similar impacts on their families, friends,
and communities. The antitorture literature documents the historical
development of torture practices and their impacts on military, scientific, and other governmental institutions. Clearly, the antitorture
opponents are the ones who really care about consequences.

Protorture theorists must abandon their use of philosophical and
legal abstraction and work with the messy empirical details. Their
lack of concern for the conceptual and empirical harms is a signal
failure. The arguments for torture work only because they ignore
all of this important work. It is only because of an ignorance of the
viciousness of torture practices that torture advocates can even conceive of such a myth as "interrogational" torture and generate a
set of unsound arguments to support it.

I do not claim that the list of harms I have described is complete.
A great deal of work remains to be done just in understanding how
terribly violent torture is. In particular, a feminist analysis of the
patriarchal structures underlying torture would be valuable. But the
additional harms will just increase the list and generate additional
reasons to oppose torture.

ABSTRACTION AND THE TICKING BOMB

We have also seen that the ticking-bomb hypothesis is a hopeless
conceptual mess. It is the paradigm example of abstract and bad
reasoning. The point is not that terror attacks do not happen or
that bombs of greater or lesser severity explode. Of course, political
violence occurs. The problem is that the ticking-bomb hypothesis
has nothing to do with such violence. It tells us nothing about violence and how to respond to it because it excludes all consideration
of historical context, and it is unsound because it excludes the entire
range of harms and the required institutional transformations that
torturing requires.

Furthermore, the ticking-bomb hypothesis offers an illusion of
coherence only because it discourages us from closely attending to

its key component elements. Once we examine each of these elements closely, we see that they just do not fit together. No possible real situation can fit the ticking-bomb hypothesis. Consequently, we cannot validly reason from it. The ticking-bomb hypothesis entails the justifiability of torture only insofar as it is completely divorced from reality. It supports torture only because it neglects even to consider the nature of torture. If it did, it would not be so blithe in its treatment of the consequences.

The caricature presented by the ticking-bomb hypothesis is even worse when we consider that its imagined interrogators and victims have neither histories nor prejudices. The interrogators are not subject to the problems of idiocy or inadequate resources that confront and mark real public officials. There is neither corruption nor incompetence, and there is no sense of the institutional nature of torture. Indeed, this last point is as fundamental as any, for the violence of torture transcends any single instance of its use, as chapters 3 and 4 demonstrate.

An argument about a state practice that excludes every significant empirical consequence and pays no attention to the practice's conceptual components is not much of an argument at all. The ticking-bomb hypothesis is a piece of sophistry that should never be employed in a debate about such a grave subject as torture. It is an argument from fear but is not any more valid for being so.

WHY TORTURE IS AN ABSOLUTE VIOLATION

There is no facet of human identity that torture fails to assault. To appreciate just how extensive are the harms arising from assaults on dignity, we need an improved understanding of identity. Arguments that defend torture assume an isolated and atomic individual and suppose that only he or she suffers from the torture. But it is incoherent to speak of state violence assaulting only a single individual. Humans are social beings with deeply entrenched social networks, all of whose members are harmed when a single individual is attacked. To attack one is to assault many. Torturing one person inevitably harms broader social networks. Although torture harms the primary victim, its trauma is transgenerational, harming the victim's family into the second generation at least. While the primary torture victim suffers terribly, his or her family members experience their own physical and psychological suffering as well. This has economic consequences for the family unit, with spin-off impacts on relatives and friends as well, since in various ways their wellbeing is tied up with that of their social networks.

Furthermore, torture undermines the ability of communities to function by destroying trust and inducing fear. Torture is a "divide and conquer" strategy, regardless of the immediate purpose of any single act. In undermining trust and inducing fear, torture must damage social, political, and economic institutions within the target community. We have also seen that it has parallel effects on the torturer and similar social, political, and legal consequences for family and home community as well. Jennifer Harbury (2005, 155–60) is thus right to assert that these are inevitable consequences of state torture. They cannot be avoided because they are essential to torture as an exercise of state violence.

Given the wealth of empirical evidence, it is not clear where the violence of state torture does not reach. Of course, it does not inflict its reach by itself. It is a particularly violent form of institutionalized wrongdoing that is used by states to impose terror in order to dominate and control others and that functions in concert with other coercive institutions. Thus the institutional prerequisites for its employment are enormous. To torture at all, states must put in place a wide range of violent practices and institutions and must organize the behaviour of substantial numbers of individuals. As we have seen, this torture has to be planned, prepared, and researched long in advance of any possible threats and thus cannot be restricted only to a specific kind of threat.

META-ETHICAL CONVERGENCE AGAINST TORTURE

As I noted in the Introduction, the strategy of this book is to demonstrate meta-ethical convergence. That is, regardless of whether one feels allied to the deontological, utilitarian, or virtue-ethical traditions, the arguments in all cases support an absolute prohibition against torture. We have already seen that everyone concedes the deontological case: torture is an evil and thus should not be done. But both utilitarian and virtue-ethical traditions are also perfectly capable of supporting exceptionless prohibitions as well.

UTILITARIANS MUST REJECT TORTURE ABSOLUTELY

For utilitarians, careful consideration of the consequences that inevitably follow from state torture, along with cautious reflection on the institutional preconditions for torture, show that torture cannot be carried out as the exceptional case and can be done only as a routine. It is, of course, possible for untrained interrogators to try their hands, but they will then be unsanctioned and maximally ineffective. The problem is that torture is a complicated skill, and like any skill it requires practice. People have to get good at it. They might have a natural disposition toward it, but like any disposition, whether in sport or anywhere else, the mere possession of the disposition is insufficient to be able to perform well. Individuals have to practise, and to do so repeatedly, in order to become skilled.

The preparations necessary to enhance torture skills impose additional harms on torturing societies that are well beyond those sketched in chapter 1. Although some defenders of torture mention the institutionalization problem, there is little sophisticated discussion of it. Seumas Miller (2005, 183) addresses it partially and draws the conclusion that although exceptional acts of torture can be morally justified, it must never become institutional. But he neglects to demonstrate either the actuality or even the possibility of noninstitutional cases. The only examples he cites are not historical instances (Miller 2005, 182). Rather, one is a straightforward ticking-bomb hypothesis and the other is a policing example that he believes to be "realistic" – a constructed example involving the torture of a Pacific Islander car thief to save the life of a three-year-old child.

In the protorture literature, there is no analysis of the extent to which institutionalization might be inevitable. It is this institutionalization problem that makes incoherent the idea that torture can be practised only in the exceptional situation. This is not just an abstract logical claim but is well supported by the history of state torture, for a hypothetical imperative operates in state torture. Assuming that the state desires to be as effective as possible in torturing, it must institutionalize it. It must turn torture into a routine and create all of the institutions, research, and logistical preconditions that give it any chance at all of achieving its torturing goals. Since the torture institutions have to develop routines and since these have to be practised independent of any specific threat, the possible purposes for which torture may be used are independent of any given threat. This means that there is at best a contingent relation between institutionalized torture and terror threats.

However, there is an inevitable relation between state torture and the deliberate infliction of widespread suffering and violence. This suffering and violence is threat-independent and is not justifiable according to any existing argument for torture. The institutional nature of state torture is logically incompatible with the model according to which any torture defender believes torture can be justified. For states to torture, they must normalize it. That is, torturing states must (and do) torture routinely. Defenders of torture do not appreciate the complexity of torture and fail to understand that it requires considerable preparation and training, all of which is independent of any threat. Defenders support the use of torture only in the exceptional situation, but state torture can never be exceptional. States face a choice whether or not to torture. If they choose to do so, they must make it routine.

Since no utilitarian defends the normalization of torture and since state torture can be only routine, they must absolutely oppose it. When we consider the inevitable and probable harms that torture inflicts and contrast these with the merely possible benefits, and when we consider as well the logical incoherence of making routinization compatible with exceptional situations, we realize that utilitarians must also absolutely oppose torture.

VIRTUE ETHICISTS MUST OPPOSE TORTURE

As chapter 4 shows, those virtue ethicists who support torture are also consequentialists. They defend torture on the grounds that, in exceptional situations, it can be the lesser evil among the available alternatives. Thus the utilitarian considerations that speak against torture also must be considered by virtue ethicists. Given that virtue ethicists are concerned with communal and national character, the impact on community life of the institutionalization and routinization of state torture is an important additional reason to reject state torture.

But there are additional problems. The dirty-hands problem, when used to defend torture, is parochial. It prioritizes the obligations of

public officials to their states. The moral public official is no cosmopolitan and owes no obligations to humanity as a whole; the moral
calculus is restricted almost entirely to a specific state or community.
Such public officials are not constrained by a cosmopolitan greatest-
happiness principle because the principle demands that equal consideration be given to all relevantly affected sentient beings and
denies that special consideration can be given to members of one
group simply because of their community membership. The only
people who really count morally are those whom the public officials represent. Thus the officials are obligated to maximize their
superiors' wellbeing but have no obligation to equally consider the
wellbeing of others – or even to consider such wellbeing at all.
Consequently, their conduct is compatible with quite enormous
infliction of suffering on the members of the target community.

Individual Virtue Cannot Constrain Torture

To prevent an explosion of evildoing, tragic-choice theorists believe
that character-based controls have to be in place. So they envision
the individual with dirty hands – the shame-faced torturer. The idea
is that dispositions like shame constrain deliberate evildoing and
help to minimize its occurrence. Otherwise, the constraint has to
be found in the just-war theoretical principles of proportionality
and military necessity or in some kind of informed public opinion.

But a careful consideration of the history, psychology, and consequences of torture shows that character cannot do the job that
tragic-choice theorists envision. It cannot constrain torture and for
clear reasons. First, torture must corrupt the torturer, as we saw in
chapters 3 and 4. The repetition of any action decreases our repugnance for it. In any routine use of torture, it is quite likely that
torturers might begin with the sense of repugnance but gradually
lose it over time. The more we deliberately do evil, the easier it is
for us to do it. But as we have seen, because torture is a complex
skill, it has to be practised. Otherwise, torturers will not become
good at it. But to practise torture is just to make it routine. Furthermore, it is a routinization requiring that we overcome our inhibitions and thus lose precisely the shame that is supposed to ensure
torture remains exceptional.

In any case, the emphasis on good character is a red-herring. There
is no reason to expect that virtuous individuals will be running

interrogation units and many reasons to believe that they will not. As Leonard Wantchekon and Andrew Healy's (1999) argument suggests, states will not seek out virtuous individuals. They will select for obedient lackeys, zealots who do what they are told. The virtuous individual will be extremely hesitant to torture and prepared to disobey orders where he or she believes it necessary. Second, virtuous individuals are not going to volunteer for torture interrogation units because of the dirty nature of the activities and because of the threats to character that torture must inevitably represent. This means that states are neither going to find nor want virtuous torturers.

But in any case, virtue is irrelevant to the debate because the state-of-exception reasoning that motivates torture prioritizes state security over character. If the calculations require torture, it will happen regardless of the character of the interrogation team. Consequently, virtue is a fifth wheel in the argument. From the point of view of a torturing state, virtue is likely to hinder torture rather than to enable it. Hence states will avoid virtuous torturers. So virtue is neither necessary nor sufficient to justify torture. Consequentialism rules, and the safety of the state trumps considerations of character.

Tragic-choice theorists, in focusing on the choices of individuals, also fail to see that torture is violence-intensifying. They miss this because they consider the behaviour of the official only in relation to his or her alternative choices in an imagined exceptional situation, not in relation to the game he or she plays with competing state and nonstate actors. The choice of violent methods by one individual compels others to use similar or still more violent methods in order to avoid suffering a competitive disadvantage. This means that choosing torture will launch some form of torture arms race – an indication that torture is hardly a lesser evil likely to minimize violence. Since virtue ethics require us to consider the complete context of policy and choice making, they prohibit us from considering the behaviour of public officials in isolation. We are obliged to consider their behaviour in relation to the probable and inevitable behaviour of allied and competitor state officials. When we do this, we realize that torture is not a lesser-evils strategy but an evil intensifier.

Just as no utilitarian defends the routine use of torture, so virtue ethicists must also oppose it. But since state torture can be only routine, virtue ethicists must absolutely oppose torture as well. State torture is character-destroying and vice-creating. It does not and cannot create good dispositions either in public officials or in the state institutions for which they work. Even on the assumption that tragic-choice situations occur, it does not follow that torture is justifiable. Quite the contrary, the routine nature of state torture is incompatible with the description of tragic-choice situations and incompatible with virtue.

PROPORTIONALITY AND MILITARY NECESSITY CANNOT LIMIT TORTURE

A state will intensify the means it employs according to the intensity of the emergency that it believes it confronts. As we have also seen, tragic-choice reasoning lacks a principled limit to its violence. Indeed, it compels state agents into violence spirals as the emergency gets worse. If there is a constraint, it is the vacuous admonition that any action chosen must be less evil than the available alternatives. But all actions are less evil than available alternatives, and all massacres and other atrocities can plausibly be described as lesser evils in comparison to the alternatives that the actors who inflicted them believed were available. These are deeply fallible and prejudiced judgments, not objective facts in the world.

Proportionality is not a moral principle, although it is prudential. It can be a moral principle only if it is tied to certain absolute prohibitions. If certain classes of actions are not absolutely forbidden, proportionality can and will justify all of them. The fact of the extremity of the violence and suffering inflicted will not count as a reason against an action. Only success at achieving the specific goal and the choice of means that are maximally likely to be successful under the circumstances will count. Every military commander will try to choose means that are appropriate to military goals, and all cases of state torture have been adopted for precisely this reason. It is difficult to avoid the conclusion that proportionality and necessity justify all state torture, at least if the justification is to be found in the situational judgments of military and intelligence officials who inflict the tortures.

Military necessity is burdened with the same problems. There will always be a specific military goal and a range of options for attaining it. Military officials never deliberately choose the least efficient option for attaining their ends. They choose the one that they believe to be the best for the given purposes. But every action is a potentially most effective means for some goal, including deliberate massacre. If the goal is the control of an unruly population, terror might be more effective than any other alternative. Historical military and intelligence officials have drawn and continue to draw these conclusions.

Proportionality and military necessity, in combination with lesser-evils reasoning and the rejection of absolute prohibitions, provide an argument for deliberate massacre. That Michael Walzer (1977) expressly justifies the use of terror bombing and that others have expressly justified atomic bombs and other horrific acts shows how plastic and dangerous this kind of reasoning is. Consequently, all violence and massacres can be justified by lesser-evils reasoning when such reasoning is not modified by certain absolute constraints like the prohibition against torture.

PUBLIC OPINION CANNOT CONSTRAIN TORTURE

Postconflict communal judgments are supposed to limit torture. The population is supposed to be given the opportunity, following a conflict, to judge the behaviour of its public officials. The hope, among torture defenders, is that postconflict opinion will suffice to ground proportionality and necessity judgments and to ensure that the behaviour of public officials was reasonable and justifiable under the circumstances. In the event that the community rejects the explanation for torture, officials are censured.

But this does not work either. First, as we have seen, the target population is always going to be some "undesirable" group. It will be an internal or external enemy. In the context of prosecuting the struggle, enormous propaganda resources must be devoted to ensuring that the home population supports the conflict. This requires racist, sexist, and other kinds of propaganda. But development of this support creates a disposition to violently judge enemy individuals and to believe them worthy of their suffering. It demands that the public come to believe that the target population is deserving of its fate. A public that has been conditioned to believe in and to accept the justice of its violence is not going to critically evaluate that violence.

Second, in the contexts in which torture is used, the home population either believes itself threatened or has only just emerged from a perceived emergency. In either case, it is traumatized. In situations like this, populations tend to close ranks and justify extreme measures. Given that many members of the public must be complicit in the violence (since state torture is so institutional), the prospects of that population critically confronting its culpability in extreme violence is low. Such a population is far more likely to deny, explain away, or excuse the violence inflicted on its behalf. It is not going to assess dispassionately the behaviour of public officials who torture in its name. This may be one of the reasons why torturers are so rarely prosecuted.

Third, torture is conducted under conditions of fear and secrecy. It is difficult for a public to gather the relevant facts about official behaviour in a crisis, for these are typically closely guarded secrets. If they emerge at all, it may be only fifty years or more after the crisis. By that time, no meaningful community judgment is possible. There is no reason to believe that such a late judgment will have any impact on agents who may currently torture since it shows that they will not bear any of the costs of their actions at all. Nor will a late judgment deter future torturers since they, too, when confronted by similar dilemmas, will likewise recognize that they are not going to bear the costs of their actions.

Finally, routine state torture compels torturing states to choose between either keeping torture secret or accustoming their community to torture. The former is incompatible with postconflict community judgment since anything other than complete repudiation will result in its continuation. The latter legitimizes torture and conditions the public to believe in the correctness of official action. Thus it will not hold officials accountable for their wrongdoing. Either way, there is no good reason to think that public opinion will work to limit torture and every conceptual and empirical reason to believe that it will not.

TORTURE IS INEXCUSABLE AND UNJUSTIFIABLE

It makes no sense to speak of an excuse for state torture. Actions are supposed to be excusable when, in an appropriate set of circumstances, no other actions are possible. The agent does something wrong but has no alternative other than to inflict the wrong. Because he or she could not have done otherwise, the actions are excused. The routine and institutional nature of state torture is logically incompatible with excusing torture, for routines are independent of any exceptional circumstances. There are always alternatives, yet torture training and research continue. The violence of state torture vastly exceeds any given instance in which torture is used. Excusing torture would be like excusing premeditated murder, which is hardly a case in which an individual lacks alternatives.

The same point applies to justifications. Defenders of torture are willing to permit its use only as an exceptional act. But states cannot effectively torture if they use torture only in exceptional cases. They can use torture only as a rule. A justification of state torture is an argument for the routinely justified use of torture, and this is incompatible even with the claim that torture is prima facie wrong.

WHY TORTURE MUST BE FORBIDDEN

Torture defenders fail to appreciate that they inadvertently defend an entire structure of routine systemic violence. This violence is necessarily threat-independent and cannot be constrained only to the ticking-bomb cases. It is bad enough that the ticking-bomb case is a fantasy, but the weaknesses are exacerbated by the failure to appreciate the core distinction between individual actions and institutional behaviour. Consequently, defenders of torture do not realize that their moral calculations are irrelevant to institutional behaviours and genuinely possible tortures.

Individuals can make choices, but states create dispositions, policies, and laws. In the context of torture, it might be possible for an untrained and inefficient torturer to act only once. But then he or she is highly unlikely to succeed. States can torture only when they create routine systems of violence. Such systemic violence has nothing to do with the fantasy of the heroic individual choosing, under exceptional circumstances, to torture one individual in order to prevent the deaths of many.

We should also recognize that the routine nature of state torture poses an additional problem for defenders of torture. They claim that although torture is a prima facie wrong, it is a wrong that public officials are sometimes obligated to commit in exceptional circumstances. But the routine nature of torture is inconsistent with its exceptional use. If defenders of torture wish to assert the prima facie wrongness of torture, they have to confront the problem of institutionalization. Institutionalized torture is incompatible with the prima facie wrongness of torture. If routine state torture is justified, state torture is in fact prima facie right. Since states can employ torture only as a rule, a justification of state torture is simultaneously a repudiation not merely of the absolute wrongness of torture but also of its prima facie wrongness.

If state torture is to be at all effective, it can never be exceptional. It can be only routine. An argument for effective state torture is an argument for routines and policies that operate independently of exceptional circumstances. These routines and policies mean that torture is in fact justifiable in normal situations, not just in exceptional cases. If a state wishes to be able to use torture, it will have to do so with all of the institutional preconditions and violence. Otherwise, the torture is maximally unlikely to be effective.

The convergence of moral views against torture is remarkable and distinguishes it from many other acts, like lying, which may turn out to be either moral or immoral depending on which position one adopts. Mainly, this is because state torture is necessarily institutional, whereas lying and other individual acts need not be. Whatever the reasons for this may be, moral convergence is a mark of the wrongness of torture. This may be one of the reasons why it was possible to get agreement on the nonderogability clause of the United Nations Convention against Torture.

Catastrophes are possible and occasionally happen. But this does not justify us in taking every possible means to try to avoid them. Doing so inevitably turns into a different catastrophe. We should also be wary of claims that torture is necessary because nobody has ever demonstrated the moral necessity of torture in any single case. Nobody in the debate even seems to try and for good reasons. The emergence of torture is a sign of individual and communal character decline as well as an indication of a loss of power and control. In the only contexts in which torture defenders conceive it to be justifiable, torture is likely to be a sign of prior state failure and incompetence rather than a sign of success.

If theorists wish to continue to defend torture, they have to do two things: first, they have to acknowledge its institutional character and construct a calculus that begins by acknowledging the necessarily far-ranging use of violence in developing and perfecting torture techniques; second, they have to play with the inevitable and highly probably real historical consequences and abandon the caricatures that currently feature in arguments for torture. Moral arguments are not going to support torture under these conditions, as chapters 3, 4, and 5 show.

So if torture is an indication of individual and cultural failure, why does it happen? Am I claiming that state agents who create torture policies and institutions, along with the torturers themselves, are irrational? I think there is a sense in which they are rational and another in which they are not. There is no question that public officials, including torture interrogators, are more or less instrumentally rational. Some believe that torture is valuable in the pursuit of various goals and choose it because they believe it to be more effective than any of their alternatives. The repetition and proliferation of torture across historical time periods also supports the idea that torture is perceived to be useful. Perception of value alone is sufficient to account for its continuation over time. There is no reason to believe that practices continue only because they are rational. They need only be believed to be so in order for them to flourish. But the oldest lesson Plato has to teach us is that we can wrongly believe something to be good and useful.

However, even if torture is instrumentally valuable, this does not mean that it has any moral justification and does not entail that torture even can serve any moral purposes. Some officials may believe that they torture for moral reasons, but they are deceived. Given that they are inflicting such savage harm, along with degrading themselves and the state that they represent, they inflict an evil in the name of a falsely perceived good.

Here, we have to be wary of the concept of effectiveness, for effectiveness always depends on a prior presumed good. We always have to ask ourselves the question "effective for what?" If the goals for which some tactic is used are themselves evil, it is no great virtue to demonstrate that the tactic is effective. A competent architect or engineer can develop a brilliant design for a death camp, but the design's effectiveness is no virtue. In the service of evil goals, effective means are particularly devastating. They make communities and the world that much worse than they would otherwise have been.

So consider some of these possible goals. Torture is used to spread terror and win wars, and it seems to have some effectiveness in achieving the former. It is unclear whether it helps to achieve victory, especially given the resultant violence and hatred that it awakens in the target population. There is historical evidence to suggest that torture is at least temporarily tactically effective in breaking a population and dividing it against itself. Thus it renders those populations vulnerable to domination and control by some other group. Torture may also be effective temporarily in allowing some specific group to preserve its own power and privilege at the expense of other groups. It may also prove effective as a technique in building troop unity and morale and, thereby, in encouraging soldiers to fight some enemy more violently. It might be effective in bringing about religious or ideological conversions. It also appears to be quite effective in extracting "confessions."

The one place where torture is maximally ineffective is in the acquisition of truth. At the least, its intelligence value is highly disputed within military and intelligence circles. Renowned former US marine interrogator Sherwood Moran (2007, 251) emphasizes that successful interrogation requires qualities like warmth, sympathy, a sense of culture, a sense of dignity, friendliness toward the captive, and frankness. Torturers cannot exhibit any of these traits. If Moran is right, torture is counter to successful interrogation practice.

Darius Rejali (2007b, 446–79) provides additional reasons why torture is ineffective for intelligence gathering. For example, torture of the ignorant commits valuable resources to tracking down false information (461), torturers have little chance of detecting deception (465), and torture damages both the ability to communicate and the ability to remember (466–7). In consequence, intelligence gleaned through torture is inevitably corrupted.

Moreover, we have no randomized clinical trials or other scientifically respectable evidence indicating that it achieves what its advocates claim. Although the supposed point of torture is to prevent an imminent terrorist threat, we have no reason to believe it can do so. Even if torture in fact succeeds in one case, it inevitably generates future threats rather than helping to eliminate the unjust and oppressive conditions under which attacks and violence happen in the first place. At the least, we have to acknowledge with William Schulz (2007, 261) that torture is a very good means to spread and perpetuate violence. Whatever torture does, it never diminishes violence.

But although these are the purposes for which torture is actually used, nobody is willing to defend them. Indeed, every defender is careful to try to distinguish between mythical "interrogational" torture, which they are prepared to defend, and terroristic and oppressive kinds of torture. Nobody argues for terroristic torture because it is an evil end. It would be self-contradictory to argue morally that we should deliberately spread evil. Furthermore, nobody argues for torture as a means of exploitation and domination. But this is the only end that torture can and must necessarily serve. Given that torture is always terroristic in intention and impact, and given that it is always inflicted against the consent of the torture victim and his or her entire network of social relations, this cannot be otherwise.

Torture may serve a variety of political purposes, and I suppose it is possible that with respect to some of these purposes, it does so effectively. But even here nobody really knows. Whether or not torture effectively supports evil ends, it certainly cannot serve any moral goals. It is necessarily an element of domination, oppression, and exploitation and has no connections to any meaningful moral theory. The scale of suffering inflicted through state torture is immense and reaches into the second generation of the families and relatives of torture victims and survivors. Torture is yet more problematic when we consider the character destruction, institutional decay, and threats to legal structure that must accompany state torture. To think that there is a sound moral justification for torture is a delusion that arises only because of a lack of attention to the demonstrable historical, medical, psychological, and social impacts of torture. Torture is an absolute violation precisely because the scale of the violence that it inflicts goes well beyond the simple violations of physical integrity that torture defenders suppose. It is not clear what parts of a society state torture fails to touch and damage. Consequently, the absolute prohibition against torture, including the nonderogability clause of the United Nations Convention against Torture, is morally sound. Hence torture must be absolutely forbidden, no matter what.

References

Alleg, Henri. 1958. *The Question*. London: Calder Books.

Allhoff, Fritz. 2005a. "A Defence of Torture: Separation of Cases, Ticking Time-Bombs, and Moral Justification." *International Journal of Applied Philosophy* 19, no. 2: 243–64.

– 2005b. "Terrorism and Torture." In T. Shanahan, ed., *Philosophy 9/11: Thinking about the War on Terrorism*, 243–60. Peru, IL: Open Court.

Amery, Jean. 1995. "Torture." In L.L. Langer, ed., *Art from the Ashes: A Holocaust Anthology*, 121–37. New York: Oxford University Press.

Amnesty International. 2000. *Torture Worldwide: An Affront to Human Dignity*. New York: Amnesty International.

Arendt, Hannah. 1977. *Eichmann in Jerusalem: A Report on the Banality of Evil*. New York: Penguin Books.

Aristotle. 1984. "Nicomachean Ethics." In J. Barnes, ed., *The Complete Works of Aristotle*, vol. 2, 1729–1868. Princeton, NJ: Princeton University Press.

Arrigo, Jean-Maria. 2004. "A Utilitarian Argument against Torture, Interrogation, and Terrorists." *Science and Engineering Ethics* 10, no. 3 (July): 543–72.

Asad, Talat. 1997. "On Torture, or Cruel, Inhuman, and Degrading Treatment." In A. Kleinman, Veena Das, and Margaret Lock, eds, *Social Suffering*, 285–308. Berkeley: University of California Press.

Bagaric, Mirko, and Julie Clarke. 2005. "Not Enough Official Torture in the World? The Circumstances in Which Torture is Morally Justifiable." *University of San Francisco Law Review* 39 (Spring): 581–616.

Baker, Ron. 1992. "Psychosocial Consequences for Tortured Refugees Seeking Asylum and Refugee Status in Europe." In M. Basoglu, ed.,

Torture and Its Consequences: Current Treatment Approaches, 83–106. Cambridge, UK: Cambridge University Press.

Bassiouni, M. Sharif. 2005. "Great Nations and Torture." In K.J. Greenberg, ed., *The Torture Debate in America*, 256–60. Cambridge, UK: Cambridge University Press.

Bauer, Peter, et al. 2006. *Statement on Interrogation Practices.* http://www. amnestyusa.org/denounce_torture/statement_on_interrogation.pdf.

Bedau, Hugo Adam. 1997. *Making Mortal Choices: Three Exercises in Moral Casuistry.* New York and London: Oxford University Press.

Bentham, Jeremy. 1973. "Of Torture." In W.L. Twining and P.E. Twining, "Bentham on Torture," *Northern Ireland Legal Quarterly* 24 (Autumn): 305–56.

British Medical Association (BMA). 1992. *Medicine Betrayed: The Participation of Doctors in Human Rights Abuses.* London: Zed Books.

Booth, Cherie. 2006. "Sexual Violence, Torture, and International Justice." In K. Roth, Minky Worden, and Amy Bernstein, eds, *Torture: Does It Make Us Safer? Is It Ever Ok? A Human Rights Perspective*, 117–30. New York and London: New Press.

Borum, Randy. 2006. "Approaching Truth: Behavioral Science Lessons on Educing Information from Human Sources." In R.A. Fein, ed., *Intelligence Science Board Study Phase 1 Report: Educing Information*, 17–44. Washington, DC: NDIC Press.

Brecher, Bob. 2007. *Torture and the Ticking Bomb.* Oxford: Blackwell.

Brison, Susan. 2002. *Aftermath: Violence and the Remaking of the Self.* Princeton, NJ: Princeton University Press.

Browning, Christopher R. 1998. *Ordinary Men: Reserve Police Battalion 101 and the Final Solution in Poland.* New York: HarperCollins.

Bunster, Ximena. 1993. "Surviving beyond Fear: Women and Torture in Latin America." In M. Agosin, ed., *Surviving beyond Fear: Women, Children and Human Rights in Latin American*, 98–125. New York: White Pine.

Bustos, Enrique. 1990. "Dealing with the Unbearable: Reactions of Therapists and Therapeutic Institutions to Survivors of Torture." In P. Suedfield, ed., *Psychology and Torture*, 143–64. New York: Hemisphere.

– 1992. "Psychodynamic Approaches to the Treatment of Torture Survivors." In M. Basoglu, ed., *Torture and Its Consequences: Current Treatment Approaches*, 333–47. Cambridge, UK: Cambridge University Press.

Camus, Albert. 1991. "On Purity and Realism." In A. de Gramont, ed., *Between Hell and Realism: Essays from the Resistance Newspaper Combat, 1944–1947*, 76–7. Hanover and London: Wesleyan University Press.

Card, Claudia. 2002. *The Atrocity Paradigm: A Theory of Evil*. Oxford: Oxford University Press.

Carlson, Eric Stener. 2006a. "The Hidden Prevalence of Male Sexual Assault during War." *British Journal of Criminology* 46, no. 1: 16–25.

– 2006b. *The Pear Tree: Is Torture Ever Justified?* Atlanta, GA: Clarity.

Casebeer, William. 2005. "Torture Interrogation of Terrorists: A Theory of Exceptions (with Notes, Cautions, and Warnings)." In T. Shanahan, ed., *Philosophy 9/11: Thinking about the War on Terrorism*, 261–72. Peru, IL: Open Court.

Cavanagh, William T. 1999. *Torture and Eucharist: Theology, Politics and the Body of Christ*. Oxford: Blackwell.

Chester, Barbara. 1990. "Because Mercy has a Human Heart: Centers for Victims of Torture." In P. Suedfield, ed., *Psychology and Torture*, 165–84. New York: Hemisphere.

Cobain, Ian. 2005. "The Secrets of the London Cage." *The Guardian Unlimited*, 12 November.

Conroy, John. 2000. *Unspeakable Acts, Ordinary People: The Dynamics of Torture*. New York: Alfred A. Knopf.

Coulam, Robert. 2006. "Approaches to Interrogation in the Struggle against Terrorism: Considerations of Cost and Benefit." In R.A. Fein, ed., *Intelligence Science Board Study Phase 1 Report: Educing Information*, 7–16. Washington, DC: NDIC Press.

Davis, Michael. 2005. "The Moral Justifiability of Torture and Other Cruel, Inhuman, or Degrading Treatment." *International Journal of Applied Philosophy* 19, no. 2: 161–78.

De Wijze, Stephen. 1994. "Dirty Hands – Doing Wrong to Do Right." *South African Journal of Philosophy* 13, no. 1 (February): 27–33.

– 2003. "Democracy, Trust, and the Problem of Dirty Hands." *Philosophy in the Contemporary World* 10, no. 1 (Spring/Summer): 37–42.

Denford, John. 1996. "The treatment of Torture Survivors." In D. Forrest, ed., *Amnesty International, a Glimpse of Hell: Reports on Torture Worldwide*, 153–66. New York: New York University Press.

Dershowitz, Alan. 1989. "Is it Necessary to Apply Physical Pressure to Terrorists – and to Lie about It?" *Israel Law Review* 23, nos 2–3: 192–200.

– 2002. *Why Terrorism Works: Understanding the Threat, Responding to the Challenge*. New Haven: Yale University Press.

– 2004. "Tortured Reasoning." In S. Levinson, ed., *Torture: A Collection*, 257–80. Oxford: Oxford University Press.

Dowdall, T.L. 1991. "Repression, Health Care, and Ethics under Apartheid." *Journal of Medical Ethics* 17, supplement: 51–4.

— 1992. "Torture in South Africa." In M. Basoglu, ed., *Torture and Its Consequences: Current Treatment Approaches*, 452–71. Cambridge, UK: Cambridge University Press.

Dworkin, Gerald. 2006. "Taking Risks, Assessing Responsibility." In Wendy Parmet and Patricia Illingworth, eds, *Ethical Health Care*. Upper Saddle River, NJ: Pearson Prentice Hall.

Elshtain, Jean Bethke. 2004. "Reflection on the Problem of 'Dirty Hands.'" In S. Levinson, ed., *Torture: A Collection*, 77–92. Oxford: Oxford University Press.

Evans, M.D., and Rod Morgan. 2007. "Preventing Torture." In W. Schulz, ed., *The Phenomenon of Torture*, 38–48. Philadelphia: University of Philadelphia Press.

Fabri, Mary R. 2001. "Reconstructing Safety: Adjustments to the Therapeutic Frame in the Treatment of Survivors of Political Torture." *Professional Psychology, Research and Practice* 32, no. 5: 452–7.

Fanon, Frantz. 2004. "Colonial War and Mental Disorder." In N. Scheper-Hughes and Philippe Bourgois, eds, *Violence in War and Peace: An Anthology*, 443–52. Oxford: Blackwell.

Felner, Eitan. 2006. "Torture and Terrorism: Painful Lessons Learned from Israel." In K. Roth, Minky Worden, and Amy Bernstein, eds, *Torture: Does It Make Us Safer? Is It Ever Ok? A Human Rights Perspective*, 28–43. New York and London: New Press.

Forrest, D. 1996. "Introduction." In D. Forrest, ed., *Amnesty International, a Glimpse of Hell: Reports on Torture Worldwide*, viii–x. New York: New York University Press.

Frey, Barbara. 2002. "Documenting a Well-Founded Fear." In Vincent Iacopino and Michael Peel, eds, *The Medical Documentation of Torture*, 45–62. London: Greenwich Medical Media.

Gibson, Janice T. 1990. "Factors Contributing to the Creation of a Torturer." In P. Suedfield, ed., *Psychology and Torture*, 77–88. New York: Hemisphere.

Gilbert, Paul. 2005. "Proportionality in the Conduct of War." *Journal of Military Ethics* 4, no. 2: 100–7.

Gorman, William. 2001. "Refugee Survivors of Torture: Trauma and Treatment." *Professional Psychology, Research and Practice* 32, no. 5: 443–51.

Greenberg, Karen, and Joshua L. Dratel, eds. 2005. *The Torture Papers: The Road to Abu Ghraib*. Cambridge, UK: Cambridge University Press.

Grey, Stephen. 2006. *Ghost Plane: The True Story of the CIA Torture Program*. New York: St Martin's.

Gross, Michael. 2004. "Doctors in the Decent Society: Torture, Ill-Treatment and Civic Duty." *Bioethics* 18, no. 4: 181–203.

– 2006. *Bioethics and Armed Conflict*. Cambridge, MA: MIT Press.

Gross, Oren. 2004. "Are Torture Warrants Warranted? Pragmatic Absolutism and Official Disobedience." *Minnesota Law Review* 88 (June): 1481–555.

Gur-Arye, Miriam. 2004. "Can the War against Terror Justify the Use of Force in Interrogations? Reflections in Light of the Israeli Experience." In S. Levinson, ed., *Torture: A Collection*, 183–98. Oxford: Oxford University Press.

Harbury, Jennifer K. 2005. *Truth, Torture, and the American Way: The History and Consequences of U.S. Involvement in Torture*. Boston: Beacon.

Hardt, Michael, and Antonio Negri. 2004. *Multitude: War and Democracy in the Age of Empire*. New York: Penguin.

Hawthorne, Susan. 2005. "Ancient Hatred and Its Contemporary Manifestation: The Torture of Lesbians." *Journal of Hate Studies* 4: 233–58.

Hinshelwood, Gill. 1996. "Women, Children, and the Family." In D. Forrest, ed., *Amnesty International, a Glimpse of Hell: Reports on Torture Worldwide*, 187–96. New York: New York University Press.

Hintikka, Jaako. 1981. "Some Main Problems of Deontic Logic." In R. Hilpinen, ed., *Deontic Logic: Introductory and Systematic Readings*, 59–104. Dordrecht: D. Reidel.

Hobbes, Thomas. 1985. *Leviathan*. Ed. C.B. McPhersen. London: Penguin.

Holmes, Robert L. 1989. *On War and Morality*. Princeton, NJ: Princeton University Press.

Holmes, Stephen. 2005. "Is Defiance of Law a Proof of Success? Magical Thinking in the War on Terror." In K.J. Greenberg, ed., *The Torture Debate in America*, 118–35. Cambridge, UK: Cambridge University Press.

Hooks, Gregory, and Clayton Mosher. 2005. "Outrages against Personal Dignity: Rationalizing Abuse and Torture in the War on Terror." *Social Forces* 83, no. 4: 1627–45.

Human Rights Watch. 1994. *Torture and Ill-Treatment: Israel's Interrogation of Palestinian's from the Occupied Territories*. New York: Human Rights Watch.

Hurley, Patrick. 2003. *A Concise Introduction to Logic*. 8th ed. Belmont, CA: Wadsworth and Thomson Learning.

Ignatieff, Michael. 2004. *The Lesser Evil: Political Ethics in an Age of Terror*. Toronto: Penguin.

– 2006. "Moral Prohibition at a Price." In K. Roth, Minky Worden, and Amy Bernstein, eds, *Torture: Does It Make Us Safer? Is It Ever Ok? A Human Rights Perspective*, 18–27. New York and London: New Press.

Jaffe, Helene. 1991. "A Response to Human Affliction and Suffering." *Journal of Medical Ethics* 17, supplement: 58–9.

Jempson, Mike. 1996. "Torture Worldwide." In D. Forrest, ed., *Amnesty International, a Glimpse of Hell: Reports on Torture Worldwide*, 46–86. New York: New York University Press.

Jones, Gary. 1980. "On the Permissibility of Torture." *Journal of Medical Ethics* 6 (March): 11–13.

Journal of Medical Ethics 17, supplement (1991).

Kadish, Sanford. 1989. "Torture, the State and the Individual." *Israel Law Review* 23, nos 2–3: 345–56.

Kagee, Ashraf. 2004. "Present Concerns of Survivors of Human Rights Violations in South Africa." *Social Science and Medicine* 59: 625–35.

Kant, Immanuel. 1998. *Groundwork of the Metaphysics of Morals*. Trans. M. Gregor. Ed. K. Ameriks and Desmond Clarke. Cambridge, UK: Cambridge University Press.

Kershner, Stephen. 1998. "An Argument for the Use of Torture as Public Policy." *Hamline Journal of Public Law and Policy* 19, no. 2 (Spring): 497–528.

– 2005. "For Interrogational Torture." *International Journal of Applied Philosophy* 19, no. 2: 223–41.

Kleinig, John. 2005. "Ticking Bombs and Torture Warrants." *Deakin Law Review* 10, no. 2: 613–27.

Kleinman, Steven. 2006. "KUBARK Counterintelligence Interrogation Review: Observations of an Interrogator: Lessons Learned and Avenues for Further Research." In R.A. Fein, ed., *Intelligence Science Board Phase 1 Report: Educing Information*, 95–140. Washington, DC: NDIC Press.

Kordon, Diana. 1991. "Impunity's Psychological Effects: Its Ethical Consequences." *Journal of Medical Ethics* 17, supplement: 29–32.

– et al. 1992. "Torture in Argentina." In M. Basoglu, ed., *Torture and Its Consequences: Current Treatment Approaches*, 433–51. Cambridge, UK: Cambridge University Press.

Krog, Antje. 2004. "The Wet Bag and Other Phantoms." In N. Scheper-Hughes and Philippe Bourgois, eds, *Violence in War and Peace: An Anthology*, 372–7. Oxford: Blackwell.

Landau Commission Report. 1989. *Israel Law Review* 23: 154–85.

Langbein, John. 2004. "The Legal History of Torture." In S. Levinson, ed., *Torture: A Collection*, 93–104. Oxford: Oxford University Press.

Leibniz, G.W.F. 1951. *Theodicy: Essays on the Goodness of God, the Freedom of Man, and the Origin of Evil.* Trans. E.M. Huggard. London: Routledge and Kegan Paul.

Lenta, Patrick. 2006. "The Purposes of Torture." *South African Journal of Philosophy* 25, no. 1: 49–61.

Levin, Michael. 1982. "The case for torture." *Newsweek*, 17 June, 13.

– 1990. "Torture and Other Extreme Measures Taken for the General Good: Further Reflections on a Philosophical Problem." In P. Suedfield, ed., *Psychology and Torture*, 89–100. New York: Hemisphere.

Lomax, Eric. 1995. *Railway Man.* London: Jonathon Cape.

Lorentzen, Lois-Ann. 1998. "Women's Prison Resistance: Testimonials from El Salvador." In Lois-Ann Lorentzen and Jennifer Turpin, eds, *The Women and War Reader*, 192–202. New York: New York University Press.

Luban, David. 2007. "Liberalism, Torture, and the Ticking Bomb." In S.P. Lee, ed., *Intervention, Terrorism, and Torture: Contemporary Challenges to Just War Theory*, 249–63. Dordrecht: Springer.

Lukes, Stephen. 2005. "Liberal Democratic Torture." *British Journal of Political Science* 36: 1–16.

Lunde, Inge, and Jorgen Ortmann. 1992. "Sexual Torture and the Treatment of Its Consequences." In M. Basoglu, ed., *Torture and Its Consequences: Current Treatment Approaches*, 310–31. Cambridge, UK: Cambridge University Press.

MacKinnon, Catherine A. 1993. "On Torture: A Feminist Perspective on Human Rights." In Kathleen E. Mahoney and Paul Mahoney, eds, *Human Rights in the Twenty-First Century: A Global Challenge*, 221–40. Dordrecht: Martinus Nijhoff.

Malinowski, Tom. 2006. "Banned State Department Practices." In K. Roth, Minky Worden, and Amy Bernstein, eds, *Torture: Does It Make Us Safer? Is It Ever Ok? A Human Rights Perspective*, 139–44. New York and London: New Press.

Marchak, Patricia. 1999. *God's Assassins: State Terrorism in Argentina in the 1970s.* Montreal and Kingston: McGill-Queen's University Press.

Marks, Susan. 2004. "Apologizing for Torture." *Nordic Journal of International Law* 73, no. 3 (August): 365–85.

Matthews, Irene. 1998. "Torture as Text." In Lois-Ann Lorentzen and Jennifer Turpin, eds, *The Women and War Reader*, 184–91. New York: New York University Press.

McCarthy, Andrew C. 2005. "Torture: Thinking about the Unthinkable." In K.J. Greenberg, *The Torture Debate in America*, 98–110. Cambridge, UK: Cambridge University Press.

McCoy, Alfred. 2006a. "The Myth of the Ticking Bomb." *The Progressive*, www.progressive.org/mag_mccoy1006.

– 2006b. *A Question of Torture: CIA Interrogation, from the Cold War to the War on Terror.* New York: Metropolitan Books.

Mendez, Juan E. 2006. "Torture in Latin America." In K. Roth, Minky Worden, and Amy Bernstein, eds, *Torture: Does It Make Us Safer? Is It Ever Ok? A Human Rights Perspective*, 55–68. New York and London: New Press.

Miles, Steven. 2006. *Oath Betrayed: Torture, Medical Complicity, and the War on Terror.* New York: Random House.

Milgram, Stanley. 2004. "Behavioral Study of Obedience." In N. Scheper-Hughes and Philippe Bourgois, eds, *Violence in War and Peace: An Anthology*, 145–9. Oxford: Blackwell.

Miller, Seumas. 2005. "Is Torture Ever Morally Justifiable?" *International Journal of Applied Philosophy* 19, no. 2: 179–92.

Millett, Kate. 2007. "The Politics of Cruelty." In W. Schulz, ed., *The Phenomenon of Torture*, 163–6. Philadelphia: University of Pennsylvania Press.

Moher, Andrew. 2004. "The Lesser of Two Evils? An Argument for Judicially Sanctioned Torture." *Thomas Jefferson Law Review* 26 (Spring): 469–89.

Mook, Douglas. 2004. *Classic Experiments in Psychology.* Westport, CT: Greenwood.

Moran, Sherwood F. 2007. "Suggestions for Japanese Interpreters." In W. Schulz, ed., *The Phenomenon of Torture*, 249–55. Philadelphia: University of Pennsylvania Press.

Nagel, Thomas. 1979. "War and Massacre." In *Mortal Questions*, 53–74. Cambridge, UK: Cambridge University Press.

Nielsen, Kai. 1996. "There Is No Problem of Dirty Hands." *South African Journal of Philosophy* 15, no. 1 (February): 1–7.

Orend, Brian. 2000. *Michael Walzer on War and Justice.* Montreal and Kingston: McGill-Queen's University Press.

Ortiz, Sister Dianna. 2002. *The Blindfold's Eyes: My Journey from Torture to Truth.* Maryknoll, NY: Orbis Books.

Osiel, Mark. 2001. *Mass Atrocity, Ordinary Evil, and Hannah Arendt: Criminal Consciousness in Argentina's Dirty War.* New Haven: Yale University Press.

Oxford Dictionary of Philosophy. 1989. Ed. Simon Blackburn. Oxford: Oxford Paperback Reference.

Oxford English Dictionary. 1989. Ed. J.A. Simpson and E.S.C Weiner. Oxford: Clarendon.

Pakar, Murat, Ozgun Paker, and Sahika Yuksel. 1992. "Psychological Effects of Torture: An Empirical Study of Tortured and Non-Tortured Non-Political Prisoners." In M. Basoglu, ed., *Torture and Its Consequences: Current Treatment Approaches*, 72–82. Cambridge, UK: Cambridge University Press.

Parry, John T. 2004. "Escalation and Necessity: Defining Torture at Home and Abroad." In S. Levinson, ed., *Torture: A Collection*, 145–64. Oxford: Oxford University Press.

– 2006. "Pain, Interrogation, and the Body: State Violence and the Law of Torture." In John T. Parry, ed., *Evil, Law and the State: Perspectives on State Power and Violence*, 1–16. Amsterdam: Rodopi.

Perry, John. 2005. *Torture, Religious Ethics and National Security.* Maryknoll, NY: Orbis Books.

Peters, Edward. 1985. *Torture.* Oxford: Basil Blackwell.

Plato. 1978. *Republic.* Ed. Edith Hamilton and Huntington Cairns. Princeton, NJ: Princeton University Press.

Pokempner, Dinah. 2006. "Command Responsibility for Torture." In K. Roth, Minky Worden, and Amy Bernstein, eds, *Torture: Does It Make Us Safer? Is It Ever Ok? A Human Rights Perspective*, 158–72. New York and London: New Press.

Posner, Richard. 2004. "Torture, Terrorism, and Interrogation." In S. Levinson, ed., *Torture: A Collection*, 291–98. Oxford: Oxford University Press.

Ratner, Michael, and Ellen Ray. 2004. *Guantanamo: What the World Should Know.* Vermont: Chelsea Green.

Rejali, Darius. 2007a. "Does Torture Work?" In W. Schulz, ed., *The Phenomenon of Torture*, 255–9. Philadelphia: University of Pennsylvania Press.

– 2007b. *Torture and Democracy.* Princeton, NJ: Princeton University Press.

Rieff, David. 2002. "The Bureaucrat of Torture." *World Policy Journal* 19, no. 1: 105–9.

Rivera-Fuentes, Consuela, and Lynda Birke. 2001. "Talking with/in Pain: Reflections on Bodies Under Torture." *Women's Studies International Forum* 24, no. 6: 653–68.

Robin, Marie-Monique. 2006. "Counterinsurgency and Torture: Exporting Torture Tactics from Indochina and Algeria to Latin America." In K. Roth,

Minky Worden, and Amy Bernstein, eds, *Torture: Does It Make Us Safer? Is It Ever Ok? A Human Rights Perspective*, 44–54. New York and London: New Press.

Rodley, Nigel, interviewed by Amy D. Bernstein. 2006. "On Negotiating with Torturers." In K. Roth, Minky Worden, and Amy Bernstein, eds, *Torture: Does It Make Us Safer? Is It Ever Ok? A Human Rights Perspective*, 106–16. New York and London: New Press.

Ross, W.D. 1930. *The Right and the Good*. Oxford: Clarendon.

Roth, K. 2006. "Justifying Torture." In K. Roth, Minky Worden, and Amy Bernstein, eds, *Torture: Does It Make Us Safer? Is It Ever Ok? A Human Rights Perspective*, 184–202. New York and London: New Press.

Salimovich, Sofia, Elizabeth Lira, and Eugenia Weinstein. 1992. "Victims of Fear: The Social Psychology of Repression." In J. Corradi, Patricia Weiss Fagan, and Manuel Antonio Garreton, eds, *Fear at the Edge: State Terror and Resistance in Latin America*, 72–89. Berkeley: University of California Press.

Saporta, Jose, Jr, and Bessel A. van der Kolk. 1992. "Psychobiological Consequences of Severe Trauma." In M. Basoglu, ed., *Torture and Its Consequences: Current Treatment Approaches*, 151–81. Cambridge, UK: Cambridge University Press.

Sartre, Jean-Paul. 1968. "On Genocide." In E. Kaim-Sartre, ed., *On Genocide and a Summary of the Evidence and the Judgments of the International War Crimes Tribunal*. Boston: Beacon.

– 1989. "Dirty Hands." In *No Exit and Three Other Plays*. New York: Vintager International Books.

– 2004. "Preface." In Frantz Fanon, *The Wretched of the Earth*. In N. Scheper-Hughes and Philippe Bourgois, eds, *Violence in War and Peace: An Anthology*, 229–35. Oxford: Blackwell.

Scarry, Elaine. 1985. *The Body in Pain: The Making and Unmaking of the World*. Oxford: Oxford University Press.

– 2004. "Five Errors in the Reasoning of Alan Dershowitz." In S. Levinson, ed., *Torture: A Collection*, 281–90. Oxford: Oxford University Press.

Schulz, W. 2007. "Tainted Legacy." In W. Schulz, ed., *The Phenomenon of Torture*, 260–66. Philadelphia: University of Pennsylvania Press.

Seelmann, Gunter. 1991. "The Position of the Chilean Medical Association with Respect to Torture as an Instrument of Political Repression." *Journal of Medical Ethics* 17, supplement: 33–4.

Sen, Amartya, and B. Williams, eds. 1982. *Utilitarianism and Beyond*. Cambridge, UK: Cambridge University Press.

Shue, Henry. 1978. "Torture." *Philosophy and Public Affairs* 7, no. 2 (Winter): 124–43.

Singer, Peter. 1993. *Practical Ethics*. 2nd ed. Cambridge, UK: Cambridge University Press.

Skylv, Grethe. 1992. "The Physical Sequelae of Torture." In M. Basoglu, ed., *Torture and Its Consequences: Current Treatment Approaches*, 38–55. Cambridge, UK: Cambridge University Press.

Smart, J., and B. Williams. 1973. *Utilitarianism: For and Against*. Cambridge, UK: Cambridge University Press.

Somnier, Finn, et al. 1992. "Psycho-Social Consequences of Torture: Current Knowledge and Evidence." In M. Basoglu, ed., *Torture and Its Consequences: Current Treatment Approaches*. Cambridge, UK: Cambridge University Press.

Staub, Ervin. 1989. *The Roots of Evil: The Origins of Genocide and Other Group Violence*, 56–68. Cambridge, UK: Cambridge University Press.

– 1990. "The Psychology and Culture of Torture and Torturers." In P. Suedfield, ed., *Psychology and Torture*, 49–76. New York: Hemisphere.

Stover, Eric, and Elena O. Nightingale, eds. 1985. *The Breaking of Bodies and Minds: Torture, Psychiatric Abuse, and the Health Professions*. New York: W.H. Freeman.

Suarez-Orozco, Marcelo. 2004. "The Treatment of Children in the 'Dirty War': Ideology, State Terrorism, and the Abuse of Children in Argentina." In N. Scheper-Hughes and Philippe Bourgois, eds, *Violence in War and Peace: An Anthology*, 378–88. Oxford: Blackwell.

Taussig, Michael. 2004a. "Culture of Terror – Space of Death: Roger Casement's Putumayo Report and the Explanation of Torture." In N. Scheper-Hughes and Philippe Bourgois, eds, *Violence in War and Peace: An Anthology*, 39–53. Oxford: Blackwell.

– 2004b. "Talking Terror." In N. Scheper-Hughes and Philippe Bourgois, eds, *Violence in War and Peace: An Anthology*, 171–4. Oxford: Blackwell.

Timerman, Hector. 2006. "Torture: A Family Affair." In K. Roth, Minky Worden, and Amy Bernstein, eds, *Torture: Does It Make Us Safer? Is It Ever Ok? A Human Rights Perspective*, 69–78. New York and London: New Press.

Timerman, Jacopo. 1981. *Prisoner without a Name, Cell without a Number*. New York: Alfred A. Knopf.

Tindale, Christopher. 1996. "The Logic of Torture: A Critical Examination." *Social Theory and Practice* 22, no. 3 (Fall): 349–75.

Twining, W.E. 1978. "Torture and Philosophy." *The Proceedings of the Aristotelian Society* 52, supplement: 169–94.

– and P.E. Twining. 1973. "Bentham on Torture." *Northern Ireland Legal Quarterly* 24 (Autumn): 305–56.

United States. *United States of America Military Commisions Act – Turning Bad Policy into Bad Law.* http://web.amnesty.org/library/index/ENGAMR511542006.

United States Army. *US Army Field Manual 34–52 Intelligence.* www.globalsecurity.org/intell/library/policy/army/fm/fm34–52/.

Vesti, Peter, and Marianne Kastrup. 1992. "Psychotherapy for Torture Survivors." In M. Basoglu, ed., *Torture and Its Consequences: Current Treatment Approaches*, 348–62. Cambridge, UK: Cambridge University Press.

Wahlquist, John A. 2006. "Educing Information: Interrogation – Science and Art." In R.A. Fein, ed., *Intelligence Science Board Study Phase 1 Report: Educing Information*, xv-xxvi. Washington, DC: NDIC Press.

Walzer, M. 1977. *Just and Unjust Wars.* New York: Basic Books.

– 2004a. "Emergency Ethics." In M. Walzer, ed., *Arguing about War*, 33–50. New Haven: Yale University Press.

– 2004b. "Political Action: The Problem of Dirty Hands." In S. Levinson, ed., *Torture: A Collection*, 61–76. Oxford: Oxford University Press.

Wantchekon, Leonard, and Andrew Healy. 1999. "The Game of Torture." *Journal of Conflict Resolution* 43, no. 5: 596–609.

Warren, Kay B. 2000. "Death Squads and Wider Complicities: Dilemmas for the Anthropology of Violence." In J.A. Sluka, ed., *Death Squad: The Anthropology of State Terror*, 226–47. Philadelphia: University of Pennsylvania Press.

Weber, Max. 2004. "Politics as a Vocation." In David Owen and Tracy B. Strong, eds, *The Vocation Lectures*, 32–94. Indianapolis and Cambridge: Hackett.

Williams, Bernard. 1981. "Politics and Moral Character." In B. Williams, ed., *Moral Luck: Philosophical Papers, 1973–80*, 54–70. Cambridge, UK: Cambridge University Press.

Winterbottom, Peter, and Matt Whitecross. 2006. *The Road To Guantanamo.* Documentary film. Channel Four Television, UK.

Index

absolutism, 12, 183–4
Algerian War, 3
Alleg, Henri, 119
Allhoff, Fritz, 5, 20, 32, 68, 137; and deontologists, 10; on restricting torture to emergencies, 137; on the permissibility of torture, 15–16, 96; on the utilitarian case for torture, 107–9; on the weak ticking-bomb case, 86
Amery, Jean, 48
Arendt, Hannah, 28
Aristotle, 141–3. *See also* virtue ethics
Arrigo, Jean-Maria, 105, 137
Asad, Talal, 182
Auld, Jim, 41

Bagaric, Mirko, and Julia Clarke, 52, 69
Baker, Ron, 58
Bassiouni, M. Cherif, 98
Bedau, Hugo Adam, 187
Bentham, Jeremy, 106–9
Benzien, Captain Jeffrey, 163
Booth, Cherie, 50

Brecher, Bob, 198
Brison, Susan, 37, 110
Browning, Christopher, 160
Bunster, Ximena, 49–50
Bush, George W., 4
Bustos, Enrique, 61

Card, Claudia, 132, 137
Carlson, Eric Stener, 38, 50, 67
Casebeer, William, 105
categorical imperative, 12
Cavanagh, William, 43
Chester, Barbara, 55
Conroy, John, 41, 119, 157
consequentialism, 7, 26, 163–5, 183, 205, 212; consequentialist calculations, 14, 17, 26, 34, 64–5, 67, 71, 78, 87–8, 101.
contagion problem, 120–1

Davis, Michael, 31, 44
demonizing function of language: and fanatic, 28; and terrorist, 10, 28, 93–4
deontology, 96, 140–1, 203–4
Dershowitz, Alan, 20, 32, 95–6, 137, 186; on Abdul Hakim

Murad, 8; on the contagion problem, 121; on inductive risk of institutionalization, 190; on the institutionalization problem, 190, 194; on interrogational torture, 190; on legalization, 186, 191, 194; on the ticking-bomb hypothesis, 68–9, 83, 193; on torture warrants, 4–5, 188–9

de Wijze, Stephen, 143–4, 146, 148, 150, 170

dignity, 12, 13, 23, 34, 38, 46–8, 69

dirty hands, the problem of, 7, 139–40, 143–6, 203; and accountability, 171–2, 175; and brutalization, 150–7, 180; and character, 147, 159–65, 178; conflicts of values, 146; and consequentialism, 7, 26–7; and constraints on evildoing, 149–50; and democracies, 171–2; and desensitization, 173; and destruction of character, 157; and destruction of shame, 151, 157; and evil dispositions, 154; and game of torture, 161–2, 169, 212; and guilt, 146; and habituation, 172; and institutionalization, 153–6, 172, 181, 214; and Kantian ethics, 144; and lesser-evils reasoning, 144, 214; and the limit problem, 23–4, 165–8; and the Milgram experiments, 157–61; and military necessity, 181–3, 211, 213–14; and moral risk, 184; and parochialism, 210; and political necessity, 165–6; and politicians and political character, 146–8; and practical wisdom, 178; and prejudice, 160; and propaganda, 173, 180, 214; and proportionality, 177–81, 211, 213; and psychological distance,158–9, 162; and public opinion, 171–6, 211, 214; and public predisposition to torture, 173; and repetition and routinization, 151–2, 211; and shame, 147–8, 150–1, 211; and situational uncertainty, 179; and triage decision making, 145; and utilitarianism, 144; and violence intensification, 168–71, 212; and zealous, professional, and sadistic character types, 152–5. See also tragic choices

doctrinal civil libertarianism, 12

Dowdall, T.L., 56–7, 59

Dworkin, Gerald, 187

Elshtain, Jean Bethke, 11, 39, 147, 168

exceptional circumstances, 36, 210. See also state of emergency

excuse, logical character of, 15–18

Fabri, Mary, 44

Fanon, Frantz, 118

Felner, Eitan, 76, 98, 166

first-person narratives, importance of, 37–8

fog of war, 22, 72, 77, 87, 189

Foreign Intelligence Surveillance Act (FISA) courts, 192, 198

Forrest, Duncan, 18
Front de Libération Nationale
   (FLN), 88, 115

Gibson, Janice, 161
Gilbert, Paul, 180
Gross, Michael, 5, 10, 20, 126,
   181; and proportionality and
   military necessity, 177–9
Gross, Oren, 15, 20, 27, 137,
   186, 197–8; and institutionalization problem, 200–1; and
   interrogational torture, 200;
   and the official disobedience
   model, 199–202; and rule
   utilitarianism and rule
   worship, 201
Gur-Arye, Miriam, 5, 186,
   188–90

Harbury, Jennifer, 67, 208
Hardt, Michael, and Antonio
   Negri, 63
Hawthorne, Susan, 44
Hinshelwood, Gill, 42
Hintikka, Jaako, 15
historical examples, role of,
   29–30
Hobbes, Thomas, 185
Holmes, Robert, 182
Hooks, Gregory, and Clayton
   Mosher, 95, 130
hypothetical imperative, 13–14,
   22, 122, 209
human identity: and ethnicity, 23;
   and gender, 23, 49–52; and
   intersubjectivity, 9, 13, 14, 23,
   36, 38, 47; and race, 23; and
   sexuality, 23; and sociality,
   36, 52

Iberico Saint-Jean, General, 21–2
Ignatieff, Michael, 178, 184
Irish Republican Army (IRA), 4;
   and the "troubles," 4

Jempson, Mike, 42
just-war theory, 150

Kadish, Sanford, 132
Kant, Immanuel, 12
Kershner, Steven, 30, 204
Kleinig, John, 198
Kleinman, Steven, 82
Kordon, Diana, 55
Kotze, Ria, 163
Krog, Antje, 120, 163

Landau Commission, 4, 76, 191
Langbein, John, 195
Lenta, Patrick, 67
lesser-evils reasoning, 26, 167
Levin, Michael, 4
Lifton, Robert Jay, 155
logical necessity, 13–14
Lomax, Eric, 42, 87
Lorentzen, Lois-Ann, 41
Lorenzo, Colonel, 165
Luban, David, 98
Lukes, Stephen, 70, 139
Lunde, Inge, and Jorgen
   Ortmann, 41, 110

MacKinnon, Catherine, 32
Malinowksi, Tom, 41
Marks, Susan, 95
Martinez, Ana Guadeloupe,
   41–2
mass screening, 88, 115, 134–5
McCarthy, Andrew, 5
McCoy, Alfred, 3, 8, 72, 124

McClean, Paddy Joe, 41
Mendez, Juan, 96, 175
Milgram experiments, 157–60
military necessity, 140, 150
Miller, Seumas, 209
Millett, Kate, 49
Mitrione, Dan, 67, 125
Moher, Andrew, 39, 198
Mook, Gregory, 158
Moore-King, Bruce, 89
Moran, Sherwood, 219
Murad, Abdul Hakim, 8
Murray, Craig, 136

Nagel, Thomas, 12, 183
Nielsen, Kai, 167

obligation, 15–18
Operation Bluebird, 124
Orend, Brian, 181
Ortiz, Sister Dianna, 56
Osiel, Mark, 118

pain: and calculus, 109–13;
    and cultural factors, 110; and
    humiliation, 110; and severity,
    11; and subjectivity of, 110
Parry, John T., 33, 45
permission, 15–18
Perry, John, 117, 120
Peters, Edward, 72, 116, 196
Phoenix Program, 115
Pokempner, Dinah, 42, 112
population: home, target, and
    third-party, 29
Portnoy, Alicia Mabel, 156
Posner, Richard, 20, 26, 32, 39,
    133–5, 137
prohibition, logical character,
    15–17

Project Artichoke, 124
pseudo consequentialism, 9, 73,
    96, 101

racism, 23, 73
Ratner, Michael, and Ellen Ray, 41
Rejali, Darius, 3, 133, 219
Rieff, David, 94
Rivera-Fuentes, Consuela, 110
rights, human, 9, 11; and prima
    facie, 11, 204, 215; and
    absolute, 11; and human
    rights advocates, 12–13; and
    nonderogability, 27
Rodley, Sir Nigel, 33
Ross, W.D., 11, 101
Roth, Kenneth, 77
Roualdes, Colonel Roberto, 165
Rumsfeld, Donald, 21

Saporta Jr, Jose, and Bessel van
    der Kolk, 45–6, 52
Sartre, Jean-Paul, 29, 58, 143
Scarry, Elaine, 43, 58, 110, 155
Schulz, William, 219
semantic cynicism, 19–20
sexism, 23, 73
Shue, Henry, 6, 60, 98
Skylv, Grethe, 48
slippery-slope arguments, 30, 72,
    120
Somnier, Finn, 55, 100, 110
sorites paradox, 18–19, 21, 74–5
state and nonstate actors, 28, 32
state of emergency, 36, 167,
    173, 203; and reasonableness,
    179. See also exceptional
    circumstances
state-of-emergency reasoning, 21,
    27, 212; and limits, 23

Staub, Ervin, 62, 155, 162; and pro- and antisocial acts, 159; and ingroup-outgroup attitudes, 160

Suarez-Orozco, Marcelo, 43, 121

Taussig, Michael, 57, 93

ticking-bomb hypothesis, 24, 108, 137, 188, 206–7, 209, 216; and appeal to fear, 99; and consequentialism, 7; and epistemic state of the interrogator, 83–8; and imminence, 74–7; and logical objections, 70–2; and necessity, 80–3; and political and empirical objections, 72–3; and pseudo consequentialism, 96; and suspect/source, 88–94; and threat, 77–80; and utilitarianism, 114

Timerman, Hector, 54, 172–4

Timerman, Jacopo, 54, 57, 174

Tindale, Christopher, 20

torture: as absolute violation, 207–8; and asymmetricality, 44; as attack on dignity, 46–7; and barbarism, 133; and coercion, 38, 59, 63; and community, ethnicity, and culture, 53–9; and complicity, 176; and cruel, inhuman, and degrading treatment, 20, 32–3; and destruction of character, 116–20, 213; and destruction of empathy, 117–18, 128; and dignity, 62–3; and domination, 38, 66; and effectiveness, 217–20; and essential properties, 37–40; and excuses and justifications, 15, 18, 186–8,

215–16; and family, 52–3, 55; and gender, 49–51, 59; and habituation processes, 128, 132; and identity, 37, 42, 47, 49, 53, 55, 59, 66, 118; and impacts on individuals, 47–59; and individualist assumptions, 9, 23, 47; and institutionalization, 10, 14, 25, 27, 59, 95, 96, 120–34, 137, 176, 207, 208, 216–17; and intentions (subjective and objective), 62–3; as interrogational, 24, 37, 60–1, 64–5, 86, 100, 206, 219–20; and intersubjectivity, 62, 100; and laws, 15, 127–8; and limits, 23; and medical personnel and practice, 123, 126–7; and the official-disobedience model, 199–201; and oppression, 220; and physical and psychological aspects, 39, 40–3, 59; and policies, 22, 30, 64, 95; and power projection, 66; and purposes, 60–7; and racism, 55–7, 59, 62; and routinization, 119, 217; and self-assertion, 38; and self-defence, 188–9; and severity, 33; and sexism, 62; and sexual violence, 49–51, 66–7; and social attachments and belief systems, 52–4, 58, 90; as terroristic, 24, 60–1, 63, 100, 220; and theatricality, 43–4; and training, 122–3, 125; and transgenerational trauma, 207; and warrants, 189–99; and will breaking, 42; and the world of the victim, 46

tragic choices, 26–7, 139–40,
    144, 146, 188. *See also* dirty
    hands
Twining, W.E., 31

United Nations Convention
    against Torture, 35–7, 192,
    205; and cruel, inhuman, and
    degrading treatment, 33; and
    nonderogability, 6, 36, 217,
    221; and public officials, 129;
    and UNCAT definition limita-
    tions, 9, 31; and United
    Nations Committee against
    Torture, 20
US Army Field Manual, 34–52,
    81–3, 89, 91–3, 135
utilitarianism, 4, 7, 10, 17, 96,
    209–10; and act utilitarianism,
    25–6, 102–4, 106–9, 115, 121,
    203; and calculating pain,
    109–13; and calculus, 116; and
    cosmopolitan values, 140–1;
    and equal consideration of
    interests, 103, 138; and ethno-
    centrism, 138; and happiness
    maximization and harm
    minimization, 7, 17, 103;
    and harms (necessary and
    possible), 113–16; and harms
    to institutions, 120–34; and
    harms to society, 134–6; and

harms to torturers, 116–20;
    and punishment, 103; and
    rejection of torture, 209–10;
    and rule utilitarianism, 102–6;
    and sentience, 102–3, 138

vagueness, 18–22, 72–4, 78–9,
    86, 165
Videla, General, 165
virtue ethics, 10, 26, 96, 140–3,
    203, 212; and consequences,
    141; and the dignity principle,
    141; and dispositions, 140–1;
    and practical wisdom, 142; and
    rejection of torture, 210–15;
    and utility principle, 141; and
    virtues and vices, 142. *See also*
    Aristotle

Walzer, Michael, 29, 214; and
    doctrinal civil libertarianism,
    12; and noncombatant immu-
    nity, 168; and obligation to
    torture, 145; and practical wis-
    dom, 154; and psychological
    distance, 158, 162; and
    supreme emergency, 149
Wantchekon, Leonard, and
    Andrew Healy, 160–2, 164,
    170, 212
Warren, Kay, 176
Weber, Max, 143, 169
Williams, Bernard, 170